Theology for
Non-Theologians

Theology for Non-Theologians

God and His Word

JAMES CANTELON

Collier Books

Macmillan Publishing Company

New York

Collier Macmillan Publishers

London

Collier Books
Macmillan Publishing Company
866 Third Avenue, New York, NY 10022
Collier Macmillan Canada, Inc.

Library of Congress Cataloging-in-Publication Data
Cantelon, James.
    Theology for non-theologians: God and His word/James Cantelon.
—1st Collier Books ed.
        p. cm.
    ISBN 0-02-084280-5
    1. Theology, Doctrinal—Popular works. I. Title.
    BT77.C223   1989   89-7299   CIP
    230—dc20

Macmillan books are available at special discounts for bulk purchases for sales promotions, premiums, fund-raising, or educational use. For details, contact:

Special Sales Director
Macmillan Publishing Company
866 Third Avenue
New York, NY 10022

First Collier Books Edition 1989

10 9 8 7 6 5 4 3 2 1

Printed in the United States of America

Theology for Non-Theologians is also available in a hardcover edition from Macmillan Publishing Company.

To Homer and Shirley,
my first teachers in theology

CONTENTS

Theology for Non-Theologians

PART I

The Existence of God

INTRODUCTION

❦ "FIRST IMPRESSIONS are lasting impressions." So goes the old saying, and I suspect in most cases it is true. My first impression of God is with me to this day. It happened at a musty old church camp in central Saskatchewan, Canada. I was five years old.

Back in those days we were into tabernacles. Not only were most of our churches called tabernacles, but our camp meeting buildings were also given this Old Testament name for tent. On one especially hot day my parents were in the adult tabernacle and I, with my fellow junior campers, was in the children's tabernacle. The teacher was taking us through Bunyan's *Pilgrim's Progress*. As she taught, something sparked within me.

After the lesson the children exploded into the sunshine to play. I lingered. Miss Brown seemed to know why.

"Can I help you, Jimmy?" she asked gently. I nodded dumbly, biting my suddenly trembling lower lip, tears welling in my eyes.

"Let's go into the back room and pray," she said. I can't explain what happened. Nor do I wish to describe it. But I will say this: at age five I suddenly felt as though I were the worst sinner who had ever lived. My sense of sin nearly crushed my little heart. The prayer, however, had not ended. It began with remorse, it grew into joy. I felt this newly discovered burden lift from my fragile soul. The presence of God overwhelmed me. Without my looking for him or asking for him—indeed, without any knowledge of my need of him—God came looking for me, asking for me, needing me, a five-year-old kid. I left that tabernacle reborn, knowing sin and knowing a savior, but not knowing that I had become a theologian.

Yes, a theologian—just like anyone else who comes to a knowledge of sin and of a savior. For as one theologian put it, the putting together of these two great truths is a beginning of theology. Just a beginning, mind you. A beginning that must be followed by a lifelong adventure in growth. The Apostle Peter in his great letter (II Pet. 3:18)* challenges us to "grow in the grace and knowledge of our Lord and Savior Jesus Christ." Paul put it another way, "And we pray . . . that you may live a life worthy of the Lord and may please him in every way: bearing fruit in every good work, growing in the knowledge of God" (Col. 1:10). Whichever way you want to put it, by acknowledging your sin and confessing Christ as Savior you have committed yourself to a life defined by theology. Nevertheless, we have a problem.

The problem is a huge communication barrier. The barrier is composed of two parts: caricature and language. In our world we do not think of every believer as a theologian. Theologians are stuffy academics who frequent moldy libraries and smoke evil-smelling pipes. Their hair is wispy, their foreheads are prominent, and they tend to sing tenor at best and monotone at worst. In fact, we see their whole lives as one colorless monotone. Then there is their language. Most people never open a book on theology, but if they do manage to get past the must and the mold, intending only a casual glance, their eyes light on something like: "In this we hold the Sublapsarian view, as distinguished from the Supralapsarianism of Beza and other hyper-Calvinists, which regards the decree of individual salvation as preceding, in order of thought, the decree to permit the fall," or "The scriptures enlarge our conception of Christ's Sonship by giving him in his preexistent state the names of the Logos, the image, and the effulgence of God." What in the world is a

*All biblical references are taken from the New International Version unless otherwise noted.

Sublapsarian? Someone who lives beneath Lapland? And effulgence? Isn't that some kind of pollution?

Little wonder the book is slammed shut. Theology and theologians seem to be woefully out of touch with the real world. But they should not be. Certainly you, as a theologian, are in touch with the real world. But I'm *not* a theologian, you protest. Oh yes you are. Maybe it will help to discuss briefly the what, why, and how of theology.

Theology, simply put, is the science of God. Science is defined by the *Concise Oxford Dictionary* as "systematic and formulated knowledge." So putting the two definitions together, theology is the systematic and formulated knowledge of God. The definition doesn't answer the questions, Whose system? or Whose formula? nor should it. Everyone has a system. Everyone has a formula, no matter how primitive or erroneous it may be. However, the work of classic theologians (wispy hair and all) has been to cut through error and arrive at a biblically grounded science of God. They have a lot to say. But it needs to be said in terms that you and I can understand today.

The communication barrier should not be attributed solely to the classic theologians. The fact is that theology deals with more unknowns than knowns. It also demands a lot. It requires exacting mental and spiritual concentration on our part and concerted revelation on God's part. Theology is like a puzzle, two pieces of which God puts together, leaving us to figure out the rest. We should expect a few blunders along the way.

There is more than one answer to the question, Why theology? Theology is as much a part of thought as physiology is a part of anatomy. If some rabid, antitheological society could succeed in destroying all theologians and theologies in this generation, new theologians and theologies would emerge in the next generation. Indeed, the antitheologians are theologians in their own right. Those who most disdain others' theology show by their convictions that they have their own theology. But there is yet another answer.

You have heard the adage, "Ignorance is the mother of superstition." Unfortunately, many people's theology is the crystallizing of ignorance more than the systematizing of God's revelation. They wander about in the theological dark, formulating doctrines that belong in the world of witch doctors. Therefore, we need to say more than that everyone has a theology when asked, Why theology? We need to distinguish between right theology and wrong theology. For theology is like a backbone. Right theology will have you walking straight and fit. Wrong theology will have you hunchbacked and paralyzed.

The biggest question is, How theology? How can I begin to develop a "systematic and formulated knowledge" of God when my intellect tells me that I cannot know God? And your intellect is telling you the truth. Even the Bible agrees: "The man without the Spirit does not accept the things that come from the Spirit of God, for they are foolishness to him, and he cannot understand them, because they are spiritually discerned" (I Cor. 2:14). Here is the place to build a case for *heart knowledge* as a counterbalance to *head knowledge.* In Old Testament terms the heart is a combination of what your senses tell you and what you choose to do about that information. What is more, the Old Testament sees your heart as an organ of knowledge. There are several references to this, among them: "I will give them a heart to know me, that I am the Lord. They will be my people, and I will be their God, for they will return to me with all their heart"(Jer. 25:7). The importance of heart knowledge is vital in the minds of the old theologians because love and faith, which seem to reside in the heart, generally precede intellectual knowledge of God. Blaise Pascal once said: "Human things need only to be known, in order to be loved; but divine things must first be loved, in order to be known."* You become a theologian with the potential to develop a correct theology if, before anything else, you have a heart of love for God.

*Quoted in *Strong's Systematic Theology* by A. H. Strong, Judson Press. p.4.

I think it necessary, however, to qualify the term *correct*. Theology has its limitations. "Correct" theology has degrees of correctness. Here is an example of why.

When a parent is teaching his preschooler to add and subtract, he uses apples or oranges. "Here is one orange, Johnny. Here is another orange. How many oranges do I have now?"

"Two."

"Very good! One orange plus one orange is *two* oranges! One plus one is two."

This seems to be a rather self-limiting exercise for the parent, especially if he is a mathematician. In order to teach a smaller mind, however, self-limitation is necessary. And a good deal of self-repression is needed as well. There is such a temptation to the teacher to answer for the student, to do his work for him. But the teacher must repress his superior knowledge and skill and be content with what at most times is a maddeningly slow pace.

The student develops from one level of correctness to another until one day he may be teaching his teacher. Until that day the teacher will have to limit himself to the student's pace. This is the way it is with theology. Its correctness is limited. One day, when God's plan for the universe has been fulfilled, we will have a perfect theology because we will know him even as he knows us. In the meantime, theology will always be lacking something. Its lack reflects our limitations as students and God's self-limitation and self-repression as teacher. This fact should not discourage us from studying and developing theology. Rather, it should encourage us to be forever growing in our knowledge of God.

That's why I'm writing this book on theology. My target audience certainly is not professional theologians, for I still have much to learn from them. My target is you, the everyday believer who has never studied theology in any formal way. At the time of writing this, I have been pastoring for sixteen years. In those years, and especially the past five years here in Jerusalem, I have seen the turmoil created in believers' lives by their inability to deal correctly with the "winds of doctrine" that afflict church doctrine today. They, you, we need a solid theological foundation. I want to introduce (if not reintroduce) sound doctrine to you.

In doing this I have committed myself to three guidelines. (1) What I write must be simple enough to be understood by young people, and even adaptable to children. (2) I will not write about anything that I myself have not grasped (to the extent that my limited abilities allow). Where I am not sure about some aspect of a doctrine, I will say so. Where possible I will illustrate the doctrines with stories, examples, and parables from real life. (3) I will try when appropriate to devote a portion of each chapter to the practical implications and/or applications of the doctrines described.

I will feel that I have failed if you do not retain most of what you read in this book. The acid test of a teacher is the student's retention. Thus I will do whatever I can within the limits of writing to stimulate your interest and engage your memory.

One final comment before we take a breath and plunge into a study of God's existence—remember that theology is like a painting of a beautiful landscape. Recently I walked from our home, just south of Mount Zion, to the archaeological dig of David's City on the southern slope of the Temple Mount in Jerusalem. It was a glorious day! The earthly swellings of spring were everywhere—buds on the olive trees, blossoms on the acacia trees, emerald shoots of grass highlighting the slopes of Mount Zion and Mount Moriah. The piping of the birds and the heady fragrance of the flowers made the walk a sensual delight. Just as I passed the Pool of Siloam, I looked up and saw an artist busily at work capturing the scene on canvas. Hesitantly, I looked over his shoulder and saw his beautiful interpretation of the scene I had just walked through. It was so lifelike I almost expected that he would have painted me, the only human in the scope of his picture, as a part of the pastoral vista. But I was not in the picture. Neither was the singing of the birds, nor the perfume of the flowers. The warmth of the sun, the cleanness of the air, the feel of the warm earth were not there either. Why? Because a painting is greatly limited. There is much in the landscape that a painting cannot capture. It is rather like theology. Theology is the image of the landscape, not the landscape itself. But the picture *is* valuable—indeed, it is worth a thousand lifetimes. For there is coming a day when we will walk through the picture into the verdant landscape of the kingdom of heaven.

CHAPTER 1

Does God Exist?

🎗 IT WAS Father's Day. I came down to the breakfast table to find three poorly wrapped gifts filling my cereal bowl. Our children (aged six, four, and two), with the early morning flush coloring their faces and excitement flashing in their eyes, gathered about me demanding that I open these treasures *now!* To squeals of delight and loud claims of craftsmanship—"I made that Dad! All by myself!"—I tore open their symbols of homage to fatherhood. Frankly, I forget what the gifts were. But I will never forget the cards.

Katie's card was your basic Picasso. At first I was holding it upside down. That didn't bother Katie. She patiently explained to me, "This line here is me, Daddy, and this line here is you, and here's us flying my kite." With this explanation the picture became clear. Short line, Kate; long line, me; longer line with the smudge at the end, kite. Then I noticed one little splotch of crayon color joining her line and mine. "What's this, Katie?"

"Oh, Daddy! Don't you see? We're holding hands!" Inside the card, in script suspiciously similar to my wife Kathy's, were the words, "I *love* you, Daddy," signed with an abstract *Katie*.

Jess's card was a bit easier to decipher. There was a smiling large-headed, stick-legged figure with arms and hands so over-sized that they looked like wings. He was standing on the grass, and above him was a small stick figure floating dangerously close to a spiky sun. "Tell me about your card, Jess," I asked.

"Well, this is you [the large-headed, big-armed one] and this is me, and you're throwing me up in the air!" he answered. Inside were the words, "I love you because you throw me up in the air! Jess."

Then there was Todd's card. With the deliberate strokes of a six-year-old, he had drawn what appeared to be an overweight bicycle with a large figure on the seat and a smaller figure riding in front. No problem.

"This is you and me on your motorcycle, Dad!" he exclaimed. Inside were the words, "You're the best dad in the world! I love you. Todd."

Three cards. Three views of Father. Three expressions of love. Showing three levels of skill in the communication of feelings.

Note that feelings of love were uppermost. Their knowledge of me was pretty feeble then. But love was strong and vital. Several years later they know me much better; you might say their knowledge is catching up with their love, to a point. Indeed, they are much better artists today, but it is still their love that moves the crayon.

Kids are good theologians. They don't limit their understanding of the world to externals. They deal with internals. Holding hands. Being thrown in the air. Riding two-up on a motorcycle. Their focus is not just on the physical contact but on the flow of love the contact allows. They see the world and experience its realities through the "eyes of their hearts" (Eph. 1:18). As one great teacher put it, "Except you become like a little child you cannot *see* the kingdom of heaven" (Matt. 18:3). Although they may not know it, kids have a high regard for intuition.

Intuition. As I said in the introduction, my first encounter with God found an immediate response of acceptance and love in a five-year-old heart. In other words, this revelation of God's love uncovered an intuitive knowledge of God already resident within me. I was like all kids and people everywhere.

There is an inner knowledge of God in man that has always been evident to any interested observer. Granted, some of the primitive views of jungle tribesmen may not include the words *God* or *gods,* but they do include *ghosts.* The overwhelming majority of humankind live with a belief in a spiritual being or beings whose goodwill must be nurtured. The fact that they may depict these spiritual beings in various and sometimes grotesque ways should not detract at all from the sincerity of their beliefs. Even the most avowed secularists have intuitive knowledge of God. All that is necessary to uncover this inner knowledge is a sudden jolt—a car crash, a dying child, an earthquake, an explosion—and the secularist joins humanity everywhere by crying, "Oh, my God!" or "God! Help me!" It is tragic, as one old poet noted, that many who cry, "God be merciful!" never cry, "God be praised!"

So what *is* this intuitive knowledge of God? First of all, intuitive knowledge of God is a bit like the apricots that are *not* growing on the apricot tree in our garden. "Huh? How's that again?" I hear you ask. Let me explain.

Kathy, the children, and I moved into a brand-new apartment here in Jerusalem a few years ago. As is the case with new buildings generally, there was much unfinished, including the "garden." Kathy let it be known that she would not feel at home until we laid some grass, planted flowers and shrubs, and built a patio in the seventy-square-meter backyard, or *gan,* as the Israelis call it. So we worked diligently and finally completed the task. A day later, Kathy came triumphantly into the house carrying a thin, scalped, strangely bent stick.

"What's that?" I asked.

"Our apricot tree," she answered happily.

"Our what?"

"This is our apricot tree. Just give it a few years, and we'll be eating our own homegrown apricots on the patio with our breakfasts!" Such vision. Without changing into gardening clothes, she went promptly to the garden and in a matter of minutes planted the apricot tree. It just stuck there in a mournful way. I didn't give it a chance.

Today that stick is three meters high. Last year it produced beautiful blossoms. This year the blossoms will produce apricots—so Kathy tells me! To this point we haven't seen any. But I've been converted. I now believe that apricots will soon appear. That's why I say that the intuitive knowledge of God is like the apricots that are *not* growing on our apricot tree. The blossoms were nowhere to be seen when Kathy planted the stick. Nor were the apricots. But both blossoms and apricots were there, somehow, even in the stick's baldness. All that was necessary to reveal the blossoms and (we hope) the apricots was a combination of planting, watering, sunshine, and time. The apricots just need a trunk and some branches. They have been there from the beginning. In a similar way, the intuitive knowledge of God is present in all men. It just needs the proper combination of time, plus circumstances, to be revealed.

So what is this intuition? It is a knowledge of God that springs out of our "branches" as sensual, thinking, choice-making beings. Our senses, thoughts, and choices are the roots, trunks, and branches that reveal our intuitive knowledge of God. And if ever you doubt that you have intuitive knowledge of any kind, ask yourself why you often see some things to be true without asking for, let alone thinking about, evidence to support your conviction. For example, why do you believe that love is better than hate? You have *always* believed this because intuitively you *know* it to be true. Your senses, mind, and will support this belief. Let's pursue this a bit further.

Hate produces pain. Sometimes, pain produces hate. In either case you associate the two because your senses tell you pain and hate go together. Somehow you know *hateful* and *happy* don't mix. Now, there may be times when we will misinterpret the information our senses send us, but generally they do give us, fairly unblemished, the facts as they perceive them. When a person feels pain, he may misread it and attribute it to the wrong cause or place, but he *knows* it is pain. An intuition, then, is an immediate perception of truth. It may be truth "in the raw," but it is truth nonetheless. Your senses tell you hate is hurtful. Therefore you prefer un-hate to hate at least, and love to hate at most.

Your mind tells you that hate is hurtful as well. What's more, it tells you that love is healthful. This is because there are some things that the mind instantly sees as true without any search for proof. No rational mind, for instance, will deny that half an apple is less than a whole apple. Nor will it insist that a curved line is a shorter distance between a person's eyes than a straight line. Like the senses, the mind has an ability to make instantaneous assessments of truth that are accurate and universal. How? Not through deduction or experience or education, but through the genius of intuition. And there is more.

Our choices get in on the act as well. When faced with love and hate we know we *should* choose love. Why? It is because we have within us, intuitively, a moral sense of right and wrong. We know it is right to love and wrong to hate. Just as we know it is right to give and wrong to steal. And if we choose to do what we intuitively know is wrong, we have a built-in kangaroo-court system. My psychiatrist and psychologist friends tell me that, immediately upon transgressing our moral code, our subconscious activates a punishment-and-atonement mechanism. We may be unaware that our sin is causing a psychosomatic affliction, but there usually is one evidence ruffling our moral equilibrium: guilt.

Guilt tells us intuitively that we are accountable to someone or something. It may be a system of law, or God, or both. Whatever it is, our moral natures tell us that truly, no one lives to or for himself. So we have an innate sense of accountability.

Added to this is an innate sense of dependence. Our senses, our minds, and our wills point us to some kind of ultimate sensualist, thinker, chooser, upon whom we are dependent. We may not refer to him or it as God. Indeed, we may choose to go no further than to say, "I believe in a higher power." But very few can honestly deny, in spite of any subsequent intellectual defense mechanisms, that at one point or another in their lives they have felt dependent upon and accountable to a higher power.

World history demonstrates clearly that this intuitive knowledge of God—call it religion if you will—is as universally common among men as are their rational and social predispositions. Even the "anti-" or "non-" religionists show the depth of their intuition by acting so strongly against those feelings in denying their existence. Indeed, secularism is a religion in its own right. Dependent on no one? Accountable to no one? No. In secular circles one is dependent on oneself and accountable to oneself. Secularism as religion places self upon the throne. For man's intuitions demand that someone be independent, someone be judge—if not God, then a substitute must be found. This is why the classic theologians call the intuitive knowledge of God necessary. Someone has got to do it. If not God, then perhaps self will have to do.

"But it's *not* necessary!" I hear someone object. "I have this atheist friend who's adamant in his refusal to believe in anything that can't be scientifically proven." Well, let me tell you about one of my atheist friends here in Israel.

Ari is a committed atheist. His atheism springs from an intellectual aversion to anything like superstition. Shoshanna, his wife, is less sure of her atheism, but defends it by saying, "God died for me at Auschwitz." Her's is a kind of post-Holocaust anger at God. Last week we had brunch together. The conversation amazed me.

They told Kathy and me about their recent adoption of an infant son. The process was full of complications, delays, reversals, and bureaucratic bungling.

"You know, the fact that we finally got David was a miracle," said Shoshanna, "if, of course, miracles exist. It was almost enough to make you believe in a God. I can still hardly believe we succeeded."

They went on to recount young David's first serious sickness. They thought he might die.

"I went into his room," said Ari, "and he was convulsing. We were desperate. I must admit," he said, with a hint of a blush, "that I called out to God and said, 'If you're there, God, we need your help now!' "

David recovered. Ari is back to his atheism. Shoshanna backslid to agnosticism. The point is this: Anyone can deny God's existence, but it is a forced denial. The power of denial (usually intellectual) is no match for the power of love—love of life, or love of a child. When one's own life or the life of a loved one is in the balance, the force of intuition overcomes the force of denial. At times like that the most powerful knowledge we have bursts through our "branches." We become more aware of God's existence than of the doctor next door or of the pills in our purse. We instinctively cry to God for help. Atheism can never stand in the presence of an anguished, "O God!"

The Bible assumes that "O God!" is universally and necessarily the cry of all men's hearts. It makes no attempt to prove God's existence. The very first statement made in the Bible does not say, "There is a God." It merely asserts, "In the beginning God . . ." Now, if it were possible to prove God through logical argument, I expect the Bible would present those proofs. But it does not. Yet it calls itself a revelation of God. How can this be?

Revelation can't occur in a vacuum. Let me illustrate. My first year in high school I took a course in electronics. I was all thumbs. I passed with a startling 51 percent and a lifetime knowledge of how to splice two wires with a Western Union joint. Electrons, amperes, and resistors are beyond me. I do, however, have a basic understanding of electricity and of the universal electrical home companion, television. And fundamentally, I know that you must have electricity before you can have television. Television presupposes electricity and can't be understood without at least a rudimentary knowledge of electricity. It's like the Bible. It presupposes an intuitive knowledge of God and can't be understood without it. Thus, there must be something there in men's hearts before the revelation of the Bible can have any effect.

"But surely there have got to be some logical proofs of God's existence," someone exclaims. Yes, there are. Although I prefer not to call them proofs. A better word might be *arguments*.

Speaking of arguments, I am sure you have heard the old story of the argument among three blind men who were attempting to describe an elephant. Seems that one guy had a hold on the tail, another on the trunk, and the third on a leg.

"An elephant is like a rope," declared the man at the hindquarters.

"No way!" said the man at the trunk. "An elephant is very much like a snake."

"Come on, you two!" chided the third man, holding on to the leg. "An elephant is exactly like a tree!"

The fact is, they were all right. Especially in that they used similes in their descriptions. Their points of view, subjective as they were, were nonetheless accurate in that they represented varying degrees of probability. If we were to follow these converging lines of description, we would come to a general picture of what an elephant is like, although we would not come to the elephant himself. This is what the arguments for God's existence are like. None of them is adequate in itself. Put them together, however, and you get a fairly general idea that points you convincingly to God.

There are four classic arguments for God's existence. They have been presented, developed, and refined over centuries. For the modern reader the language used by the composing philosophers and theologians has been so intimidating that the common everyday believer has ignored these arguments. But they are worth considering. They deserve a second look. One may describe the "tail" and another the "trunk," but together they are impressive.

First, there is what is known as the *ontological* argument. Forget you ever saw the word. Just remember this: the very *idea* of God suggests there *is* a God. Simple. The classic presentations of this argument have focused on three propositions. First, as God's existence is known intuitively to all people, and is necessary, therefore what is necessary is actual. Second, since we are finite beings we have no natural ability to create the idea of infinity—the idea must have come from some infinite source who is other than man. Third, like love and marriage, or a horse and carriage, finity and infinity are correlatives—you can't have one without the other. This argument tells us we should take seriously the fact that all of us have this innate idea of an infinite being. It doesn't describe this being nor does it suggest a holy tree is any less valid than a golden statue as its personification. Indeed, it doesn't suggest it is even necessary to worship this other. It is just there—impassive, impersonal, detached, and probably not too smart. But there nonetheless.

Ready for another forgettable word? Would you believe *cosmological?* This word has been used by the classic philosophers and theologians to describe the second argument for God's existence. Chopping through the haze and tangle of their verbiage, we come to this distillation: All beginnings have a cause. Not *everything* has a cause, but *all beginnings.* If everything had a cause, God would have a cause. And God cannot be God if he too had a beginning. This argument from causation says nothing about a first cause or an uncaused cause, it just suggests that what *is* must have been started by something, if not someone. That force, whatever or whomever it may be, need not be infinite—it just has to be big enough to cause the universe to come into being. If we demand that this force be uncaused, we can do so, but not by any rational process. It has to be by intuition. The value of the first argument is that it suggests God is there. The value of this second argument is that the God who is there is also infinitely great—a force strong enough to cause a universe. Whether or not he or she or it is intelligent or personal remains to be seen.

Perhaps we should not dismiss the word *cosmological* too quickly. It does have a smaller word in it which most of us recognize: cosmos. According to the dictionary, *cosmos* refers to the universe as an "ordered whole." The word *order* suggests "rank, row, sequence, arrangement." The word *whole,* of course, refers to an integral, a complete entity made up of one or more units. So what am I getting at? Simply this: the word *cosmological* implies that there is order and wholeness in the universe. How did this happen? By chance? The answer brings us to the next argument for God's existence.

The third argument says the order and wholeness in the universe demand an inventing, designing intelligence as the cause. What's more, it says there must be a purpose behind it all, which suggests that this intelligence has a will. This is called the *teleological* argument. It doesn't insist that this inventing, designing intelligence be all-knowing, it just has to know enough to be able to invent and design our universe. Beyond our universe this intelligence may get only *C* grades in celestial sculpting classes. But its abilities were adequate to think through and design our part of the heavenlies. Nor does the argument demand that this intelligence have a personality. At best it is still a force, a "smart" force.

Before we look at the fourth argument, let's briefly summarize the first three. So far we have a God who is there somewhere, mainly because he, she, or it is there intuitively in men's hearts. And, the very idea of God, in people's minds, underscores his "thereness." This God is also indefinitely great, a force powerful enough to cause our universe, because every beginning must have a cause. Then, this God is intelligent because the design of the universe demands an intelligent designer. He, she, or it also must possess a will, for the design implies inventive purpose. But does this force have any personality? More important, is it good or bad? Or both?

I have read that one of the toughest jobs on earth is to be an intelligence agent. Apparently the factor making it so difficult is that intelligence people are generally creating, stealing, and keeping secrets. Therefore, a big part of their job is telling lies in order to acquire and protect those secrets. This puts them under strain over the long run, because people's intuitive moral nature doesn't want to tell lies. It wants to tell the truth and be told the truth. People have a very distinct moral nature. It is part of our design. Does this mean our designer was/is also moral? The fourth argument for God's existence says yes.

The fourth argument is called the *anthropological* argument. It is the most complex of the four. It argues from the mental and moral nature of man. Man's mental nature includes not only rationality but self-consciousness as well. His moral nature includes awareness of right and wrong. Because he is mentally self-aware (with both good and bad desires wrestling within his "aware" self) and because he chooses to indulge or deny self in terms of those good and bad appetites, we can say that man is a *personality*. He is a person who has his own self-awareness and makes his own moral choices. But there is more.

When man violates his own moral law, he tends to feel remorse and to fear judgment of some kind. If this were not true, guilt would not exist. This moral law and fear of judgment are not self-imposed, they are just there. They suggest the existence of a righteous will that has imposed the law and a punitive power that will perform justice. To summarize, man is intelligent, self-aware, and has a conscience—or, he is a personality. Because man is an *effect*—that is, he has had a beginning—and because that effect is a person (possessing intelligence, self-awareness, and conscience), the cause of this effect must also be a person who has imposed conscience (that is, moral awareness) out of his own moral nature. In other words, the anthropological argument says: because man is a personal being with a sense of the superiority of right over wrong, he must have been caused by a personal being who is righteous and demands righteousness of his effects. Is this still a little fuzzy to you? Read on.

Do you have a conscience? I suspect you do. A conscience is simply an awareness of right and wrong. When you violate your conscience, you experience guilt. "But what kind of guilt are you talking about?" someone asks. "Haven't you heard about true guilt and false guilt?" Yes, I have. I know psychiatrists call it false guilt when we transgress the laws or expectations of others and feel guilty about it. True guilt occurs when we transgress the law of God written on our hearts. The point is this: conscience does not dictate law, but it warns us of the existence of law. It also warns us of purpose, not ours but someone else's, whose will we must obey. Thus, your conscience suggests *Conscience*. Your will suggests *Will*. Your person suggests *Person*.

Notice the anthropological argument says nothing about *eternality*. It just adds to the ideas of causative power (cosmological) and inventive intelligence (teleological) the wider ideas of personality and righteousness.

So, does God exist? Before I go out on a limb and answer, I will ask another question. What do you think of the picture I have drawn? It is probably like Katie's picture of me, "your basic Picasso." But let me tell you about my picture. Before I even picked up the "crayon," I loved God. My picture is very much a Father's Day effort. This "short line" over here says somebody is there. This "long line" says the thereness is at least strong enough to cause our universe. It is also intelligent and makes choices. The "longest line" says it is righteous and personal. It may be a poor picture. But it is an expression of my ideas of power, reason, perfection, and personality. Does God exist? My picture really doesn't portray him very well. But yes, for me he does exist. And for you, too, I think. It could very well be that your picture is much better than mine, but let's face it: none of us are very good artists.

CHAPTER 2

A Case for
Unbelief

🦋 IT WAS the first time I had ever been in a traffic jam of tanks. Twenty of them, to be exact. And one of me, in my Volkswagen. It was a sultry summer morning in 1982. The Israeli war against the PLO in Lebanon had just begun—on the very day when it was *my* turn to do the morning shift at a radio station in southern Lebanon. One of the tanks had lost a track, and the following tanks would not go around the disabled machine for fear of antitank mines—thus, the traffic jam. I also thought it wise to avoid the mines, so I stopped too.

One of the tank commanders came over to me with an amused look on his face. "What's this? You took a wrong turn at the Lebanese border?" he joked.

"No. I'm a broadcaster at the station just up the road," I answered.

"So you know this part of Lebanon? Where's Marjayoun?"

As I showed him Marjayoun and Khleia on the hills across the valley, the young Israeli tank crew gathered around. For most of them this was their first time in Lebanon. I was the veteran. Pointing to the hills directly behind us, I said, "And there is El

Khayam, a ghost town. It used to house fifteen thousand people."
I sounded like a tour guide.

Just then a series of mortar shells burst in the valley about three
hundred meters away. They had been fired from the ruins of
Beaufort Castle, a PLO stronghold, on the highest mountain just
two kilometers distant. This old Crusader fort had become the
symbol of PLO stubbornness. It refused to fall. Sitting there like
a jagged tooth on the horizon, it defied conquest and almost
casually spewed its shells into southern Lebanon and northern
Israel.

In the flurry of activity following the explosions, I noticed
one young soldier seemingly unperturbed. He was standing by
himself in the shadow of an Israeli tank, a brilliant white and blue
tallith, or prayer shawl, over his head and shoulders. Facing
toward Jerusalem, he was praying. The beauty of his tallith
against the dull gray-green of the killer tank caught my breath.
But this moment was short-lived. Screaming overhead, a second
barrage of mortar shells slammed into the hills behind us. We
were in Beaufort's sights. Every shell seemed to shout, *"Allah hu
akbar!"* ("God is great!") No matter that the shells were made
in Russia. The Islamic fervor of the various factions of the PLO,
the Shiites, and the Sunnis seemed, in spite of their factional
differences, to be as much a propellant as the technology of the
communist manufacturers. Their targets were the Jews in the
tanks and the Maronite Christians in Khleia and Marjayoun. Jew,
Christian, and Moslem all killing and being killed in the name
of God.

A week later I wrote an article for a Toronto newspaper.
"Monotheism is facing troubled days," I began. "In the seething
cauldron that is Lebanon the three great religions, Judaism, Christianity, and Islam, are giving God a bad name. The greater irony,
however, is that God is being besmirched by default."

Whether one sees God as besmirched, misrepresented, or

simply misunderstood, there is very little about his "representatives" in the Middle East that makes him appealing to the noncommitted. Indeed, there seems to be more than enough evidence to build a case for unbelief.

Unbelief exists in many guises. Atheism, agnosticism, skepticism, materialism (or secularism), and even pantheism are some of the clothes it wears. In this chapter I am going to introduce you to some of these. Call them anti-God theories, unbelief systems, or alternate religious beliefs. Whatever they are called, they are alive and well and deserve our attention.

The "bad guy" in these unbelief systems is the atheist. Usually the word *atheist* is a term of reproach. In fact, most real atheists resist the title. They say that a real atheist is someone who believes in a God, but in entirely nonbiblical or nonreligious terms. Yet I saw a psychologist on TV recently who referred to himself as "an atheist who writes religious books." He was acknowledging that his anti-God stance demanded that he be pro whatever God he put in the "religious" God's shoes. Now, these comments come from atheists who have thought through their atheism. It is only the uninformed, or nonthinking (dare I say ignorant) atheist who dogmatically declares there is no God of any kind.

Before I look at these dogmatic atheists, let me briefly outline the basic tenets of atheism. In the context of the Middle East with Judaism, Islam, and Christianity at one another's throats, one of the claims of atheism has a lot of weight—the claim that belief in God does real harm in terms of war and persecution. Who can argue with this one? Perhaps the only valid comment is that God should not be blamed for those whose view of him is so terribly warped by selfish interests. Besides, I think it can be shown that as much harm has been done in history by "un-God" philosophies. Marxist-Leninism is just one case in point. The problem here is not the existence of God. The problem is the existence of evil.

Then there is the claim that science offers an adequate explanation of the world without need for any supernatural trappings. This is a view seeing the universe in natural terms only. It denies the reality, let alone the involvement, of the supernatural in our world. Scientific explanation is enough. But is it? Scientific *description* might be better. To explain something means, among other things, to answer the question Why? Science can't tell us why life exists. It can't say why you are reading a book such as this. It can only suggest theories as to how. In other words, science describes rather than explains. It describes theories as to how life began. It describes, in psychological terms, how you became religiously predisposed and the spiritual momentum, in terms of heredity and environment, that led to your reading this religious book. But it can't answer Why? Description, after all, is not synonymous with explanation. Explanation of the world and human nature in terms of why? seems to call for a response from the supernatural, because the answer is beyond our natural abilities. Which brings us to the next basic tenet of atheism.

It focuses on natural abilities—not those of the scientist, but those of the theologian. It says that not only are there many flaws in the traditional proofs of God's existence, but the word *God* is meaningless because no one can verify his existence in practical terms. To put it another way, the atheists say theologians do not provide a convincing case for God's existence. There are too many holes. And I agree, about the holes, that is. That's why I said in the preceding chapter that the "proofs" for God's existence are better termed *arguments.* I also pointed out that none of these arguments is sufficient in itself. Put them all together and the cumulative picture is appealing. But it is still a poor picture. The major flaw in this atheistic focus on theological flaws is that the atheists treat the idea of God as if it were a species of animal that can be scientifically identified, described, and cataloged. They speak of the supernatural in terms of the natural. They might just as well try to explain love in terms of nerve endings.

The real atheist, as I said, admits there are serious deficiencies in his denial of God. The dogmatic atheist, on the other hand, says unequivocally, "I *know* there is no God!" This is a tall order. To say that you know there is no God is to say you know at least three other things: You must know what God would be like if he were to exist; you must know that all believers in God everywhere, throughout the centuries, are/were all mistaken; and you must know that no evidence for God exists anywhere in all corners of the universe. Let's face it, no one knows all this. If you did, you would be God.

Dogmatic atheists doggedly insist that there is no God. And it's an uphill struggle, a struggle of faith. Yes, *faith*. They desperately want to believe in a Godless universe, and they do. They accept by faith that the description they give of the God-who-is-not-there is the correct description; they would certainly recognize him, were he to exist. They accept by faith the denial that no believers throughout history had even the faintest clue to support their belief in God. And they take a great leap in the dark by affirming that "God" has not left any footprints anywhere in the whole, almost completely unknown, universe.

Adding to the strain of their struggle is that atheists must attempt to deny their own moral natures in taking a stand against God. Remember the anthropological argument? Man's moral nature demands an absolute of some kind. He has an innate sense of right and wrong. To be an atheist means to believe that no absolute exists. This is tough. If you believe in no absolute, how do you determine that an act of terrorism, for example, is right or wrong? Innocent people killed. Families broken. Society outraged—except the atheist, that is. He has no basis on which to be outraged. But common decency demands it. So in this case common decency becomes Common Decency, the missing absolute in the atheist's life. In fact, whenever he makes a moral decision or faces a moral crisis, the atheist engages one absolute or another, be it common decency, common sense, or the common good. A man may think he can free himself from the conviction that there is a personal being to whom he is responsible and by whom he is judged for his misconduct; but he cannot free himself from his conscience. Whether he likes it or not, his conscience speaks to him of Conscience. If, for some reason, his conscience becomes hardened, it is not an irreversible condition.

A big enough shock will bring him back to his need for a standard to live by and for.

So you have got to be a "true believer" to be an atheist. It requires commitment, determination, and an affinity for hard work. For, as one theologian has suggested, dogmatic atheism requires proof of a negative, and no debater is ever asked to do this. The Bible puts it less gently, "The fool says in his heart, 'There is no God'"(Ps. 14:1). Little wonder atheists backslide to agnosticism—there's a bit more room to maneuver as an agnostic. Or so they think.

Whereas a dogmatic atheist says, "I know there is no God," an agnostic says, "I know that God's existence cannot be established." This, at first glance, seems rather appealing for a cornered atheist. But it is almost as difficult to defend as atheism. Agnosticism is immediately on thin ice, for anyone who says man can't know anything about God seems already to have some sort of knowledge about God—at least an intellectual capacity to grasp what God means. So if he has this intellectual capacity, he can't be a complete agnostic—at best he is a partial agnostic. A complete agnostic ("Man cannot know *anything*") is really brave. He lives with constant contradiction—to know that you can't know is an impossibility. When you get right down to it, atheists and agnostics have bitten off more than they can chew. They can't defend their "religion." All they can defend is a sort of tentative skepticism. The skeptic says, "I am not convinced, and I am not sure."

A few years ago a terrorist planted a bomb on a bus here in Jerusalem. Eight people were killed, including two sisters, five and seven years old. It was the same bus route that our six- and nine-year-old sons took to school every day. We grieved for the bereaved parents, and we decided then and there that Todd and Jess would never take a bus in Israel again. But in a few days we relented. In the long run you can't live defensively. If you do, you might as well roll over and die right now. Nevertheless, we have become very alert. Like all Israelis our eyes are open to spot suspicious objects and persons. We've become full-time skeptics.

For the sake of illustration let's pretend the object of our atheism, agnosticism, or skepticism is not God, but terrorism. And we have just heard that a terrorist has planted a bomb somewhere in the Zion Square area of Jerusalem. How do we respond? The atheist, who knows terrorism does not exist, does nothing. The agnostic, who knows we can't establish the existence of terrorism and by extension any individual act of terrorism, also does nothing. The skeptic, who is always alert to the facts and will make every effort to know the truth about terrorism (thereby being prepared to be convinced and to be sure), will do everything he can to ascertain that there is a bomb. If he can't find it, he will still run (slowly rather than quickly) to safety. The ones who run quickly are the believers—those who have had some personal experience with terrorism in the past.

There is one further point. When the explosion occurs, those who have not been killed will run. The skeptic, of course, is already running. But he'll increase his pace from slow to quick to avoid being run over by the fleeing atheists and agnostics.

In terms of God, atheists and agnostics have a closed mind. They are consistent with their position if they deny themselves any thoughts of, or desire to search for, God. Skeptics, on the other hand, do not deny themselves thoughts of God. They have open minds. And they are consistent with their position if they are prepared to close their minds once sufficient data has been gathered. One old preacher put it this way: "The purpose of an open mind is to close it on something."

But there's more to it than merely an intellectual opening and/or closing of minds. The denial of God has as much to do with our wills as with anything else. To put it simply, belief in God demands responsibility and accountability on our part. It challenges our selfishness. It cramps our style. It demands dependence. And this offends the rebel in all of us. We want to be independent. Free. Unattached. Calling our own shots, doing our own thing. Being our own end and beginning—our own God. That's why John Lennon's song "Imagine" had such appeal.

Imagine a world with "no religion," no "God." Lennon also imagines no war, universal peace, utopian health and fitness. Strange. On the one hand we want freedom from God. On the other hand we want peace—the one thing that only God can give. We want to have our cake and eat it too.

So people opt for an atheistic world view. Not because they've thought it through, but because it "frees" them to pursue their own pleasures. If they were honest, they would have to admit that they are not really atheists or agnostics at all. And they are not even skeptics—for their minds are not open. Rather, they have chosen to be secularists.

"What's a secularist?" you ask. Let's go back to Zion Square for a moment. The bomb has yet to explode. The atheist and agnostic are doing nothing, the skeptic is searching, the believer is running—but at least they are all involved, positively or negatively, in the issue. The secularist on the other hand says, "Hey! I don't even live near Zion Square! What's it to me? I live in Tel Aviv. Let's get on with living." He lives as though any God-awareness in mankind does not exist. He lives in terms of protecting his own interests. There's nothing else.

Secularism has its roots in materialism. By materialism I don't mean consumerism. Rather, I refer to the religion or philosophy that has developed over the centuries which has its roots in the teaching of a man called Epicurus. Other men such as Hobbes, Locke, Hartley, and Comte have built on Epicurus's foundation. You and I live with the superstructure.

Before we look briefly at the tenets of materialism, let's review. The atheist says, "I know there is no God." The agnostic says, "I know the existence of God cannot be established." The skeptic says, "I'm not convinced. I'm not sure. But I'm open. The secularist says, "I don't care." So what does the materialist say?

Essentially he says the same as the secularist. But his lack of care is not so much apathy (as is the case with most secularists) as it is sensual. No, I'm not referring to *sensual* as sexual. I'm thinking of sensual in terms of *sensational*. For the materialist, sensation is the only source of knowledge. He sees the mind and the soul as purely material (there is no spiritual dimension). The senses (by way of sensations) agitate the brain and, like a computer, the brain stores these sensations and codifies them. Repetition of these agitations or vibrations produces thought and feeling. Thus, sensation is the real basis for every mental operation. Even the origin of ideas is sensation plus reflection. According to materialism, the only eternal reality is matter and motion, thought is nervous response to stimuli, the soul is simply the sum total of our nerve endings, our will is the most powerful of our sensations, and the standards of our morality are determined by what makes us happy. In other words, we are not independent, free, or moral. We're victims of our senses. Stimulus and response define and imprison our lives.

You might say the materialist banishes everything to the physics department. Comte went so far as to say that because everything is controlled by physical laws and because there is no more freedom in human acts than in the motions of the stars, therefore man's actions can be predicted with the same certainty as the stars' actions. What this means, of course, is that all freedom of action for mankind is nonexistent. Thinking is nothing other than the molecular motion of the brain. Where's the freedom in that? Materialism, then, in denying freedom of thought in man, denies mind in man. This leaves man not only an automaton, but also accountable for nothing. How can man be held accountable for an action about which he had no choice because of his molecules? And in denying all mind in the universe (only matter and motion are eternal), materialism leaves no being to whom man is accountable. But man cannot give up his sense of accountability. The authority of conscience is one of the constants of what it means to be human. A man will sooner give up sense and reason than his conscience.

Prisoners of conscience have been receiving a good deal of media exposure over the past decade. Indeed, fourteen years of imprisonment for conscience' sake ended just a few months previous to this writing right here in Jerusalem. To the emotional cheers of thousands of Israelis, Anatoly Shcharansky was carried on the shoulders of his new countrymen to the Western, or Wailing Wall, in the center of the Old City. He had been a prisoner of conscience in the Soviet Union. As he told his story on television to a fascinated population, the deprivation and suffering he had endured (and which is still endured by many who have yet to be freed) clearly illustrated the power that conscience has over the body and the brain. Prisoners of conscience throughout the ages have undergone unspeakable physical and mental horrors when a simple statement of recanting could have freed them to comfort and their families. But conscience would not allow it.

It would be absurd to speak of Shcharansky's courage and stubbornness as merely the product of the molecular motion of his brain. Yet this extreme position is consistent with the philosophy of materialism. But it is absurd. Just as absurd as it is to say that all artistic efforts, all acts of heroism, all expressions of love are the work of unintelligent physical force. How much greater the absurdity to attribute to blind, unintelligent force the marvelous, complex, and beautiful works of God!

Now, the secularist may find it absurd too. Indeed, many a fine secularist considers himself to be a religious person, a believer. Nevertheless, his values, his everyday world view, have a materialist basis. He may not see matter and motion as the only eternal factors in the universe, but he lives as though his possessions and his pleasures were the only truly valuable factors in the world. He may dream a few dreams, speculate occasionally about God, but the bottom line of his life is survival, survival of the fittest, and that fitness comes not through God, but through the manipulation of money, sex, and power. If religion can make this manipulation any easier, fine. Unfortunately, many religions do just that.

So far I've been talking about unbelief systems that either deny or exclude God's existence. Now I want to look briefly at one that purports to include God, but ultimately denies and excludes him as well. Pantheism is the most persistent and universal form of human thought about the origin and nature of the universe. The pantheist says, "The universe is God, and God is the universe."

Pantheism is also known as monism, the "all one" doctrine. It teaches that there is only one substance in the universe, only one real being. Everything is made up of the same stuff. Thus, there is in reality no distinction between finite and infinite, God and the world, body and soul, matter and mind. What's more, there is no distinction between good and evil. Man himself is not even distinct. He is merely a fleeting millisecond in the life of God. And what is this "life of God"? Pantheism doesn't know. For the very idea of God has no meaning other than in the context of this little globe we call earth. Before the earth existed and outside of the earth's atmosphere, the infinite has no existence. In other words, the idea of infinity, or God, is merely a human invention and has no objective reality or relevance outside human experience.

Pantheism says the finite created the idea of the infinite, and any idea of an infinite being excludes intelligence, consciousness, or will. God has no personality, nor can he say "I" or be addressed as "you." God simply is. And his is-ness has no meaning, at least no meaning that man can discover. Man can no more know the mind of God (if he has one) than a fingernail can know the mind of its owner. Nor can man choose freely. His acts are acts of God. The soul of man is a spiritual automaton.

This, of course, means that sin does not exist. If we are only milliseconds in the life of God, then we are and do nothing that is not God. And evil, as an objective reality, does not exist. Yes, there is sickness and suffering in the world, but these are the result of man's limitations. A child runs out on the road and is hit by a car. He suffers severe injury or death. This is an evil, but only because the child was limited in his awareness of danger. An adult would not have done the same. The child's limitation produced and was the evil. Thus, if limitation is evil, it follows naturally that un-limitation is good. To be unlimited is to be strong and powerful. This is the only good. Indeed, for the pantheist, might is right.

The significance of this theory is that the most powerful are seen as the most moral. The greater a man's power, the more divine he is. This not only deifies self, but it potentially deifies evil. In pantheism an evil person or act is only one way of God's self-manifestation. By logical sequence, if God is everything and if there is a Devil, then God must also be the Devil.

You may have read one of the several books or articles about the great Indian leader, Mahatma Gandhi. It's no secret that this famous Hindu was an ardent admirer of Jesus Christ. In fact, it is sometimes held by the more idealistic opponents of religious intolerance that Gandhi's love for Jesus somehow qualifies him as a "Christian" of sorts. They don't understand. The very fact that Jesus claimed to be God makes him most appealing to a Hindu. Why? Because Hinduism, which is based on pantheism, sees man's highest development when he becomes aware of his identity with God. When man is able to say, "I am Brahma," he has finally beat the seemingly endless cycle of reincarnation and is about to become lost in God. (I said *lost—extinguished* might be a better word.) Hindus have an affinity to Jesus because he seems to be the only man in history who has practiced what they preach, for he said, "I and the Father are one." He showed the way. But he was no different from any other man in his potential. Anyone else, including any modern-day, high-caste Hindu, could do and say the same.

Jesus, however, taught many things that are absolutely denied by Hinduism (pantheism). For instance, Jesus said, "If the Son sets you free, you will be free indeed"(John 8:36). Pantheism says, "No way! Man is not and cannot be a free agent. Whatever we do, good or evil, is all an outworking of God's activity in and through us. We're puppets." Jesus taught that there is a very real difference between good and evil. Pantheism says no. Sinful acts are acts of God. In fact, in Hinduism, gods who represent evil are honored. Jesus taught that God is not just personal, he is also our Father. "Impossible!" says pantheism. It denies that God can be a person, or intelligent, or self-aware, or righteous. God has as much about him that is worthy of worship as does radiation or analytical geometry. Ironically, pantheism, as a religion that sees God in everything because God *is* everything, actually denies the existence of God. Not God as an extension of man's need to have a god, but God as an objective, personal, intelligent, distinctly eternal being. "Herein," as Shakespeare said, "lieth the rub."

The rub is this. We are faced with basically two choices. Either we trust in God as the Bible reveals him, or we trust in ourselves. On the one hand we trust a powerful, intelligent, personal, and moral creator. On the other we trust the creature, ourselves—weak, stupid, selfish, and immoral as we may be. In trusting the creature, we may refer to ourselves as atheists, agnostics, skeptics, secularists, or materialists. But in the final analysis we've become pantheists. Be you atheist or whatever, you must replace God with someone else. Ultimately, as is the case with all pantheists, that replacement will be yourself. So beware any religions (including many "Christianities") which say, "You have the power in yourself." It's pantheism. It's independence. The only true Christian stance is dependence. To paraphrase the words of one biblical author, when we are weak, then we are strong. For then our strength lies in his grace.

I like the story of a very rich man who employed the world's leading scientists to build the biggest and smartest computer the world had ever known.

"When it's finished," he said, "I want to ask it the most important question ever asked."

When the giant electronic brain was completed, the rich man came to it and asked, "Is there a God?" There was a momentary pause, then came the answer, "There is now!"

As we've seen in this chapter, when God's existence is denied (by an unbelief system), there is need to replace him. When his existence is affirmed (by our Jewish, Christian, and Moslem neighbors in the Middle East, for example), there is a desire to dominate him. Either way, God's name is besmirched. Not only by default, but by man's refusal—be he unbeliever or true believer—to do the one thing God requires of all men. "What's that one thing?" you ask. It's certainly not to deny him. Nor is it to dominate him. It is to love him.

PART II

The Nature
of God

CHAPTER 3

What's God
Like?

✥ JOE BURNHAM was the town fool. He used to ride around
our little town in central Saskatchewan on a bent bicycle with
rags stuffed in the shredded tires. As he rode, he wore a leather
flying helmet with goggles and made spit-flecked motor noises
as if he were piloting a biplane in search of the Red Baron. When
he talked, his cleft palate made him sound like he was speaking
out of an empty garbage can. At night he slept between two
musty mattresses in a leaky shed outside his two spinster sisters'
house. They treated him like a stray dog. But Joe never complained. He wasn't smart enough to complain. He *was* smart
enough to be content. And to love God.

Joe used to call God Father. I know this because ours was the
only home in town open to Joe. Dad was the local preacher, and
Joe would come by every week for a visit and prayer. Dad liked
Joe. So did I. We seemed to be on the same wavelength. Every
visit he would pat me on the head, say "Hello, Jimmy!" then
reach into his pocket and pull out a linty stick of stale gum, gum
that seemed as hard as rock. I would dutifully apply my young
teeth to the offering and sit down to listen to the conversation.
It usually began with, "Well, Brother Cantelon (he always called

Dad Brother), let's talk about the Lord." It was then the transformation would take place.

The rheumy eyes would start to shine. The weathered face would shed its age. Even the voice would change its timbre, like the transformation in a saxophone's voice when taken from a novice and given to a master. He would lift his head and hands to heaven and pray. Usually he prayed for my father, as though Dad were the junior and Joe the senior. There was no question in my mind—when Joe prayed he was the guide, the leader, the one who knew the way. In my six-year-old heart I knew that God existed and that Joe Burnham was his friend.

How can this be? A young preacher, a child, and a simpleton praying together. Each overwhelmed in the presence of an invisible God. And the simpleton the most godly of all. How could we love a God we had never seen? How did we know God was lovable? Indeed, how did we know what God was like? And how was it that the town fool seemed to know more about God than the town preacher and his son?

Theologians tell us that we use two methods to augment our intuitive knowledge of God. One is the rational method. The other is the biblical method. Strangely enough, Joe Burnham used both. First of all, he used the biblical method, which is simply the inductive method. What is induction? Let me illustrate.

A psychiatrist friend of mine and I were weight lifting one day at the Jerusalem YMCA. As we were hard at it, an off-duty Israeli paratrooper struck up a conversation with my friend.

"Boy! You guys sure go at it. Especially your friend there (meaning me). You both Jewish?"

"I am, but not my friend," said Paul. "He's Christian."

"No kidding! Well, one thing you gotta say about Christians—they sure take their weight lifting seriously!"

The paratrooper was using the inductive method. When you induce, you start with a particular instance (or weight lifter?) and infer a general law (Christians are serious weight lifters). Thus, in the biblical method, you start with specific facts, statements,

and descriptions of God in the Bible, and infer a general picture
of what God is like.

Joe Burnham, though he was a simpleton, had clear intuitive
knowledge of God, and he could read. Joe's intuition told him
there was a personal, creative God upon whom he depended. He
saw God as infinitely great and perfect. The Bible told Joe his
intuitions were true.

Amazingly, Joe also used the rational method in discovering
what God is like. Here are three of Joe's statements that demonstrate his use of the rational method:

"Ah, yes, Brother Cantelon, it's a shame Mr. Wright has that
bad leg. Let's pray to God. He's got two *good* legs. He can help
Mr. Wright!" Now, Joe's induction leaves a bit to be desired if
you wish to be technical—we all know a spirit doesn't have legs.
But the Bible does talk about God's hands, eyes, and ears—these
are called anthropomorphisms or human being-isms. Nevertheless, notice Joe's view of God's perfection. Mr. Wright has a bad
leg, but God has perfect legs! In other words, Joe saw God as free
from the imperfections that plague created things. Theologians
call this negation. Joe simply called it common sense.

Another example is the way Joe would say, "Look at these
boys of yours [my younger brother and I]. Look at their strong
legs and their fair skin. Why, in their faces I see the face of God!"
Here Joe saw my five-year-old brother and me as near perfect in
our young bodies. His idea of perfection, however, had its roots,
not in the ideal of youthfulness, but in the ideal of God's wholeness. Whereas many older people see in the blush of unmarred
childhood their childhood past, Joe saw childhood future. That
is, he saw God. He attributed to God the ultimate perfection of
a child, a flower, a sunset—every perfection he saw in his simple
world spoke to him of the infinite perfection of God. Theologians call it climax when you attribute ultimate perfection to
God. Joe called it only natural.

Other times Joe would say, "God knows I needed a friend.
That's why he brought you here, Brother Cantelon." Like all of

us, Joe had a need for love. There wasn't any, until Dad came along. He didn't see Dad's arrival in town as anything other than God's answer to his need for a friend. In Joe's thinking, God was the root cause of every good thing. Theologians call this causality. Joe called it Father's love.

Call it negation, climax, and causality; or call it common sense, only natural, and Father's love. Regardless of the terminology, the rational method has the creature starting with himself and his perceptions of the world, and projecting to the creator. As such it has a major flaw: the creature tends to create the creator in his own image. Joe did it. You and I do it. We forget that we bear God's image, he doesn't bear ours.

This forgetfulness is understandable because we're "here," locked in space and time, and God is "there," freewheeling in eternity, as well as here. We're limited, he's unlimited. There doesn't seem to be much potential for a meeting of minds, at least from any effort on our part. The onus seems to be entirely on his shoulders. The only way we can avoid creating him in our own image is if he uncovers or reveals part, if not all, of himself to us. He must take the initiative. That's why the Bible is so important. It is there God has spoken and given us vital information about himself.

I trust the Bible. A few chapters later I'll tell you why. But, for this chapter's purposes I will refer to the Bible as the authoritative Word of God. With the Bible as my base I will be less likely to create God in my own image. I will also be free to do some reasoning gymnastics (very basic exercises) and to refer to a few intuitive and experiential insights as well.

First of all, I think it necessary to point out that we are dealing with two dimensions, the eternal and the temporal, when we discuss what God is like. On the eternal plane we are studying the absolute qualities he possesses, qualities which exist independently of his creation. On the temporal plane we are looking at the relative qualities he possesses, qualities which relate to his creation. To put it another way, we want to discuss what God is like in two ways: first, God in relation to himself (who he is), and second, God in relation to his creation (how we see him). In terms of God's relation to himself, we'll look at his spirituality, his infinity, and his perfection. In terms of his relation to his creation, we'll look at how he relates to time and space, to the world, and to moral beings (you and me). In both cases I will appeal to the authority of the Bible.

Authority is a nasty word in our scientific age. The scientific method demands tangible verifiability and repeatability as a prerequisite to establishing proof. It's not enough that Scientist A discovers and defines gravity by observing an apple fall from a tree. He must present his experiment, observations, and conclusions in such a way that Scientist B can verify gravity's existence by repeating the experiment. Any appeal to authority—"If Scientist A says it's true, that's good enough for me!"—is invalid. Thus, it's not enough in the scientific context for me to say, "The Bible says so, therefore it must be true."

But, what is authority? The *Concise Oxford Dictionary* refers to it as "power, right to enforce obedience; personal influence; weight of testimony." A person with authority is someone who knows what he's talking about. Scientists speak with authority. And they appeal to authority—the authority of other scientists and their theories (Charles Darwin, for example, and his *Origin of Species*). I read a best-selling science book recently in which the author gave a stunning overview of the universe and stressed the exclusivity of the scientific method in ascertaining truth. However, in the final chapter, he encouraged the readers to cuddle their infants and to allow teenage premarital sex in order for the next generation to be nonviolent. He did this by appealing to the authority of a social scientist's theories.

Theologians also appeal to authority. The question then is, Which authority is valid? Many scientists and theologians reject out-of-hand the authority of the Bible. They do not believe that God, if he exists, inspired it. On the other hand, there are many scientists and theologians who do believe in the inspired word of God. So the former group embrace the scientific method and reject the Bible outright; the latter group embrace the Bible and also accept the validity of the scientific method. (There are, unfortunately, some Bible-believers who reject science, seeing the Bible and science as mutually exclusive.) Personally, I relate to those who accept both the authority of God's Word and that of science, though both authorities have their limitations. Nevertheless, let's not focus on limitations. Let's focus on horizons.

Opposite is a diagram to help keep you on track for the rest of this chapter. My discussion of what God is like will follow these headings:

So what does the Bible say about God's nature? The second sentence of the Bible says, "Now the earth was formless and empty, darkness was over the surface of the deep, and the Spirit of God was hovering over the waters"(Gen. 1:2). Sometime later, Jesus said, "God is Spirit, and His worshippers must worship in spirit and in truth" (John 4:24). In the original Bible languages the words translated *spirit* speak of air in motion or activity and movement. *Spirit* speaks to us of energy, activity, and movement. Or in other words, *spirit* means life. According to most conservative theologians, this life of God includes intellect (the ability to think), affection (the ability to love), and will (the ability to make moral choices). To say God is spirit is to say God is alive. It is also to say that God is a person.

The fact that we are personalities means, among other things, that we can think, love, and make moral decisions about ourselves. That is, we have the ability to objectify ourselves. We're conscious of what we do and who we are, and we're aware of the self that does and is. This, of course, is something that mere animals cannot do. We can also think, love, and make moral decisions about others. We can say, "I" and "I am, I think, I love, I do." To put it another way, we have the ability to be self-aware and self-determined. Similarly, God is in the ultimate sense self-aware and self-determined. When he says, "I am who I am" (Exod. 3:14) he is telling us that he is both present with himself and his creation, and is what he has chosen or decreed to be. So, our idea of God's personality springs not only from awareness of

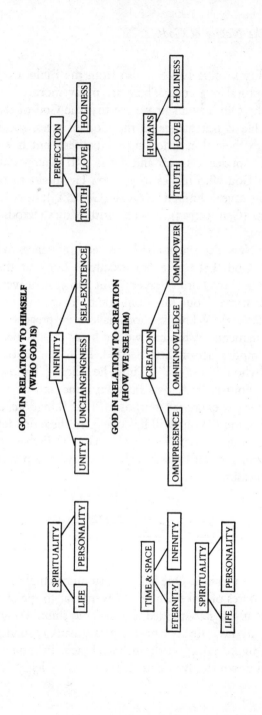

personality in ourselves but also from the Bible. I've given you one scriptural reference. There are many more.

In the Old Testament we see that the God of the Bible is a person. He is not named as the God of trees, rocks, and hills (although these things do sing his praises), but he's called "the God of Abraham, Isaac, and Jacob" (II Kings 18:36). He's a personal God who relates to persons. He speaks to Adam (Gen. 3:8–9); he reveals himself to Noah (Gen. 6:13); he covenants with Abraham (Gen. 12:1–3); he talks with Moses (Exod. 3)—person to person.

The New Testament also has several references to the personality of God. Let's take one example. Look at the first four statements of the Lord's Prayer: "Our Father in heaven. Hallowed be Your name. Your kingdom come. Your will be done . . ." (Matt. 6:9–13). Whole sermons have been preached on each of these statements. What can we see here? First, God is a Father, which implies personality. Second, he is immaterial, that is, a spirit ("who is in heaven"). Third, he is holy ("hallowed be Your name"). Fourth, he knows his own mind and out of that self-awareness has expressed purpose (*"Your* kingdom come") and determination ("Your will be done"). In these first few words of Jesus' famous prayer we see that God is Father, spirit, holy, self-aware, and self-determined. He's alive and personal, a spirit above measure.

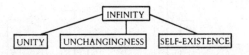

Above measure. One beautiful summer's night at our cottage on the shores of Lake Ontario, I went out to spend a little time looking at the star-studded sky and the shimmering waters. As I sat at my favorite spot on the grassy bank, I suddenly noticed a small figure lying on the pebbly beach. In momentary shock I rushed down to investigate. My concern quickly fled. It wasn't some unfortunate drowned child. It was Jess, very much alive.

"Hi, Dad!"

"Jess! What are you doing here? I thought you were in bed."

"I couldn't sleep," he said.

"So how come you're down here? And why are you lying on your back?"

"I'm counting the stars," he explained. "Dad, how many is infinity?"

I paused for a moment. The beauty of the scene was almost overwhelming—a little guy of five lying on the shores of space and time, wrestling with the awesome question of beginnings and endings. My own childish wonder was awakened. I lay down beside him, and we talked.

"Infinity can't be measured, son," I said. "It's limitless, boundless, endless."

"I don't understand," he replied.

"You asked how many is infinity. You can't ever answer how many. Say you thought one million was infinity. Well, you could always add one more. There's no number that is infinite because there's always room for one more."

"So can one more be added to everything?" he asked.

"Yes," I answered, "everything, except God."

There was silence for a moment.

"Dad? If infinity means one more can always be added, and you said nothing can be added to God, well, doesn't that sorta mean that God isn't infinite?"

There was more silence. Not from the beauty of the moment as much as from my lack of an answer.

"I think it's this way," I finally said. "Infinity is a term that has meaning only for this universe, this world, and the people in it. Infinity for us is an endless number. But however far we count, God is there and beyond. Our numbers can never catch up with him. There may be one more star. There may be one more number. But there isn't one more God. He's the only one to whom infinity doesn't exist."

"I don't understand," he said.

"Remember the Santa Claus parade a couple of years ago in Toronto?" I asked.

"Yes. It was huge!"

"It sure was. We stood there and watched it for over two hours. It seemed to go on forever. But do you remember that police helicopter up in the sky?"

"Yep."

"Well, he was the only guy who could see the beginning and the end of the parade at once. Infinity is a bit like that parade. To us it's endless. But not to God."

"So is God infinite?" he asked.

"Yes, he is," I answered. "We're standing somewhere near the beginning of the parade of the stars. It's endless. But for God, the parade is small enough to take place in his living room. All infinity leads to God. He is the only endless one."

"I still don't understand," he said.

"If it's any comfort, Son, neither do I," I confessed. "Infinity is not really understandable at all. But it comforts me to know that God, who is infinite, understands infinity. What's more, he understands you and me."

Our conversation gave way to the whisper of the waves and the silence of the stars. Jess rested his head on my shoulder and fell asleep. As I carried him to his bed, my eyes brimmed in the presence of the Holy.

King David said, "Great is the Lord and most worthy of praise; for his greatness no one can fathom" (Ps. 145:3). The prophet Isaiah quotes the Lord as saying, "Heaven is my throne and the earth is my footstool" (Isa. 66:1). King Solomon, when dedicating the wondrous temple he had built for the Lord, said, "But will God really dwell on earth? The heavens, even the highest heaven, cannot contain you" (I Kings 8:27). One old theologian, in less poetic language, simply observed that not only is there no infinite number, there is no infinite universe (because it's conceived as an infinite number of worlds); God is the only real infinite. The universe is simply a temporal expression or symbol of his magnitude.

In order for the infinite God to relate to our finite universe, he has to limit himself. One of the psalmists put it this way: "Who is like the Lord our God, the One who sits enthroned on high, who stoops down to look on the heavens and the earth?" (Ps. 113:5–6). This suggests that God's creation requires of him some kind of self-limitation. If he has to "stoop" or humble himself (KJV) to simply look at the heavens and the earth, how far did he have to stoop in order to make the heavens and the earth? (And, how far does he have to stoop to redeem the heavens and the earth?) Thus, God is infinite whether the universe and you and I exist or not. But we do exist. And infinity exists. Albeit a "stooped" infinity. Still, it boggles the mind.

Infinity, then, tells us God has limited himself in creating a finite universe. But it also tells us God is not self-limited in terms of his oneness, his unchangingness, and his independence. These three are all included in his infinity. Let's look briefly at each.

The unity of God is the cornerstone of Judaism. Daily in Jerusalem and around the world you will hear Jewish people declare, *"Shema Yisrael, Adonai elohenu, Adonai echad"* ("Hear O Israel, the Lord our God, the Lord is one" [Deut. 6:4]). This confession, according to Jesus (Mark 12:29), is also the foundation of Christianity. God's unity includes both a numerical factor (denying that another God can exist) and a wholeness factor (denying that the one can be divided into two or three). The great Shema of Israel tells us God's nature is undivided and indivisible. He is one. And he is unchanging.

It's at this point that we often object. We can't see how God can be infinitely the same when he seems so often to change his treatment of us. One day he seems to bless us, the next to ignore us. Sometimes it even appears that he's out to make us unhappy. He seems whimsical.

Recently I was in Eilat, Israel's southernmost city. Situated on the Red Sea, it's a port city as well as an active resort and water sports center. I was walking along the beach on a very windy day and saw a young girl of about twelve sailing a small boat. At that moment she was sailing into the wind. The boat was bucking and tossing like a mad horse, with foam and spray sometimes obliterating the small craft. The sail was so full of wind that it seemed stretched to the point of bursting. Suddenly, she "came about" (sailor's jargon) and began to sail in the opposite direction, "before the wind" (more sailor's jargon). An instantaneous transformation occurred. The girl's long hair, which a moment ago had been streaming at right angles to the sea, suddenly fell to her shoulders. The foam and the spray disappeared. The sail stopped bending the mast and took on an unconcerned, almost lazy appearance. The whole scene had changed from furious competition to peaceful recreation. What had happened? Had the wind suddenly stopped or changed direction? No. The girl had changed *her* direction.

We're the whimsical ones. "OK! So maybe we do change," someone says, "but why does God seem to bless some and hurt others?" Let's go back to Eilat. As I walked the beach that day, I saw several people who had been badly burned by the torrid sun. I hurt for them as I imagined their pain. Others were nicely tanned and feeling no pain. Does this mean the sun is fickle? No. It just means that some people are foolish and some are wise.

In Malachi chapter 3, verse 6 the Lord says, "I the Lord do not change." He can neither increase nor decrease. His power can never be diminished or augmented. He can't be holier or more righteous than he is. How can perfection be better or worse? So in his nature he is changeless. But in his treatment of humankind, he will make any midcourse correction he chooses in response to our selfishness (see Gen. 6).

So in terms of God's infinity, he is infinitely One and he is infinitely unchanging. He is also infinitely independent. I have already referred you to God's description of himself in Exodus chapter 3, verse 14 ("I am who I am"). Contrast this with the Apostle Paul's words to the men of Athens when he said, "For in him we live and move and have our being" (Acts 17:28). Whereas we are dependent, God is independent. We exist. He self-exists. The basis of our existence is God. The basis of God's existence is himself.

Self-existence seems beyond understanding. Yet a self-existent person is no more beyond comprehension than is a self-existent universe, as many atheistic scientists think it to be. But it's a mystery nonetheless. The farthest we can go in comprehending it is to say that if God is God, his existence is uncaused. It simply is his nature to exist.

Before we go any further, let's review. So far we have looked at two of the three major headings in the diagram. In terms of God's eternal qualities (who he is) we have seen: (1) he is spirit; as such he has life and personality; (2) he is infinite in his unity, unchangingness, and self-existence. Now let's look at his perfection.

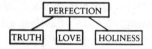

When we talk about God's perfection, we are talking about his flawless spirituality. We've already seen that *spirit* means life. And the life of God includes intellect, affection, and will. In the diagram I've related intellect to truth, affection to love, and will to holiness. You might say that truth, love, and holiness are moral attributes. So we're talking about moral perfection in this part of the diagram.

Over the years I have spoken at several youth retreats. On one occasion I wandered down to the waterfront area of the retreat center. There was a long dock jutting out over the water. Sitting at the end of the dock, their feet in the water and backs to me, sat two fifteen-year-old boys. Not realizing I was within hearing distance, they began to talk about a girl. One boy was full of superlatives. Her beautiful face. Her slender figure. Her long legs. Her wonderful personality. Her sultry voice. "She's got it all!" he exclaimed. The other boy was full of negatives. Point, counterpoint. Her face without the "tons" of makeup. Her figure without all the fashionable clothes. Her grouchy home behavior. Her screeching at her parents. "What a loser!" he groaned. I wondered how they could possibly be talking about the same girl. Only later I discovered that the former boy was a would-be boyfriend. The other boy was her brother!

One boy saw her as perfect, the other as flawed. One saw her as the sum of her parts ("She's got it all!"); the other saw her quality of character ("What a loser!"). When we discuss God's perfection, we're speaking of both quantitative and qualitative excellence. He is perfect truth, love, and holiness.

Moses, in one of his poetic songs, sang, "I will proclaim the name of the Lord. Oh, praise the greatness of our God! He is the Rock, his works are perfect, and all his ways are just" (Deut. 32:3–4). David sang, "As for God, his way is perfect; the word of the Lord is flawless" (Ps. 18:30). Jesus said, "Be perfect, therefore, as your heavenly Father is perfect" (Matt. 5:48). And the Apostle John, referring to God's flawless spirituality, said, "The Spirit is the truth" (I John 5:6). The quantity of God's perfection includes greatness, justice, flawless ways and words. The quality of his perfection includes truth.

God is not only true in his words and deeds, he is true in his being. From our limited perspective we see God as the truthful one. From God's unlimited perspective he is the truth, and as such is the source of truth. This is one reason why I admire the scientists of our world, be they believers or unbelievers. Their focus is the truth. The truth about mathematics, space, atoms, or whatever. The more they uncover the truth, the more they uncover God. One scientist put it this way, "The heavens are crystallized mathematics." Plato simply said, "God geometrizes."

The quality of his perfection also includes love. John tells us, "God is love" (I John 4:8). Love is alive. Its aliveness seeks the highest good for the person loved. It seeks to give of itself and to be united with the loved one. It desires response. It also suffers. Why? Because love exists only between persons, and persons (other than the "persons" of the Godhead) are imperfect. This imperfection hinders the flow of love. Love often has to back up and start again.

"What about the Holocaust?" many of my Israeli friends ask. "How could a God of love allow such a tragedy to happen?" Six million Jews and four million gypsies and Christians wiped out by a madman and an equally mad Nazi regime. Why does God allow such things? Why does he allow suffering and evil?

As far as the Holocaust is concerned, I can only suffer with my Israeli friends and say this, "God loves the Jews." The Bible is the story of the greatest love affair of all time. God cries out again and again of his love for the sons of Abraham, Isaac, and Jacob. That's why I believe that the greatest sufferer in the awful carnage of the Holocaust was God himself. He loves Israel as a father. As a mother wails at the suffering of her children, so God sorrows at Jacob's troubles. And more so. For I think he suffers in proportion to his magnitude, as a mother suffers more than the sick or dying child she holds in her arms.

He suffers because we suffer. But we must remember one thing. There is an element of self-limitation in God's suffering. Death to him is not a tragedy. Death is only the open door to God's eternity. To us, however, death is the great leveler, the ending of life, the ultimate loss. We suffer. And because God loves us, he suffers too.

Why does God allow suffering and evil? Especially when he is the greatest sufferer, and therefore the most greatly offended by evil. And he's also the one who has the greatest motive for setting things right and vindicating the righteous. He allows it because of his great mercy. We are free moral agents—he's made us that way. We are not puppets. Nor will he be a puppeteer. Our selfishness will kill us, and others. But he's not willing that any should perish. Thus he withholds his anger and extends forgiveness and salvation to whoever asks it of him. There is coming a day of justice and accountability. Until that day we should do all we can to see humankind turn from its selfishness. And we should ask ourselves the question, "Why do *we* allow suffering and evil?"

The third factor in the quality of God's perfection is holiness.

In Isaiah's vision he saw "the Lord seated on a throne, high and exalted. Above him were two seraphs. . . . And they were calling to one another: 'Holy, holy, holy, is the Lord Almighty; the whole earth is full of his glory!' " (Isa. 6:1–3). God's holiness is at the very core of his being. Some theologians even suggest that God is holy before he is anything else. That holiness means he is morally perfect and much more. Ultimately it means that he is forever distinct from his creation. He is not, as pantheism says, the universe. The universe is distinctly separate from God. The universe and all that is in it is flawed. It's running down. Just a few more billions of years and it will undergo its "heat death" and forever pass away. God, however, is the same "yesterday, today, and forever" (Heb. 13:8). He is forever apart from his creation. Indeed, his holiness is, in the final analysis, his "apartness."

In the context of his perfection, God is holy before he expresses holiness. He is loving before he expresses love. He is truthful before he expresses truth. In other words, his nature determines his action. Holiness consists in God's will conforming to God's being. His will expresses his nature. Similarly, in you and me, any holiness we might possess is active, not passive; positive, not negative. I remember a group of believers in Saskatchewan who used to focus on the outward show of things. Holiness to them was keeping their women as homely as possible and the chrome on their cars painted black. But they weren't active in the world. They were reclusive, self-righteous, and self-absorbed. If we are truly to be holy, we must be active in the world. We are to be out there actively, positively following God's lead. As the Bible says, those who "are without fault before the throne of God" (Rev. 14:5b) are those who "follow the Lamb whithersoever he goeth" (Rev. 14:4, KJV). Holy action expresses holy being.

So in terms of what God is like, we've briefly looked at God in relation to himself—that is, who God is. He's a spirit who is alive and personal. He is infinitely One, unchanging, and self-existent. He is perfectly true, loving, and holy. He is all this whether we're in the picture or not. But, we *are* in the picture. Therefore God must relate to us and to all else he has made. That's why how we see him is vital in discovering what God is like. We're seeing "but a poor reflection" (I Cor. 13:12), but a reflection nonetheless. Let's take a look at that reflection.

Scientists tell us that a beam of light travels 186,000 miles in one second. That's 300,000 kilometers. Seven times around the earth in one second! In a year it travels almost six trillion miles (ten trillion kilometers). This is called a light-year. Our earth, which is part of the Milky Way Galaxy, is thirty thousand light-years away from the center, or star cluster, of the Milky Way. Other galaxies, stars, planets, and black holes are trillions of light-years away. This means the light we see from distant stars is old; that is, it's taken perhaps hundreds, thousands, or even millions of years to reach us. This also means that if we could travel at the speed of light, we could literally pursue history. We could go back in time and see how it all began. At the speed of light past becomes present. Time stands still.

Anybody who could travel at the speed of light would have no problem understanding eternity. None of us can, however. And so we have a huge difficulty whenever eternity is discussed. Our lives are framed by beginnings and endings. We've no experience with timelessness. To us there is no meaning to the question, "What was God doing before creation?" This question suggests that there was time before time. Although it's possible, it's not probable. All we know is what God's word tells us. The very first thing he said after creating the heavens and the earth was, "Let there be light" (Gen. 1:3). He might just as simply have said, "Let there be time." For light is time.

Time and space are among the "all things . . . made" (John 1:3) by God. Time and space are not older divinities. They are created by the God whose nature is beginningless and endless. He is the cause of time, the creator of space. Beginnings and ends have their source in him and exist as a blip in the eternity of God.

Moses said, "Before the mountains were born or you brought forth the earth and the world, from everlasting to everlasting you are God" (Ps. 90:2). An anonymous psalmist agreed with Moses: "In the beginning you laid the foundations of the earth, and the heavens are the work of your hands. They will perish but you remain; they will all wear out like a garment. Like clothing you will change them and they will be discarded. But you remain the same, and your years will never end" (Ps. 102:25–27). Isaiah put it this way: "This is what the Lord says—Israel's king and Redeemer, the Lord Almighty: I am the first and I am the last; apart from me there is no God" (Isa. 44:6). Peter expressed God's eternity differently by using a simile, "With the Lord a day is like a thousand years, and a thousand years are like a day" (II Pet. 3:8). Past, present and future are human terms that express our bondage to time. As we look at God we see him limiting himself to our language when he is communicating with us. To us he says, "I was, I am, I will be, I will do." But to himself he says, "I am, I do." God lives in the eternal present. He is eternal. He is also immense.

Whereas eternity is infinity in its relation to time, immensity is infinity in its relation to space. Yuri Gagarin, Russian cosmonaut and the first man in space, is reported to have said that he looked carefully on his voyage for any signs of God's existence, but didn't see him anywhere. One old astronomer once said he swept the heavens with his telescope, but nowhere could he find any trace of God. An equally old preacher snorted, "He might just as well have swept his kitchen with a broom!" Remember Solomon's prayer? "The heavens, even the highest heaven, cannot contain you" (I Kings 8:27). God's nature cannot be extended nor diminished (unless he chooses to "empty himself"). He is not limited to space, but rather is himself the cause of space. He is not in space, but space is in him. He is immense. He is Lord of space.

So in terms of how we see God, from our vantage point in time and space, he is infinitely free from the limitations to which we are subject. Relative to time we are temporal, he is eternal. Relative to space we are finitely small, he is infinitely immense. But in terms of his general relation to creation, he is more than eternal and immense. He is present everywhere, he is all-knowing, and he is all-powerful.

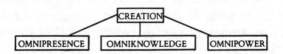

The God of the Bible, unlike pantheism, is not the "all." But he is all- (or omni-) present. His omnipresence means the whole of God is present in every place. Not just a part of him here, and a part of him there. Rather, all of him here, and all of him there. In the book of Jeremiah God asks, "Am I only a God nearby . . . and not a God far away? Can anyone hide in secret places so that I cannot see him? . . . Do not I fill heaven and earth?" (Jer. 23:23–24). King David wrote, "Where can I go from your Spirit? Where can I flee from your presence? If I go up to the heavens, you are there; if I make my bed in the depths, you are there. If I rise on the wings of the dawn, if I settle on the far side of the sea, even there your hand will guide me, your right hand will hold me fast. If I say, 'Surely the darkness will hide me and the light become night around me,' even the darkness will not be dark to you; the night will shine like the day, for darkness is as light to you" (Ps. 139:7–12). A little later in the same psalm, David said, "How precious to me are your thoughts, O God! How vast is the sum of them!" (verse 17).

How vast indeed! The Bible tells us that God "determines the numbers of the stars [trillions upon trillions] and calls them each by a name" (Ps. 147:4). He "forms the hearts of all [people]" and "considers everything they do" (Ps. 33:15). He even watches the fall of a sparrow (Matt. 10:29). From the names of trillions of stars to the dying flutter of a sparrow, God is aware and knows all. It's beyond human understanding—"Such knowledge is too wonderful for me . . ." (Ps. 139:6). He knows the past and the future, for all things are present with him.

A few paragraphs ago I mentioned the speed of light. We all know that light travels faster than sound. One simply has to observe lightning flash and listen to the thunder rumbling through the darkened sky a few seconds later. Similarly, in terms of God's future knowledge, he's given us just a few flashes of that knowledge in some of the predictive passages in the Bible. He speaks, for instance, of the "day of the Lord" and the rejoicing at the "marriage supper of the Lamb" which will take place on that day. We've seen the flash of light in his word; now we have to wait merely a few days, months, or years and we'll hear the heavens rejoice at the wedding feast.

Omnipower often brings to us a certain discomfort. It confronts us with our weakness. We feel powerless in the light of his infinite strength. Our only recourse is to attempt to make God look powerless in some way. And so the seemingly clever question arises, "Can God make a rock so big he can't lift it?" This question, of course, suggests that omnipower is capable of doing something which is not an object of power. There's a built-in contradiction in the question. God, all-powerful as he is, will not release his power on something that is not a proper object, such as lying, or sinning, or contradiction. God will not lie, nor will he sin. He cannot. It is not in his nature. Omnipower means that God has power over his power. He controls his power. Just as you do when you hold a newborn baby or caress a fragile flower. God is able to do what he chooses, but he chooses not to do all he is able to do. Otherwise he'd be a slave of his power, just as humans are slaves of the minor powers (sex, status, or money, for example) that strive for limitless indulgence. When God said to Abraham, "I am God Almighty" (Gen. 17:1), he was saying a lot. Among other things he was claiming almighty power held under almighty control.

This almighty control brings up one vital point. I've already discussed it earlier in this chapter when looking at God's infinity.

I quoted Psalm 113, verses 5 and 6, "Who is like the Lord our God, the One who sits enthroned on high, who stoops down to look on the heaven and the earth?" The point taken was God's self-limitation. God's omnipower tells us that he has the power of self-limitation. If he hadn't limited himself (see Phil. 2:7–8) and had spoken to us in human terms, I wouldn't be writing this book and you'd have no interest in theology whatsoever.

God's relation to creation, then, is described to us and by us in very human terms. We see ourselves as finite and limited. We see God as infinite and unlimited. Whereas we occupy only one little space for a fleeting moment in space and time, God is present everywhere, both in space and in time. His omnipresence takes in the whole scope of the universe and beyond. Whereas we are feeble in our knowledge and understanding, God is all-knowing. Whereas we are weak, he is strong—immeasurably so. He's awesome. Intimidating. Nevertheless, he chooses to relate to us as human beings with human needs. He does so in his truth, love, and holiness.

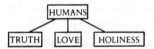

Human beings have a fundamental need to trust and be trusted. Relationships are built on trust. And trust is built on faithfulness. That's why sexual unfaithfulness in marriage is so deadly. Unfaithfulness shatters trust. Once trust is gone, the relationship falls apart. The Bible tells us God is faithful and trustworthy. "God is not a man, that he should lie, nor a son of man, that he should change his mind" (Num. 23:19). "God . . . is faithful," says Paul (I Cor. 1:9). Peter calls God a "faithful Creator" (I Pet. 4:19), and the writer of the book to the Hebrews says, "It is impossible for God to lie" (Heb. 6:18). Therefore, as puny mortals we can nonetheless be secure when we put our trust in a faithful God. His word is his bond. He speaks and is the truth, thereby proving his faithfulness and vindicating our trust.

But we mortals are a demanding lot. We not only need to trust and be trusted, we need to love and be loved. Not just to love and be loved by humans, but to love and be loved by God. The latter is a tall order. How does one go about loving a Spirit who is infinitely One, unchanging, and self-existent, perfect, eternal, immense, present everywhere, all-knowing, and all-powerful? One might just as well try to love the almost equally incomprehensible universe with its trillions of galaxies, planets, stars, and seemingly infinite distances. It may be possible to think one does love the universe, but how is one loved *by* the universe? Unless the universe reveals its love for us, we'll never know. God, however, *has* revealed his love for mankind. The Bible says, "This is love: not that we loved God, but that he loved us and sent his Son as an atoning sacrifice for our sins" (I John 4:10). Jesus said, "For God so loved the world that he gave his one and only Son, that whoever believes in him shall not perish but have eternal life" (I John 3:16). Both these Scriptures introduce the subject of sin and salvation. Suffice it to say that God loves us, keenly. For some reason he has a high view of us and has gone to extraordinary lengths to communicate his love. John puts it very bluntly, "God is love" (I John 4:8). He's approachable.

So when we approach the approaching God, we approach truth and love. Both are compelling qualities. Not so compelling, however, is God's third means of relating to humans: his holiness.

A few years ago I made a personal pilgrimage to Tekoa. Today it's a barren, windswept hill a few miles southeast of Bethlehem. In Bible times it was the home of Amos, perhaps the first prophet to record his prophecies in written form. I made this pilgrimage because I have for years been a great admirer of Amos and his insights. He was a shepherd and a fruit-picker. He protested against any suggestion that he had sought to be prophetic, claiming that he "was neither a prophet nor a prophet's son" (Amos 7:14). He was a reluctant spokesman. But he knew the Lord well enough to know when he was beaten: "The lion has roared—who will not fear? The Sovereign Lord has spoken—who can but prophesy?" (Amos 3:8). Leaving his sheep and figs behind for a short while, he walked up to the northern kingdom of Israel and spoke the word of the Lord to a fat and prosperous nation. King Amaziah was not pleased.

The powerful imagery and gripping content of Amos's message is worth a study in itself. For this discussion of holiness, however, let me focus on what I consider to be the ultimate distillation of Amos's words: "But let justice roll on like a river, righteousness like a never-failing stream!" (Amos 5:24).

Amos thunders these words after expressing the Lord's hatred of holy events, like religious feasts, assemblies, offerings, and hymns (verses 21–23). Why should God despise such holiness? Because it's not holiness at all. Holiness, in God's terms, is found in justice and righteousness.

Some theologians see righteousness as God's demand for moral perfection on our part, and justice as his judgment of imperfection. I prefer to look at it another way. First, let me list some Bible references for you: Job 29:12–16; Psalms 37:16, 21, 25–26; Proverbs 10:7, 12:10, 14:34, 16:8, 23:24. When you read these verses, you'll discover that a righteous man cared for the poor, the fatherless, and the widow, gave liberally, counted righteousness better than wealth, lived in peace with his neighbors, exalted the nation, was a joy to his family, and his very memory was a blessing. Here's another list: Psalms 5:7–12; 14:6; 36:7; 51:17; 52:6, 7; 69:6, 36; 71:5, 14; 94:12; 103:11, 13, 17; 143:8. All these verses from the Psalms describe a righteous man's view of God. He's a man who waits for God, hopes in God, seeks after God, trusts in God, fears God, and loves God. God is his fortress. In a world of spiritual and physical warfare, the Lord is his only refuge. Thus, he acknowledges his sin and his need. He offers God a broken spirit and a contrite heart. He turns to God in faith.

So how do I see righteousness and justice? This way. Both words come from the same Hebrew word *zadik*. This means that righteousness and justice are two expressions of the same idea. As you study the use of *zadik* in the Old Testament, you discover that it refers to the fulfillment of the demands of relationship. To the extent that a man fulfills those demands, in terms of man and in terms of God, he is declared *zadik*. As he fulfills the demands of his vertical relationship with God, he is righteous. As he fulfills the demands of his horizontal relationship with his neighbor, he is just. This is why Jesus himself said the bottom line of faith is not only the great Shema ("Hear, O Israel, the Lord our God, the Lord is one") but also love for God and love for neighbor (Mark 12:29–31). Holiness is lived in the context of relationships.

God is not interested in your personal piety. He's not impressed with the outward show of things. He is holy. And he wants us to be holy. How? By seeking to love and obey him and committing ourselves to seeking the highest good for our neighbor. This isn't easy, day in and day out. Holiness seems to be constantly challenging us to transformation. And transformation is never easy.

A summary is in order. What is God like? In terms of who he is: he is a spirit possessing life and personality. He is infinitely one, unchanging, and independent. He is perfect in truth, love, and holiness. In terms of how we see him, he is eternal and immense, omnipresent, omniknowledgeable, and omnipowerful. He is truth, love, and holiness.

Joe Burnham could never have described God in these terms. But he knew God and loved him. He also lived his love. I'll never forget the only time I ever saw him in church. It was for Rainer and Gilley Armstrong's funeral. Nine and six years old, they had drowned in a stagnant pool outside of town. After the service I saw a tentative Joe approach their grieving mother. As he touched her gently on the arm, I heard his hollow old voice say, "Don't cry, Mrs. Armstrong. Rainer and Gilley are with Father." Tears of joy suddenly welled in his old face, and he whispered, "They're where I want to be. And it's where I will be someday. With Father!"

CHAPTER 4

One Plus One Plus One Equals One

🌿 THE MAN blew bubbles for a living. Literally. Dressed immaculately in a tuxedo, he stood facing the BBC television cameras. His only props were a common plastic bottle of bubble soap, two bubble wands, a lit cigarette, and a glass drinking straw. He blew bubbles like you've never seen! Bubble chains. Bubble clusters. Bubble carousels. Bubbles within bubbles within bubbles. But his most astonishing feat was a bubble cube.

Before blowing the cube, he told us about a performance of his to a group of mathematics, engineering, and physics students at a university. "Is it possible for a bubble to be in the form of a cube?" he asked his audience.

"No way!" came the reply, "It won't work. Impossible. It's bad math."

"Well, I'll show you that sometimes your math is wrong," he said. He then proceeded to blow his amazing bubble cube.

Here's how he did it. First, using the two wands, he blew a cluster of six bubbles. Dipping the glass straw into the soap (so it wouldn't break the bubbles), he then inserted the straw into the cluster at the very point where the six bubbles converged. Then, inhaling a small amount of cigarette smoke, he blew through the straw. To our complete wonder a small, smoky cube appeared in the middle of the cluster! It was beautifully formed, with each of its six sides borrowed from a part of each of the six bubbles. To help you picture this unusual bubble, I've drawn a rough diagram.

The six bubbles suddenly became seven. And the seventh, unlike any other bubble in the world, was made up of six. It defied the bubble laws, yet was dependent on them at the same time. Remove any one of the six and the cube was no more. It was six but one. Or one but six. In its case, one plus one plus one plus one plus one plus one equaled one. Incredible but true. And very bad math. Sort of like the Trinity.

A writer once stated, "The doctrine of the Trinity is a contradiction in arithmetic." So it appears. Try to make mathematical sense out of this:

Whoever would be saved, must first of all take care that he hold the Catholic [that is, universal] faith, which, except a man preserve whole and inviolate, he shall without doubt perish eternally. But this is the Catholic faith, that we worship one God in trinity, and trinity in unity. Neither confounding the persons nor dividing the substance. For the person of the Father is one; of the Son, another; of the Holy Spirit, another. But the divinity of the Father, and of the Son, and of the Holy Spirit, is one, the glory equal, the majesty equal. Such as is the Father, such also is the Son, and such the Holy Spirit. The Father is uncreated, the Son is uncreated, the Holy Spirit is uncreated. The Father is infinite, the Son is infinite, the Holy Spirit is infinite. The Father is eternal, the Son is eternal, the Holy Spirit is eternal. And yet there are not three eternal Beings, but one eternal Being. As also there are not three uncreated Beings, nor three infinite Beings, but one uncreated and one infinite Being. In like manner, the Father is omnipotent [all powerful], the Son is omnipotent, and the Holy Spirit is omnipotent. And yet, there are not three omnipotent Beings, but one omnipotent Being. Thus the Father is God; the Son, God; and the Holy Spirit, God. And yet, there are not three Gods, but one God only. The Father is Lord; the Son, Lord; and the Holy Spirit, Lord. And yet there are not three Lords, but one Lord only. For as we are compelled by Christian truth to confess each person distinctively to be both God and Lord, we are prohibited by the Catholic religion to say that there are three Gods, or three Lords. The Father is made by none, nor created, nor begotten. The Son is from the Father alone, not made, not created, but begotten. The Holy Spirit is not created by the Father and the Son, nor begotten, but proceeds. Therefore, there is one Father, not three Fathers; one Son, not three Sons; one Holy Spirit, not three Holy Spirits. And in this trinity there is nothing prior or posterior, nothing greater or less, but all three persons are coeternal, and coequal to themselves. So that through all, as said above, both unity in trinity and trinity in unity is to be adored. Whoever would be saved, let him thus think concerning the trinity.*

Certainly doesn't seem to add up, does it? At least at first reading. Yet this creed has for fifteen hundred years been the Church's commonly accepted statement of doctrine about the Trinity. Which may be fine for theologians. But for the average person? Just a bit too complex, I think. Nevertheless, let's take a look at trinity and try to keep it simple.

First of all, the term *trinity* does not appear anywhere in the Bible. The idea is biblical (as we'll see later), but the word itself is never used by the biblical authors. So when we say there is one God in whom there are three coeternal and coequal persons, the same in substance but distinct in subsistence, we are using nonbiblical language. Indeed, in the Bible there is no evidence that the idea of trinity had emerged. Before you object, let me say the idea *is* there, in *solution,* but it took a few hundred years for it to be crystallized by the Church. Thus, when we read the Scripture we see the Trinity jumping out at us, but it's because we've

*The "Athanasian Creed," A.D. 5th century, quoted in Hodge's *Systematic Theology,* vol. I, part I, ch. 6.

inherited the fruit of centuries of arduous study and debate on the part of some of the best theologians who have ever lived. In the times of the apostles no trinity doctrine was being taught. They *were,* however, worshiping Father, Son, and Holy Spirit from the very depths of their hearts; and only time was necessary to see their threefold worship-focus justified and dogmatized.

So, after three or four centuries and a few Church councils, the trinitarian doctrine had been developed to the point where the Athanasian Creed (which you've just read) was composed and accepted by the Church. But its philosophical form was a far cry from the earlier simplicity of the apostles' generation. It had shifted from a simple subjective awareness of God on the part of the early Church to a complicated, metaphysical doctrine attempting to describe the very nature of God's inner life itself. This complicated, philosophical language underscores the fact that whenever there is communication between God and us, we stretch (sometimes too far), while he stoops.

God stoops because we are so limited. As we've seen in earlier chapters, God must limit himself in order to reveal some of himself to us. There is no doubt that a good deal of self-limitation on God's part was necessary to reveal just a hint of the complexity of his nature. Even the terms *Father* and *Son* are metaphorical. As for *Holy Spirit,* there would be no need for the adjective *holy* if God weren't revealing himself to an unholy world. But we don't learn anything about God unless he uncovers himself. Certainly, the doctrine of trinity is discovered not by reason, but by revelation. One old theologian suggested that reason shows us the unity of God and revelation shows us the Trinity of God. That's why analogies are not much help.

Analogies argue from reason. Not from revelation. Thus, every analogy one uses to "prove" the Trinity fails even before it begins. Trinitarian analogies are good only to a point, a very small point—they demonstrate that in the natural world there are examples of unity in diversity, or complex unities. Yet most theologians have used them—even such worthies as Martin Luther and St. Augustine.

Augustine used the analogy of the root, trunk, and branches of a tree; Luther, the form, fragrance, and medicinal effect of a flower. Someone used a candle—wax, wick, and flame. Someone else used water, steam, and ice. Then there are sunlight, rainbow, heat ("As the rainbow shows what light is unfolded, so Christ reveals the nature of God. As the rainbow is unraveled light, so Christ is unraveled God, and the Holy Spirit, figured by heat, is Christ's continued life"). There's a gaping flaw, however, in all of them. None of them addresses the revealed truth of tri-personality. The root of a tree does not have a separate personality from the trunk of a tree. Nor the trunk from the branches. The form and fragrance of a flower do not address themselves and each other as "I" and "you." Nor does water to steam, or sunlight to rainbow. So the best we can do with analogies is demonstrate the commonality of complex unities in everyday life. In my opinion, no one has done it better than C. S. Lewis. I'll let him speak for himself.

You know that in space you can move in three ways—to left or right, backwards or forwards, up or down. Every direction is either one of these three or a compromise between them. They are called the three dimensions. Now, notice this. If you are using only one dimension, you could draw only a straight line. If you are using two, you could draw a figure: say, a square. And a square is made up of four straight lines. Now a step further. If you have three dimensions, you can then build what we call a solid body: say, a cube—a thing like a dice or lump of sugar. And a cube is made up of six squares.

Do you see the point? A world of one dimension would be a straight line. In a two-dimensional world, you still get straight lines, but many lines make one figure. In a three-dimensional world, you still get figures but many figures make one solid body. In other words, as you advance to more real and complicated levels, you do not leave behind you the things you found on the simpler levels: you still have them, but combined in new ways—in ways you could not imagine if you knew only the simpler levels.

Now, the Christian account of God involves just the same principle. The human level is a simple and rather empty level. On the human level one person is one being, and any two persons are two separate beings—just as, in two dimensions (say on a flat sheet of paper), one square is one figure, and any two squares are two separate figures. On the Divine level you still find personalities; but up there you find them combined in new ways which we, who do not live on that level, cannot imagine. In God's dimension, so to speak, you find a being who is three Persons while remaining one Being, just as a cube is six squares while remaining one cube.*

"So what?" someone exclaims. "Why don't Christians forget about this murky area of the Trinity and stress the unity of God? After all it's the bedrock of Christianity, just like its parent, Judaism. Why all the fuss?" Well, forgive me for passing the buck, but you should ask Jesus. He started it.

It's a fact that no one who has focused solely on the Old Testament (in Judaism, for example) has ever come up with a doctrine of trinity. Until Jesus came on the scene no one had developed any complex-unity analogies about God's nature. Jesus, however, changed all that. His words and his deeds were charged with a Father, a Holy Spirit, and his own claims to deity. The early Church leaders (who initially were all Jewish) picked up on this, and their prayers and worship were similarly charged with Son, Father, and Holy Spirit. I say "Son, Father, and Holy Spirit" in that order purposely. Without question, Jesus dominated the thinking of the early believers. For instance, Paul in Second Corinthians concludes the letter by saying, "May the grace of the Lord Jesus Christ, and the love of God, and the fellowship of the Holy Spirit be with you all" (II Cor. 13:14). Paul was a monotheist, as were all in the Church. Doctrinally they were theocentric (God-centered). But in light of Jesus' resurrection and the outpouring of the Holy Spirit at Pentecost (Acts 2), their theology, historically, became Christocentric (Christ-centered).

Let's take a look at some of Jesus' words and deeds in the gospels of Matthew, Mark, and Luke (the synoptics, as theologians call them), and the Gospel of John. First, the synoptics.

Notice two aspects of Jesus' teaching and life. In the first

*C. S. Lewis, *Mere Christianity*, Collier Books, pp. 137–38.

place, Jesus claimed an exclusive sonship to God and a perfect mutual knowledge between himself and his Father (Matt. 11:27): "All things have been committed to me by my Father. No one knows the Son except the Father, and no one knows the Father except the Son and those to whom the Son chooses to reveal him" (compare Luke 10:22). In the second place, the term *Son of God* was used of Jesus and accepted by him without objection. It's interesting to note, by the way, that Satan and his angels were among those convinced of Jesus' sonship (Matt. 4:5–6): "Then the devil took him to the holy city and had him stand on the highest point of the temple. 'If you are the Son of God,' he said, 'throw yourself down.' " Then there is this passage from Matthew (8:28–29): "When he arrived at the other side in the region of the Gadarenes, two demon-possessed men coming from the tombs met him. They were so violent that no one could pass that way. 'What do you want with us, Son of God?' they shouted. 'Have you come here to torture us before the appointed time?' " (compare Mark 3:11 and Luke 4:41). Jesus' human enemies also called him Son of God: "And when the centurion, who stood there in front of Jesus, heard his cry and saw how he died, he said, 'Surely this man was the Son of God!' " (see also Matt. 27:40, 43, 54). So in terms of Jesus' own words and the testimony of his sworn enemies (both physical and spiritual), his relationship to God was utterly unique.

This unique sonship really comes through in John's gospel. Here are three of Jesus' own comments about himself: "I tell you the truth, a time is coming and has now come when the dead will hear the voice of the Son of God and those who hear will live" (John 5:25). "When he heard this, Jesus said, 'This sickness will not end in death. No, it is for God's glory so that God's Son may be glorified through it!' " (11:4). "What about the one whom the Father set apart as his very own and sent into the world? Why then do you accuse me of blasphemy because I said, 'I am God's Son'?" (10:36). In the Semitic culture of his day, Jesus' words had a powerful effect in polarizing his hearers. His peers believed a son was equal to his father. Indeed the son possessed what the father possessed and vice versa. Jesus himself said it: "All that belongs to the Father is mine . . ." and "All I have is yours [the Father's], and all you [the Father] have is mine . . ." (16:15; 17:10). Thus the animosity: "For this reason the Jews tried all the harder to kill him; not only was he breaking the Sabbath, but he was even calling God his own Father, making himself equal with God" (5:18). He became a target for assassination: " 'We are not stoning you for any of these,' replied the Jews, 'but for blasphemy, because you, a mere man, claim to be God' " (10:33). Jesus warned his disciples that even they would face hatred and persecution "because of my name" (15:21). And what was his name? Son of God.

Not only did Jesus declare himself God's Son, he also claimed he and the Father were one (John 10:30; compare 17:11, 21–22). What's more, he said to see him was to see God (14:9); and there was some kind of flowing identity, "the Father is in me, and I in the Father" (10:38), between the two. He said he shared God's glory (17:5) and God's attributes (in this case, eternality). " 'I tell you the truth,' Jesus answered, 'before Abraham was born, I am!' " (8:58; see also 6:62 and 17:5). Yet at the same time, he saw himself as personally distinct from his Father: "They knew with certainty that I came from you, and they believed that you sent me" (17:8). He described his presence on earth as coming both from the presence of God (16:30; 13:3) and from out of God himself (8:42; 16:28). In other words, at this point Jesus was confronting the world with a God who was at least a dyad (two persons) if not a triad (three persons).

The dyad, however, quickly became a triad—again, because of Jesus' teaching. In the conversation with his disciples during the Last Supper, he introduced the "counselor" to them by saying, "And I will ask the Father, and he will give you another Counselor to be with you forever—the Spirit of truth" (John 14:16–17). Jesus' choice of the adjective "another" suggests the counselor is distinct from Jesus—that is, both of them are distinct personalities. He then said, "The Counselor, the Holy Spirit, whom the Father will send in my name, will teach you all things and will remind you of everything I have said to you" (14:26). So this counselor is the Holy Spirit who is sent to Jesus' followers in his name by the Father. And these three personalities all share a common life. Jesus is the "truth" (see his own words in 14:6). The Holy Spirit is "the Spirit of truth" (14:17), suggesting that Jesus physically was what the Spirit is spiritually. And the Spirit "goes out from the Father" (15:26). Each of them, Father, Son, and Holy Spirit, is distinct, yet together they are one Lord. Frankly, my mind clouds at the idea. But to Jesus' mind it seemed perfectly clear.

Perhaps we should look briefly at some of what the Bible says about the personality factor in this third person of the Trinity, the Holy Spirit. First of all, as we've just seen, Jesus' comments about the Holy Spirit suggest personality. Second, the Bible presents the Holy Spirit as doing things that suggest personality—things like locking minds with mortals and telling people what to do. "Then the Lord said, 'My Spirit will not contend with man forever, for he is mortal' " (Gen. 6:3); "The Spirit told Philip, 'Go to that chariot and stay near it' " (Acts 8:29. If you would like to study a few more, look at Luke 12:12; John 16:8; Acts 2:4; 10:19–20; 13:2; 16:6–7; Rom. 8:26; I Cor. 2:10–11; and II Pet. 1:21). Third, the Holy Spirit is mentioned in some kind of intimate relationship with other persons, suggesting personality. For instance, we see him as partner with Jesus and counselor to the apostles: "He [the Spirit] will bring glory to me [Jesus] by taking from what is mine and making it known to you" (John 16:14); "It seemed good to the Holy Spirit and to us not to burden you with anything beyond the following requirements . . ." (Acts 15:28). Fourth, the Bible portrays the Holy Spirit as an emotive person affected by the acts of other persons: "Yet they rebelled and grieved his Holy Spirit. So he turned and became their enemy and he himself fought against them" (Isa. 63:10); "And do not grieve the Holy Spirit of God, with whom you were sealed for the day of redemption" (Eph. 4:30); "In the same way, the Spirit helps us in our weakness. We do not know what we ought to pray, but the Spirit himself intercedes for us with groans that words cannot express" (Rom. 8:26; see also Rom. 15:30 and Acts 5:3–9). The Holy Spirit empathizes with humans and, remarkably, it appears his feelings can be hurt (or "grieved"). One writer commented that selfishness can be angered, but only love can be grieved. Whichever way you put it, the Holy Spirit has an emotional nature. He's a person.

As I said earlier, if it weren't for Jesus, we wouldn't have a trinity controversy to deal with. It all began with him. But I also said the trinity doctrine is, in Scripture, "in solution." So where is it? Is it even hinted at in the Old Testament? Let's look.

If you were to open the Old Testament and study it cold, that is, without any New Testament knowledge or help from commentators, you would not discover the doctrine of trinity. No one ever has, and no one ever will. On the other hand, if you approach the Old Testament with New Testament exposure, you will discover several things that imply trinity. The first thing you will notice is the plural nouns, pronouns, and verbs used for God.

In the very first verse of the Bible, the third word (in Hebrew) is *elohim*. It means "God." And it is plural. Genesis doesn't say why the word is plural, it just is. What's more, there are several instances where plural pronouns are used by God when speaking of himself: "Then God said, 'Let us make man in our image, in our likeness . . .' " (Gen. 1:26); "And the Lord God said . . . 'Come, let us go down' " (Gen. 11:6–7); "Then I heard the voice of the Lord saying, 'Whom shall I send? And who will go for us?' " (Isa. 6:8). These plural nouns and pronouns aren't alone. Sometimes even plural verbs are used. They don't surface in the English translations, but in the Hebrew they are there. (If you have a Hebrew Bible and can read Hebrew, take a look at Gen. 20:13 and 35:7.) And then there are the very curious distinctions in the Bible between God and God.

Here are two of those strange references: first, in one of David's psalms, he says, "The Lord says to my Lord . . ."(Ps. 110:1); and in the book of Hosea, the Lord says, "Yet I will show love to the house of Judah; and I will save them—not by bow, sword or battle, or by horses and horsemen, but by the Lord their

God" (Hos. 1:7). The implication of these Scriptures is that there is some kind of interchange between persons within the one God.

This suggestion of plurality makes something jump out at you that otherwise might have no impact: the threefold liturgical formulas in the Old Testament. Here are two: "The Lord bless you and keep you; the Lord make his face shine upon you and be gracious to you; the Lord turn his face toward you and give you peace" (Num. 6:24–26); "Holy, holy, holy is the Lord Almighty; the whole earth is full of his glory" (Isa. 6:3). In the context of the Old Testament alone, these three *Lord*s and *Holy*s have little significance. But in the light of the New Testament, they take on special meaning.

Without question, however, the most fascinating suggestion of plural personality in the Old Testament is the mysterious angel of the Lord. Both Moses and Samson's parents, were participants in two of the many appearances of this unusual person. The appearance to Moses occurred on the occasion of the burning bush in the third chapter of Exodus. "Now Moses was tending the flock of Jethro his father-in-law, the priest of Midian, and he led the flock to the far side of the desert and came to Horeb, the mountain of God. There the angel of the Lord appeared to him in flames of fire from within a bush. Moses saw that though the bush was on fire it did not burn up. So Moses thought, 'I will go over and see this strange sight—why the bush does not burn up.' When the Lord saw that he had gone over to look, God called to him from within the bush, 'Moses, Moses!' And Moses said, 'Here I am!' 'Do not come any closer,' God said. 'Take off your sandals, for the place where you are standing is holy ground.' Then he said, 'I am the God of your father, the God of Abraham, the God of Isaac, and the God of Jacob.' At this, Moses hid his face, because he was afraid to look at God" (Exod. 3:1–6). The fascinating and puzzling thing about this account is the shift, without explanation, from the "angel of the Lord" (verse 2) to "I am the God of your father" (verse 6). It's the same person, but the titles seem interchangeable. God is the angel of the Lord and vice versa. It's as though the angel of the Lord were God's self-manifestation in Old Testament times. This certainly was how Samson's parents saw it.

The story of Israel's infamous strongman is recorded in Judges, 13 through 16. Samson was a hero of almost mythic proportions. He was made for great exploits. Not surprisingly, there was divine intervention throughout his life, even before he was born. In chapter 13 we read how his mother-to-be was sterile. But "The angel of the Lord appeared to her and said, 'You are sterile and childless, but you are going to conceive and have a Son' " (verse 3). Her husband, Manoah, after hearing the report of this amazing event, prayed that God would teach them how to raise the boy. The Bible says, "God heard Manoah, and the angel of God came again" (verse 9). After receiving the requested information from the angel, Manoah asked him his name (he thought the angel was a man). The angel replied, "Why do you ask my name? It is beyond understanding" (verse 18). At this point Manoah had no idea with whom he was dealing. In gratitude he prepared a sacrifice—and here the story becomes fascinating: "The Lord did an amazing thing while Manoah and his wife watched: As the flame blazed up from the altar toward heaven, the angel of the Lord ascended in the flame. Seeing this, Manoah and his wife fell with their faces to the ground. When the angel of the Lord did not show himself again to Manoah and his wife [he had disappeared], Manoah realized that it was the angel of the Lord. 'We are doomed to die!' he said to his wife. 'We have seen God' " (verses 19–21). In Manoah's thinking the angel of the Lord and God were the same person. So in the case of the burning bush, we have the angel of the Lord saying he is God; in the case of Samson's prenatal days, we have Manoah saying the angel of the Lord is God. Remarkable! An angel who sometimes looks like a man, talks to people, appears and disappears in flames, and says he is God. Little wonder some later New Testament theologians saw this angel as the Son of God.

Speaking of the Son of God, a very interesting implication of plurality (if not trinity) within God's nature is found in Isaiah's writings about the Messiah. "Therefore the Lord himself will give you a sign: The virgin will be with child and will give birth to a son, and will call him Immanuel," which means "God with us" (Isa. 7:14); "For to us a child is born, to us a Son is given, and the government will be upon his shoulders. And he will be called Wonderful, Counselor, Mighty God, Everlasting Father, Prince of Peace" (Isa. 9:6). Living here in Jerusalem, I am very aware of the great difficulty observant Jews have with the Christian teaching of God becoming man. "If God became man, even for a moment," one Jewish friend of mine commented, "the universe would be without an all-present God. How can God be eternal king and a baby in Bethlehem at the same time?" Good question. I can't answer it. Nevertheless, the Jewish Bible unapologetically speaks of a human son called "God with us," a child with "shoulders," called "Wonderful Counselor, Mighty God, Everlasting Father, Prince of Peace." Isaiah apparently had no problem with the idea of God becoming man. And, by extension, no problem with a God with multiple personalities.

The implications of trinity in the Old Testament, then, are more accurately implications of plurality. Plurality of personality. We see it in the plural form of God's name, in plural pronouns used by God about himself, and in plural verbs used of him. We see it in the distinctions made between God and God. We see it in the threefold liturgical formulas. We see it in the enigmatic angel of the Lord. And we see it in the deification of Messiah. We don't see trinity, but we do see, at least, that the God of the Old Testament is not a simple monad. There's more to him than meets the eye.

So trinity *is* hinted at in the Old Testament. What about the New Testament? As I've already pointed out, neither the word nor the doctrine of trinity appears anywhere in the New Testament. Like the Old Testament, it's there, but in solution. Before we crystallize it, I want to make a few general observations.

First of all, trinity is presupposed in the New Testament. It's presupposed not because of any word on the subject, but because of Jesus' life, death, resurrection, and ascension. The incarnation of God the Son and the outpouring of the Holy Spirit require a view, like Isaiah's, of a multipersonal God. In the New Testament God is One, yet Jesus Christ and the Holy Spirit are each fully God. Significantly, Father, Son, and Holy Spirit relate to each other as persons. There's an "I, you, he" interplay between the three, yet they are one. What fascinates me is that the New Testament authors, in spite of their presentation of Father, Son, and Holy Spirit, seem blissfully unaware of being "setters forth of strange gods." They don't create two new gods and place them on the right and left hands of Israel's God. Rather, they worship the one God of Israel and view him as Father, Son, and Holy Spirit. And they show no sign of second thoughts.

As you might expect, the crystallization of trinity in the New Testament requires an examination of Jesus. For our purposes we need look only at Jesus' conception, baptism, transfiguration, crucifixion, and resurrection. In each milestone experience of his life, we see an interplay of persons within the one God of Israel. The Scriptures speak for themselves: "The angel answered, 'The Holy Spirit will come upon you, and the power of the Most High will overshadow you. So the holy one to be born will be called the Son of God' " (Luke 1:35); "As soon as Jesus was baptized, he went up out of the water. At that moment heaven was opened, and he saw the Spirit of God descending like a dove and lighting on him. And a voice from heaven said, 'This is my Son, whom I love; with him I am well pleased' " (Matt. 3:16–17); "While he was still speaking, a bright cloud enveloped them, and a voice from the cloud said, 'This is my Son, whom I love; with him I am well pleased. Listen to him!' " (Matt. 17:5); "Now my heart is troubled, and what shall I say? 'Father, save me from this hour?' No, it was for this very reason I came to this hour. Father, glorify your name! Then a voice came from heaven, 'I have glorified it and will glorify it again.' The crowd that was there and heard it said it had thundered; others said an angel had spoken to him" (John 12:27–29). At his conception we see the Holy Spirit, the Most High, and the Son of God. At his baptism, Jesus, the Spirit of God, and a voice from heaven. At his transfiguration, a bright cloud, a voice from the cloud, and the Son. Just prior to his crucifixion, Jesus and a voice from heaven. And after his resurrection, we have the astonishing words of Jesus himself in what has become known as the Great Commission.

Here it is: "Then Jesus came to them and said, 'All authority in heaven and on earth has been given to me. Therefore go and make disciples of all nations, baptizing them in [or into] the name of the Father and of the Son and of the Holy Spirit, and teaching them to obey everything I have commanded you. And surely I will be with you always, to the very end of the age' " (Matt. 28:18–20). Why is this astonishing? Because of the name Jesus gives to God.

Look at the name. The name is, "of the Father and of the Son and of the Holy Spirit." Long name! Notice he doesn't say, "in the names of," nor does he say, "in the name of the Father, and in the name of the Son, and in the name of the Holy Spirit," as if they were three gods. Nor does he designate a single person by saying "in the name of Father, Son, and Holy Spirit." Rather, he combines all three within the parameters of a single name, and at the same time underscores the personal distinctiveness of each by repeating *of the*.

Judaism in Jesus' day was no different from today when it comes to the name of God. I was at a Sabbath service in a local Jerusalem synagogue recently, and as we read the Hebrew Bible together, we pronounced the name Adonai (Lord) every time we came to the written name YHWH, the reason being that in Judaism the name of God expresses and involves the very being of God. To pronounce the name YHWH is to encounter and be enveloped by the presence of God. No man can do this and live. This is why Jesus' command to his disciples to baptize "into the name" had terribly significant meaning. Instead of substituting *Adonai* for *YHWH*, he was substituting "of the Father and of the Son and of the Holy Spirit." This must have meant that YHWH was now to be called by a new name. Otherwise it would have meant that Jesus was introducing a new God. But to Jesus, the foundation of truth was, "Hear, O Israel, the Lord our God, the Lord is one" (Mark 12:29).

So the God with the long name had a job to do. He wanted to save man from his sin. He wanted to restore man to fellowship with his creator. How to do it? If man couldn't live if he even pronounced God's name, how could he survive an encounter with God himself? There was only one solution: God must become man, dwell among us, and show us the way to the Father—the ultimate self-limitation. You might call it stooping as low as you can go. Thus, God the Son became man. And this Son, as man, said, "The Father is greater than I" (John 14:28). He also said, "By myself I can do nothing" (5:30). This doesn't mean Father and Son were not equal. What it *does* mean is the Son was in "the days of his flesh." God had limited his own person as Son, and during that period the Son was dependent upon Father and Spirit for power. Rather like us when, for a period of time, a broken limb or some other afflicted part of our body is dependent on our heart and strength of will for power and healing. The fact that a broken leg is dependent for a time doesn't make it any less a part of the body. Similarly, Jesus' limitation on earth made him no less God. On one occasion he said, "Moreover, the Father judges no one, but has entrusted all judgment to the Son, that all may honor the Son just as they honor the Father. He who does not honor the Son does not honor the Father, who sent him" (John 5:22–23). His disciples got the point, eventually. John, in his first letter (2:22–23), said, "Who is the liar? It is the man who denies that Jesus is the Christ. Such a man is the antichrist—he denies the Father and the Son. No one who denies the Son has the Father; whoever acknowledges the Son has the Father also" (2:22–23). In the context of his plan for saving man, God put Father first, Son second, and Spirit third. And this is completely consistent with equality. After all, priority doesn't mean superiority.

As I said above, crystallizing trinity in the New Testament involves examining Jesus. So far we've examined some of the milestones in his life. We've looked at the Great Commission and its remarkable new name for God. And we've discussed Jesus'

equality with Father and Holy Spirit. There's just one more
aspect of his life I want to explore: his eternality.

The very first verses of John's gospel speak about Jesus'
eternal existence with the Father. John uses a Greek word for
Jesus that translates into the English *Word.* "In the beginning was
the Word, and the Word was with God, and the Word was God.
He was with God in the beginning" (John 1:1–2). We know John
means Jesus when he uses *Word* because a little later he says, "The
Word became flesh and lived for a while among us. We have seen
his glory, the glory of the one and only Son, who came from
the Father, full of grace and truth" (1:14). John goes on to
emphasize Jesus' eternality by stating, "No one has ever seen God,
but God the only Son, who is at the Father's side, has made him
known"(1:18). He even says that the world was created by Christ.
"Through him all things were made; without him nothing was
made that has been made" (1:3). Jesus himself speaks of his
eternality by praying, "And now, Father, glorify me in your
presence with the glory I had with you before the world began"
(17:5). What this does, of course, is further emphasize the multiple personality of God. Only God is eternal. If the Son is eternal,
he too must be God. Like I said, this whole trinity discussion
began with Jesus.

As you might suspect, this fuss over trinity has led some
people to adopt incorrect, or heretical, views. Generally, there
have been two classic misrepresentations. These emerged in the
first few centuries of Church history. One is called Sabellianism,
the other, Arianism. If you want to study them in detail you can
look up Sabellius and Arius in a dictionary of Church history.
Their respective errors, however, are simply put. Sabellius could
not accept tri-personality. He saw Son and Spirit, as mere modes
of God's expressing himself. God was Father. Sometimes, for our
benefit, he appeared as Son or as Spirit. But there was no "I, you,
he" interplay between them. Arius, on the other hand, could not
accept the eternality of the Son and Spirit. Logic told Arius that
a son must be younger than his father. Jesus was God only because

the Father made him so. But he was a God whose existence had a beginning and therefore could come to an end. Martin Luther used one Scripture to expose the error of both heresies. He alluded to John 1:1 and said, " 'The Word was God' is against Arius; 'the Word was with God' is against Sabellius."

I was a Sabellian for years and didn't know it. I used to use the analogy of my being a father, a son, and a husband to explain the Trinity. To my children, I'm father. To my parents, I'm son. To my wife, I'm husband. I thought this effectively demonstrated the possibility of the existence of trinity. But it doesn't. Like Sabellianism it does not include tri-personality. The father in me does not address the son. Nor the son the husband. My triple identity is relative. It all depends on who is relating to me. As for me, I'm only one person, not three. Many cults, of course, are Arian. In fact, it's difficult to find any cult that does not represent Jesus as a created being—he may be a great teacher, great leader, great son, but not God.

To wrap up, let's get back to bad math. I've entitled this chapter, "One Plus One Plus One Equals One." My daughter Kate, who's in grade two, read the title on the manuscript and said, "Daddy! Don't you know how to add?" I hemmed and hawed, and fortunately at that point one of her friends came calling. Certainly my math would be more than bad—it would be heretical—if it meant that God was three in the same numerical sense that he is one. What I'm saying is that the one God of Israel is three internally. I'm not saying he is three gods, nor that one person is three persons. Nor am I saying three gods are one god. Rather, I'm saying there is one God with three distinctions in his being. His name is the key. His name is "of the Father and of the Son and of the Holy Spirit." What's in a name? Everything, and *every one.*

PART III

The Decrees and Works of God

CHAPTER 5

His Mind Is Made Up

❧ PRESIDENT REAGAN had just been shot. I sat staring dumbly at the television replays. Reagan exits from building. Crowds of security men and journalists surge around him. He's smiling. Waves to the crowd. Walks to the limousine. Even as he raises his hand for a final wave, a young man darts out of the crowd. Shots are fired. Reagan falls, or rather is pushed into the car's open door. One of his aides lies severely wounded, face down on the ground. The next few moments are a blur of screaming, shouting, and chaos. Then the TV announcer says the president is being rushed to the hospital. One's mind flashes back to a sunny day in Dallas, November 22, 1963, President Kennedy assassinated. Now Reagan? The jarring jangle of the phone jolts me back to the present.

"Hello?"

"Hello, Pastor?" a broken, weeping voice whispers.

"Yes," I answer, a stab of "What now?" slicing my throat.

"Can you come over to the hospital right away? Artie Allison's been killed!"

"What now?" How often have I felt the sudden anxiety of these words. The tragedies of the answer live with me still.

Walking a cold hall to a morgue where a mother and father bend over the body of a twelve-year-old daughter hit by a car. Driving on a windswept winter's day to a secluded farm where an elderly couple's twenty-two-year-old son lies in a rotting barn, his tortured brain blown away with his own gun. Huddling around a small, rain-soaked hole committing the body of a three-day-old baby to the ground—her parents childless for fourteen years, burying their only hope. Their dreams and answered prayer lifeless in a tiny casket. "The Lord giveth and the Lord taketh away. Blessed be the name of the Lord." Really? Sometimes the words stick in the throat.

At the hospital, I asked the grieving widow and daughter for permission to be alone for a moment with Artie. He was one of those sixty-five-year-olds who looked fifty and acted forty. "Healthy as a horse, Pastor," he reported proudly to me after his last checkup. Now as I touched his cold hand, I groaned at the vulnerability of life. Just forty minutes ago, about the time President Reagan was shot, Artie had climbed a tree to trim a few branches. A branch broke, and he fell to the ground. At the very moment of impact, his doctors later theorized, his heart pumped. The combined pressure of the heartbeat and the jolt of the fall was too much for his aorta. The artery burst, and his life fled. What an irony. Who of us, if given the choice, would choose being shot rather than falling out of a tree. Not one. But the fact is, Artie died. Reagan lived. The crack of a branch was more lethal than the crack of a gun.

"The Lord giveth and the Lord taketh away. Blessed be the name of the Lord," said Job, a man who had lost everything (Job 1:21). And countless believers down the centuries have said much the same in the face of tragedy. Of course many others, like Job's wife, have reacted with, "Curse God and die!" But whether we bless or curse God for our sorrows, in either case we acknowledge him. Animals don't. They live in a world of hardship, violence, and sudden loss, accepting it all with stoic reserve, blaming no God for their troubles. Not us. We intuitively believe there is rhyme and reason in the universe. If we didn't, we wouldn't feel unfairly or unjustly singled out when tragedy strikes. Nor would we bless or curse. The rhyme, the reason, are there because there's a mind behind it all. (We've already looked at this in a former chapter). But we strongly disagree, sometimes, with what that mind has planned. There appears to be so much that's unfair, unjust, and unloving in the world. If there *is* a plan it seems to be out of whack. Indeed, God seems to have lost control.

Nevertheless, there is a plan (perhaps I should capitalize it, Plan). The Bible says so. It uses several intimidating words to present the Plan. Theologians love them! Words like *foreknowledge, foreordination* or *predestination,* and *election.* And the big word, in terms of making the Plan work, is *sovereignty.* I'll define these words later. Before we look at several Biblical references to them, however, I must remind you of something I've stressed in preceding chapters. Whenever we talk of God, we stretch. We try desperately to get airborne. We stand on tiptoe, while God stoops. In trying to understand foreknowledge, for instance, we're like blind men who can be seen by others but who can't see themselves. Even though we're blind, we're living in a world of timeless sight. We do the groping. God does the seeing. We're on earth. He's in heaven. And there's a "great gulf fixed" between the two. In spite of this, the Bible encourages us to reach out and up.

The focus of our unfocused eyes is the Bible. Here is some of what it says about the Plan of God. You may not like all you read.

I make known the end from the beginning,
from ancient times, what is still to come.
I say: My purpose will stand,
and I will do all that I please.
From the east I summon a bird of prey;
from a far-off land, a man to fulfill my purpose.
What I have said, that will I bring about;
what I have planned, that will I do. (Isa. 46:10–11)

Forget intimidating words for the moment. How about intimidating statements? These two verses appear blatantly belligerent. If you or I were to say such things, our friends would react, and rightly so, with, "Who do you think you are? God or something?"

Here's another example:

> All the peoples of the earth are regarded as nothing.
> He does as he pleases with the powers of heaven
> and the peoples of the earth.
> No one can hold back his hand
> or say to him: "What have you done?" (Dan. 4:35)

Never mind that these words were uttered by a chastened and humbled king with the ungainly name of Nebuchadnezzar. The point is that God is unchallengeable. He does what he pleases. Nobody can stop him. He knows and makes known "the end from the beginning" and "what is still to come." Past is the same as future to him. So what to us is an act in the past is a present act to him. What is yet to be is a present fact to him. He lives in the eternal now. Being all-powerful he "does what he pleases with the powers of heaven and the peoples of earth." Just by speaking he makes things happen: "What I have said, that will I bring about." What he plans he does.

And he has a strange sense of humor. We expect his Plan to be consistent with our perceptions and assessments of fairness, justice, and religious purity. But no. What does he say? "I will call them 'my people' who are not my people; and I will call her 'my loved one' who is not my loved one" (Hos. 2:23, quoted in Rom. 9:25).

He keeps reversing field on us. In working his Plan, he uses "heathen" kings from Persia (the bird of prey in Isaiah 46 and the "man to fulfill my purpose" are references to King Cyrus) and Egypt ("For the scripture says to Pharaoh, 'I raised you up for this very purpose'" [Exod. 9:16, quoted in Rom. 9:17]). And as we've just seen, he even uses a Babylonian king to declare what, by rights, some Israelite prophet should be saying (Dan. 4:35).

So while you and I make feeble attempts to get airborne, we're swept off our feet by the blast of God's godness. With our little personal histories, needs, and aspirations, we're like specks of dust caught in the vortex of a universal tornado. Whirling beside us are Hebrew prophets, heathen kings, good men, bad men, and the debris of human glories. Rather depressing. Except . . .

Except that in the midst of all this God has taken the initiative to reach out to us. He has revealed some of himself. Not a lot, mind you. Just enough to give us hope. And hope, for humans, is the first blush of eternal spring.

Before we go any further looking at God's Plan, let me tell you about my plan for the rest of this chapter. First, I'm going to pry into the mystery of God's foreknowledge. Tough subject, but vital. In the course of this I'll look at foreordination (or predestination) and election. And as you read, questions will occur to you. Objections, too. You'll wonder how God's Plan relates to free will and fate. You might even object that if God's Plan is so comprehensive, then it makes him the author of sin. I'll try to help you gain some perspective on these reactions. Then, in conclusion, I'll give you an overview of God's sovereignty.

One more thing before starting. No one knows God's Plan completely. Our knowledge is severely limited. If it's any consolation, the "rulers and authorities in the heavenly realms" (Eph. 3:10–11) don't know much, either. We're all in the same boat, a crude craft plying the waters of a darkened lagoon. So don't expect easy sailing.

Foreknowledge simply means to know in advance. There's a two-pronged implication here. It means to know in advance of the event, and in advance of man's knowledge of the event. And there's a complication here, too. God has foreknowledge only in terms of our perception of him. It's *fore* knowledge to us, *knowl-*

ledge to him. For as we've already seen, he lives in the eternal now. Future events are as certain to him as past events are certain to us. You might say he lives at the speed of light, where past and future have no existence. Everything is now.

One of David's psalms expresses his wonder at God's foreknowledge:

> O Lord, you have searched me and you know me.
> You know when I sit and when I rise;
> You perceive my thoughts from afar.
> You discern my going out and my lying down;
> You are familiar with all my ways.
> Before a word is on my tongue
> you know it completely, O Lord.
> You hem me in—behind and before;
> You have laid your hand upon me. (Ps. 139:1–5)

"You hem me in," says King David," behind and before." God's presence not only fills heaven and earth (remember *omnipresence?*), but he also fills past, present, and future—not *his* past, present, and future, mind you, for he has none; rather the past, present, and future of the universe and its created inhabitants. Because of this there is no uncertainty for him, nothing unexpected, no surprises. He lives in the *certain present* (certain as in for sure). So in terms of our past and present we humans have and create a history. In terms of the overall (including future) we have a destiny. But in the context of God's foreknowledge (in his certain present) we have a predestiny. You might say, to use an equation, that foreknowledge plus certainty equals predestination: $F + C = P$.

More about predestination in a moment. For now, let me summarize the preceding paragraph by drawing a diagram. If you're like me, you probably dislike diagrams. Sometimes they're more confusing than helpful. But, we've had a pretty heavy go these last few pages. Your eyes and mind need a break, if not a change of pace. So here goes.

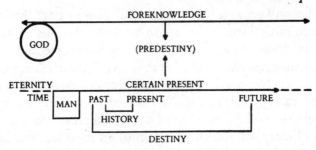

OK. So here's predestination. It has a lot to do with God's certain present. From his perspective, what is, is. There's no past or future about it. In fact, even the word *present,* if not unnecessary, is at most a relative term. What is, is. But from our point of view (locked in space and time), we use the past tense and say, "What is has been determined." Or, "it's been predestined." There are several implications. Before the implications, however, I want to give you a biblical example. Let's look at Jesus.

As you read the New Testament, it becomes very clear that Jesus' life is seen as a fulfillment of God's Plan. And is seen as you'll see, the New Testament has a high view of the Plan's spokesmen, the prophets. Paul speaks of "the gospel he [God] promised beforehand through his prophets in the Holy Scriptures regarding his Son" (Rom. 1:2–3a). There are plenty of other references. Matthew speaks of Jesus' birth this way: "All this took place to fulfill what the Lord had said through the prophet"; " 'In Bethlehem in Judea,' they replied, 'for this is what the prophet has written' "; "And so was fulfilled what the Lord had said through the prophet"; "Then what was said through the prophet Jeremiah was fulfilled" (Matt. 1:22–23; 2:5–6, 15, 17). During the events preceding his death, Jesus himself says that "the Son of Man must suffer many things and be rejected by the elders, chief priests and teachers of the law, and . . . must be killed and after three days rise again" (Mark 8:31). Notice the word *must*—there's an agenda to be filled. At the Last Supper Jesus says, "The Son of Man will go, as it has been decreed" (Luke 22:22). And in the Garden of Gethsemane he says to his sleepy disciples, "The hour is near" (Matt. 26:45). His approaching death upset him, "Now my heart is troubled, and what shall I say? 'Father, save me from this hour?' No, it was for this very reason I came to this hour" (John 12:27). (Fascinating. "I *came* to this hour." As if Jesus traveled from the dimension of the certain present to the dimension of space and time with a destination in mind, "this hour.") The disciple Peter sees Jesus' betrayal and crucifixion as the result of "God's set purpose and foreknowledge" (Acts 2:23). And in one of the first recorded public prayers of the early Church, the conspiracy against "your holy servant Jesus" is interpreted this way: "They did what your power and will had decided beforehand should happen" (Acts 4:27–28). (There's that past tense again.) Peter gives an overview of Jesus, "He was chosen before the creation of the world, but was revealed in these last times for your sake" (I Pet. 1:20). There are so many more Scriptures, but you've seen enough here to get the point. Jesus came to earth because God the Father planned it. His knowledge of the certain present demanded it. The birth in Bethlehem, the death at Calvary, and everything in between and after, were predestined. F + C = P.

Now to some of the implications. F + C = P means, first of all, that we're usually boggled by it all. There are moments, like now, when you focus in on the subject and begin to come to grips intellectually with foreknowledge and predestination. But out there where life goes on, it's very hard at best, awkward at worst, to make theological sense out of a man falling out of a tree to his death and a president getting shot and surviving. Our fickle present overwhelms any "certain present." And when someone, like me, tries to relate the two, it grates. It's much more palatable to say, "God ceased to exist at Auschwitz," than to say, "The Lord giveth and the Lord taketh away. Blessed be the name of the Lord." Simpler, too. It has an unboggled clarity.

F + C = P also means there's a determiner, a predestinator, a personality behind our fickle present. Not fate. More of this later. For the moment I'll just say there's a huge difference between fate and God. The difference? In a word, personality. Fate has no personality, no mind, no feelings. On the other hand, God is a person who knows and who determines. He has priority. His decisions precede ours. But they don't cause ours. It's just that he has the inside track. He knows what we'll decide before we do, and he orders things, or plans, accordingly.

Third, F + C = P means we're catching up, in more ways than one. There's a lot going on in the universe. Much more than our own feeble development. So we're catching up, or at least trying to keep pace, with God's Plan for a universe (on a grand scale) and a few billions of people (on a "small" scale). We're also catching up with our destiny. In one sense our destiny is a present unfolding. But in another sense our destiny has already been determined. So we are engaged in the past tense becoming present tense. What about the future tense? Well, I suppose we'll keep catching up until we're caught up.

Now for another theological word the Bible uses in presenting the Plan of God. The word is *election*. Basically it means that those who one day are caught up to God's certain present will be those whom God "elects" or "chooses" to be his eternal children. A bit confusing, no? Confusion of "the chicken or the egg" variety. Which comes first? Predestination or election? If we look at it from the eternal perspective, neither comes first. They just are. From our space and time vantage point, however, I think the only possible answer is that they are simultaneous. In predestining us to be his children ("adoption," says the Bible), God chooses us. Or in choosing us, he predestines us. So what's the difference? Frankly, I don't know. Let me appeal to Scripture. Then *you* decide. "For he chose us in him before the creation of the world . . . In love he predestined us to be adopted as his sons . . . in accordance with his pleasure and will"(Eph. 1:4–5). The only variable factor here seems to be God's "pleasure and will." He does what he pleases. Indeed, his elect ones are caught up because his mind is made up.

Perhaps the only difference between election and predestination as they relate to us is that election may be generic and predestination specific. Huh? How's that again? Well, generic is inclusive, specific is exclusive. Uh huh. Let's put it this way: Election determines the extent of God's family, predestination determines the course each member will take. In other words, election is the content and predestination the style of God's Plan for us. Questions, please.

"If God's mind is made up on who his family is and the route each one will take, what's the point of making any effort to be good or whatever?" someone asks.

"Forget apathy, what about fate?" another objects.

"You guys are missing the real question. How does God's Plan relate to my free will?" yet another questions.

"Oh, no you don't. There's a bigger question still," says another. "If God's mind is made up, and the world, which is in his hands, is full of sin, well, doesn't that make him the author of sin?"

There you have it—classic questions all. Questions focusing on apathy, fate, free will, and sin. And rightly so. These questions deserve answers. The question now is, Can I answer them? Let's give it a go.

Apathy asks, Why try? Maybe it's God's Plan for me to do nothing, to be a bum. But isn't doing nothing doing something? We're all doing something if we're alive, even if it's nothing. And nothing brings its consequences. Suppose as a passenger on a 747 aircraft you were to refuse to fasten your seat belt in turbulence as a protest because you were being flown to a destination by forces beyond your control. "What will be will be," you say, as you refuse to secure your seat belt. For sure. Including one potentially creased pate. The apathy stance sees the end as independent of the means. The plane will reach London, and so will I; I can do nothing about it. Therefore I'll do nothing. But suppose a terrorist bomb is discovered beneath the seat in front of you. Everyone else moves away, except you. The bomb explodes, punching a hole in the side of the plane. You're sucked out and fall to a cold Atlantic grave. The plane limps to London.

You swim with the fishes. Why? Because you made a fund
tal error. You assumed that God determines his ends without
reference to the means, whereas the opposite is true. In his certain
present, God determines the ends in accordance with the means.
Ends and means are always connected. So maybe my making this
fundamental error was God's means for getting me to free-fall
into the Atlantic? No. He simply foreknew that your fatalistic
obtuseness would make you fish-food. You lose. So much for
apathy, now fate.

Fate says everything happens via a blind and certain necessity.
Fate and Plan are similar in terms of the certainty of events. But
they differ greatly in every other way. I've already pointed out
the lack of personality in fate. Fate has no mind. No feelings. No
moral ideals, ideas, or ends. God's Plan, on the other hand,
because it is an expression of God's will, is also an expression of
personality, mind, and feeling. Not only does the Plan have moral
ideals, ideas, and ends, it makes them into vital law. Thus, the
Plan makes a place for reward and punishment. The Plan is just.
Fate is unjust and totally unreliable. In fact the only dream for
those who believe in fate is escape. Their bondage is blind, utterly
untouchable, and unreasonable. There's no love, no goodness, no
hope. The Plan, however, cries out lovingly to man, "Come. Let
us reason together." And the most profound words ever uttered
with regard to God's Plan for man begin with the words, "For
God so loved the world . . ." (John 3:16). This is a love song.
Fate never sings.

Free will. What is it? Some think it's the freedom to do
whatever you want to do. Perhaps. Until you want to fly without
wings or breathe underwater without an air hose. Free will is
choice within boundaries. Better yet, it's self-determination by
universal ideals—love for God and love for neighbor. These
ideals have a boundless character. One might even say that the
only way to be boundless, the only way to explore the outer
reaches of freedom, is in the act of loving. Nevertheless, the
objection is put forward: a set plan and free will cannot coexist.
How can we be free if God foreknows the choice we will make?

How indeed? The fact God knows our choice in advance has no relevance to our free choices. He won't make our choices for us. But his Plan includes the certainty of the decisions we do make. Let me illustrate.

A nickel is larger in size than a dime. Find yourself a nickel, a dime, and a one-and-a-half-year-old boy or girl. Your plan is to demonstrate that a child's decision is based on size rather than purchasing power. You offer in your open palm a nickel and a dime to the child. He makes the choice. He chooses the nickel because it's more attractive. His motive? To put it in his mouth. He has no motive to purchase or save. By knowing his motive we can predict his action, but our certainty of what that action will be in no way affects his freedom to choose. Our plan does not say, "The child *must* choose the nickel." Rather, it says, "The child *will* choose the nickel." Are we then "tempting" the child? From his perspective we may be, because he has an appetite for shiny, bright things. From our perspective we're not. We're merely demonstrating his freedom to choose and the predictability of his choice. Does this make the child a laboratory experiment? From his perspective, no. He has no critical faculties developed to the point of even framing the question. He is dominated by his appetite. He asks no larger question than, "What will please me now?" From our perspective, yes—if he's merely an experiment. No, if he's our son, whom we love. Then the experiment becomes part of the nurturing, loving process. As his mind, body, and spirit mature in the context of that nurturing, there will come a day, if not in his youth then in his elder days, when the mind of the child will meet the mind of the parent, and there will be understanding.

As in the question of fate, so in the question of free will: love is the key. The disciple John put it this way: "Whoever lives in love lives in God, and God in him" (I John 4:16). I could paraphrase it, "Whoever lives in love lives in God's Plan, and God's Plan in him." Our will is never freer than when it loves. Now for the big one: sin.

Have your ever noticed that none of your friends has ever

called a newborn son Judas? His name is forever associated with treachery. Adolf is another no-no. Hitler and Holocaust have become synonymous. However, in terms of the question regarding God and his role in the existence of sin, Judas is a fascinating case. Look at what Jesus said about him during the Last Supper: "The Son of Man will go as it has been decreed, but woe to that man who betrays him!" (Luke 22:22). On one hand you have the decree or order, springing out of God's Plan, sending Jesus to his death. On the other hand you have "that man," Judas, who "betrays him." But look! Judas is simply doing what God has already decreed, or predestined. Why should Jesus pronounce "woe" on a guy who's playing the only part available to him? Should an actor ignore the script and write his own lines? How can Judas be held responsible for the author's caprice? Without doubt the greatest sin committed by man was that committed against God's own Son. And if the blame lies at anyone's door, it has to lie at the very portals of heaven. Or so it seems. Is God the author of sin?

Usually people blame Satan for sin. Some find a convenient escape from personal responsibility by saying, "The Devil made me do it!" There's no question Satan is the master franchiser of sin. In fact, the Bible tells us God has given him a long-term lease on the world's evil by allowing him to be "the prince of this world" (John 12:31; 14:30). Yet sin, like the Devil, is not eternal. It had a beginning. Where did it come from? Did God invent it and decide to paint some of his creatures black and others white? No. Not directly. Indirectly. Let me explain.

God invented free will at great personal risk. He'd never heard a no before he created angels and humans. He wasn't used to being opposed. Nor was he used to being loved. This we suspect was why God created angels and humans. He wanted to be loved, to be praised, to be worshiped. He wanted fellowship with other personalities. But who wants love or fellowship with automatons? There's no value in the love of someone who has no choice in the matter. Indeed, unless love is a function of choice, it isn't love at all, so God had to give us the freedom to say no. And because the love was to be reciprocal, he had to provide a context in which we could, if we chose, change our no to a yes. How tempting just to wipe out anyone who dared to say no. Amazing as it is, he chose to try to win, or woo, the nay-sayers. He chose to suffer the personal consequences of loving sinners in order to extend mercy to the reluctant. The short-term pleasures of sin had to be tolerated. He could not sour sin. Sin had to sour itself. First of all, however, it soured the beauty of God's creation and broke the very fellowship God had intended with his creatures in the first place. The universe was now more than empty. It was decayed and detached. God had suffered a cosmic rejection.

"Didn't he foresee this?" Yes. "Isn't he eternal?" Yes. "So what's the big deal? A thousand years is like a single day in God's sight, right? So maybe he goes through a little discomfort over all this. But in the eternal present it's no sweat at all." Not really.

God chose to enter space and time. He chose to limit himself to walking on one little speck of dust whirling around a mediocre star in the Milky Way Galaxy. He became one of us. He allowed his immortality to be soured by our mortality. On top of that, he set himself up for more rejection. How awesome must our value be in God's eyes! To endure such humiliation, such rejection, such pain. All for the sake of a free yes from you and me. A *free* yes, mind you. Our acceptance of his love still isn't automatic.

But I stray from my point. God invented sin by inventing freedom. Sin is incidental to freedom. It's part of the risky gift of free will, said one author. God had to permit sin if he was to permit choice. Nevertheless, he wasn't saying, "Man shall, or must, sin," as if man had no choice in the matter. Rather, he was saying, "Man *will* sin." In other words, he was including sin in his Plan, for the sake of freedom. He foreknew man, as a free agent, would do as he pleased. He also foresaw the result. But he was prepared to pay the price, as steep as it was. A free yes was all he wanted.

Thus, in his certain present, God foreknew that both Jew and

Gentile would reject and crucify his Son. He also knew Judas
would betray Jesus. So he included both realities in his Plan. He
included woe for Judas and death for Jesus, but he also included
something else. Resurrection! Salvation! Eternal life! And one
depressed Devil.

So far we've looked at foreknowledge, predestination, election, and some of the questions and objections these intimidating
words evoke. But the scariest word faces us now. Sovereignty.
You know a sovereign is a king or queen. You also know most
monarchies today are titular. That is, they rule in name only.
There are, however, a few active rulers still very much alive. And
their subjects toe the mark. Unlike most of us, who will never
have the experience of being subject to the whim and fancy (or
pleasure) of one individual. Living under a sovereign can be scary
business. That's why one of the slogans of the American War of
Independence was, "We serve no sovereign here!"

This raises a bit of a problem. Most of us "serve no sovereign"
here. We live in democracies. No one individual is sovereign.
The people are. The idea of a monarch controlling our lives is
passé. We find it difficult, therefore, relating to a sovereign God.
God as Father, OK. God as creator, all right. But God as king?
Does that mean I've got to worship and obey? I'd rather debate
and vote.

Unfortunately, the polling stations are closed. In fact, they
were never open. God disregards consensus. He does what he
wants. He pulls rank. "Our God is in heaven; he does whatever
pleases him," says the psalmist (Ps.115:3). He holds all the cards:
"From him and through him and to him are all things" (Rom.
11:36). Even the infinite expanses of space and the dark, cold
depths of the oceans are subject to his pleasure, "The Lord does
whatever pleases him, in the heavens and on the earth, in the seas
and all their depths" (Ps. 135:6). He's king of space, king of oceans,
king of earth, and King of Kings. Take a look at this:

> For God is the King of all the earth;
> sing to him a psalm of praise.
> God reigns over the nations;

God is seated on his holy throne.
The nobles of the nations assemble
as the people of the God of Abraham,
for the kings of the earth belong to God;
he is greatly exalted. (Ps. 47:7–9)

Yes, he is greatly exalted, and he makes unilateral decisions, to use a contemporary term. We'd prefer he make bilateral decisions, which brings up the central issue facing us in sovereignty: the relationship between God's and man's responsibility in history. To put the question simply, Who's in charge here?

To answer that question, the first thing we've got to do is review where we're coming from. God's coming from his certain present. We're coming from our fickle present. Our view is like my aunt's films of her first trip to Florida. She'd never used a movie camera before. One film is entirely of the trip from Toronto to Miami, by car. Most of it is of telephone lines, sky, and an occasional billboard flashing by. Peppered, by the way, with several swooping shots of the car's dashboard. Her still shots of gardens, ocean, flowers, and palm trees are enough to bring on a minor case of whiplash. She has no concept of panning, that is, moving the camera slowly from subject to subject. She just jerks the camera here and there, and as you try to keep up you involuntarily begin to experience soreness in your neck.

Similarly, our view of life is a pandemonic blur of highs, lows, and in-betweens. We rush from one focus to another with seeming disregard for panning skills. The jostling speed of our daily life distorts the picture to the point of breathlessness. Yet in this crazy careening we still make decisions. Some small decisions, some large, but decisions nonetheless. Decisions that demand or elicit response from our own lives and the lives of our families, friends, and neighbors. Little wonder we have self-image problems and relationship problems. Trying to hit the mark, we're as inaccurate as if we were trying to hit the bull's-eye with a target pistol while riding at full gallop on a bucking bronco. We're certainly "trying," but we usually miss the mark. Most of our energy is spent just trying to hold on.

Now, from pandemonium to panorama. From fickle present to certain present, from full gallop to quietly unfolding plan. Remember the conversation with my son Jess in chapter 3? We talked about the Santa Claus parade. How there's so much action, excitement, and surprise at ground level, and such serene movement from helicopter level. We were discussing infinity, but we could have been talking about God's attributes generally. For now, three come to mind: his omniknowledge, his unchangingness, and his love. His omniknowledge includes foreknowledge. He foresees what we call the future, and his knowledge of the future is complete. There are no surprises for him. This is consistent with his unchangingness. What he does, he always planned to do, and he follows through. But his follow-through is tempered by love. He won't let mere created man take the controls of even this single speck of dust in the galactic expanse. He won't let us career uncontrolled into a physical or spiritual black hole. He gently, but firmly, takes the wheel. He wants to lead us home.

So who's in charge here? For sure, we're in charge of our choices, but he's in charge of the range of choice. We're in charge of our thinking, but he's in charge of the brain's limits. We're in charge of our money, but he's in charge of its value—indeed, there have been times of famine when a bag of gold would be traded eagerly for a moldy loaf of bread. We think we're in charge of our living, and we may even be in charge of our dying, but at the point of death, he takes charge, eternally. Death, for us, is the great leveler. For him it's merely a change of clothes.

"Was God in charge of the Holocaust?" I hear some of my Jewish friends ask. This is a very relevant question here in Jerusalem, and it's a loaded question—loaded with emotion, and the overwhelming number of six million. If only six had died in Nazi ovens, the question might be easier to deal with—for us anyway, not for the families of the sacrificed six. But let's remove the six zeroes for a moment. In fact, let's deal with only one or two persons. And let's vault ahead in history to 1982. Israel's "Peace for Galilee" operation is in full swing, and a young Israeli named

Dov is rumbling past the radio station in southern Lebanon where I'm broadcasting. His tank smells of new paint.

Suddenly the tank column stops. As the hatches pop and Israeli heads emerge, I rush back into the studio to put on a long-play tape of prerecorded songs. I run back out. Now there are about thirty or more tank crewmembers milling about. Several ask me for a drink of water. Some ask questions about the radio station.

One of them introduces himself as Dov. Asks me if I'm Jewish.

"No, I'm a Christian, from Jerusalem," I answer.

"You're born in Israel?"

"No, Canada."

Casting his eyes past the valley to the ugly specter of Beaufort Castle silhouetted against the sky, he says, as if to himself, "I could have been born in Poland."

Just then a call rings out, "Five minutes more, then we move!"

"What do you mean?" I ask.

"My parents. Before they were married. They were teenagers who managed to escape Kraków before Auschwitz. They ran for three years. At one point my mother nearly died, but at least they escaped the ovens."

I'm speechless. The rumble of starting engines fills the silence.

"They made it to Palestine, on one of those leaky boats. Then they fought for Israel's independence. I was born in fifty-two, a freeborn Israeli," he says with pride. "You know, Prime Minister Begin's right."

"What about?"

"About the Holocaust. It was an awful chapter in our history. But without it Israel might never have existed."

Suddenly, Dov's crew calls to him to return. He shakes my hand, "Well, I'm off to the Bekaa. Maybe I'll see you on the way back. *Shalom!*"

Begin's analysis of the Holocaust is certainly not the only

one. There are many Jews who disagree, violently. Nevertheless, Dov's commitment to Israel, as he and his mentor Begin see it, is to a land whose life has sprung out of unspeakable death. I think of Samson's riddle, "Out of the eater, something to eat; out of the strong, something sweet"(Judg. 14:14).

No, I don't believe God caused the Holocaust. But I do believe, I *must* believe he permitted it. And he used it to the advantage of his people. Do you think Hitler and Nazi Germany would ever have begun exterminating the Jewish people if they had known that they were forever establishing the Jewish nation as a world power in the Middle East? Even as I write these words, the people who were nearly wiped out by Hitler's men have begun the trial of the man accused of being one of his most evil servants, the man known as Ivan the Terrible. Today in Jerusalem his lawyers made their opening remarks. They don't deny the deeds of Ivan the Terrible. They just say Israel's got the wrong man. Whether they are right remains to be seen. But the point is this: any Nazis still alive are old, guilt-ridden, and wracked with fear of exposure; Israel, on the other hand, is young, visionary, and alive. Very much alive.

Who's in charge here? The evil of the Holocaust seems to call for a vote of no confidence in God's ability to govern. But, "out of the eater . . . something sweet," something very good has arisen. The iron jaws of Hitler's demonism have been broken by God's Plan for his people. His sovereignty can never be successfully challenged. He's in charge. It's scary, but it also brings a deep sense of security. We're cared for.

There's just one more thing I want to say. It has to do with the why of God's Plan. The answer is expressed quaintly in the *Westminster Shorter Catechism.* "The decrees of God are his eternal purpose, according to the counsel of his will, whereby for his own glory He hath foreordained whatsoever comes to pass." The why of God's Plan is "his own glory." Seems a mite egotistical. Egotism, for us, is frowned upon. Perhaps we frown because we see in the egotist some vain attempt to be godlike. We allow no one to be God, except God himself. He is the only one who has a right to be glorified, because he's the only one without sin. He's the only one worthy.

> You are worthy, our Lord and God,
> to receive glory and honor and power,
> for you created all things,
> and by your will they were created
> and have their being. (Rev. 4:11)

And God, for his own reasons, will allow no one else to receive glory or honor. The Bible says he's a jealous God. He's always first. His creation is always second.

> For my own sake, for my own sake, I do this.
> How can I let myself be defamed?
> I will not yield my glory to another. (Isa. 48:11)

Frankly, there's a lot about this I don't like. Mainly because there's something competitive in me. Looking at the history of just this century, it seems to me a lot of things could have been handled differently by our sovereign God. And I don't see what possible glory has accrued to him in two world wars. But I have to remember I'm seeing things from a fickle present, from the back of a bucking bronco. Maybe I should be thankful that God is applying his certain present lovingly to our undulating world. Whether I agree with him or not at the time. Because the world is certainly *not* in my hands. It's in his. And his hands know what they're doing.

CHAPTER 6

The Lord God Made
Them All

❧ THE WEDDING was about to begin. I had performed a lot of them in the past, but this was a first. There were familiar aspects. A groom and best man standing in front of me. A happy group of friends and relatives sitting behind them. A processional. A glowing bride on the arm of a grim-faced father. A beaming mother. The suffused flush of not-too-successfully suppressed excitement on the faces of the young couple as the processional ended and they joined hands facing me. But there were differences, too. The chapel was outdoors, a blue sky above, a brisk wind playing havoc with hair, flowers, and veil. The music flowed from a guitar rather than a pipe organ. The unique factor, though, was the location. As I lifted my eyes above the heads of the people, I saw the Mount of Beatitudes. Behind me, not more than ten feet away, crisp waves slapped the shore of the Sea of Galilee. We were at Tabgha, the site of one of Jesus' miracles of creation. The place where five loaves and two fish had fed five thousand. Not your average miracle. Nor your average wedding chapel.

The most famous wedding of all also included a miracle of creation. In fact, it was Jesus' first recorded miracle. The venue wasn't quite as romantic as the Sea of Galilee. Rather, it occurred in Cana, a sort of nondescript village about fifteen miles west of Tabgha. But it was a genuine miracle. Jesus turned water into wine. You can read about it in the second chapter of John verses 1 through 11. What interests me, as I write this chapter, is the creative aspect of Jesus' act. It wasn't magic or illusion. It was creation reflecting creation recorded in the very first verse of the Bible, which says, "In the beginning God created the heavens and the earth" (Gen. 1:1).

Before I go any farther, I've got to make a confession. I've never been too keen on discussing creation. Why? Because I've always been a bit thrown, if not intimidated, by the theory of evolution. It was taught to me, uncriticially, all through my school years. And, all my friends accepted it. Again, uncritically. Now scientists of every religious and nonreligious predisposition are asking hard questions of Darwin and his "natural selection" description of how life evolved on earth. It's about time. But there's no cause for creationists to rejoice. All that's happened is balance. It's now in style to ask the same critical questions about evolution as have been asked, forever it seems, about creation. It no longer is sour grapes to say, for instance, that Darwin describes the survival of the fittest but draws a blank on the arrival of the fittest. The latter is Genesis' domain.

So what is creation, anyway? In the last chapter I discussed God's plan. Well, creation is the plan in action. It's an exercise of both God's mind and will. A will, by the way, that's personal and free. It's a making to exist of that which once did not exist by means of nothing else than the desire and power to call things into being. And it's making existence without the availability of preexisting material. Creation is not God, nor God creation. Creation may feebly manifest God, but it comes nowhere near expressing his totality. Mind you, what is manifest in creation is great enough for mere mortals like you and me to exhaust our poetry and singing. We worship the Creator and bow down, but so does he—bow down, that is. I keep getting back to this "stooping" theme, but it applies here. To create, God had to voluntarily limit himself. Self-limitation, of course, is a sign of power. So while we weaker ones stretch, the Greater One stoops.

Here's how I'll approach creation in this chapter. First I'll give you an overview of what Genesis says about it. Second, I'll look briefly at ways of interpreting creation and include some of the opposing theories. Third, I'll discuss the why of creation. Finally, I'll make some general observations on the subject. Incidentally, I won't be attacking evolution. Mainly because I'm not qualified to do so. Besides, there's enough in the Bible to keep us occupied. Open yours to Genesis, chapter 1. I'm asking you to read two books at once for a few minutes.

If I was to ask you what God created on the first day of creation, you'd probably answer, "The heavens and the earth." But look. The first day isn't described until verses 3 through 5. What we have in verses 1 and 2 is a prologue, an introduction.

"In the beginning God created the heavens and the earth" is really more than an introduction to the creation account, it's an introduction to God, first and foremost. Notice it doesn't say "There is a God" or attempt to prove God's existence. It simply acknowledges God's presence and sees him as the creator of all. And he has no beginning. The universe, on the other hand, has a beginning, a history; it *started* at some point. "In the beginning" means the universe did *not* preexist, but in its created primeval state it was "formless and empty," or chaotic. It was raw material, in the dark. "Darkness was over the surface of the deep" tells us there was no light, no life, and no time. What's more, everything was water, "the deep," a sea no one could sail. Except the Sailor, the "Spirit of God . . . hovering over the waters." He was about to bring cosmos out of chaos.

The first day (verses 3 through 5) begins with God's voice, "And God said, 'Let there be light.' " God's word was not a magic incantation, but an expression of will. I think of the Thirty-third Psalm verse 9, "He spoke, and it came to be; he commanded, and it stood firm." To create light is to create life and time. Light, life, and time, all created before the sun. But these are relative terms. The Bible tells us "God is light; and in him there is no darkness at all" (I John 1:5–6). Which means light exists in God's eternal now simply because he is there. In "creating" light, then, he created life and time in the context of a limited chaos. A chaos fast becoming a cosmos. But a limitation, indeed, a *self*-limitation, nonetheless. So what about the sun? How can you have light in this world without the sun?

Before the sun, God was the light of the world. In a sense he still is (see John 8:12). One day in eternity when we are forever in his presence, he'll be all the light we need (Rev. 21:23). As for now, the sun does the job. It's rather like a battery.

Recently our neighbor's burglar alarm went off. I rushed over to see if there had been a break-in only to discover another neighbor with a key. He opened the door and shut the alarm off. "This thing's been malfunctioning all week!" he said glumly. "Sure wish the Goldbergs would get back from their trip." The next day it went off again. This time nobody was around with a key. The ear-piercing sound, "whoop-whoo-oop-whoop!" was enough to drive the neighborhood mad. Suddenly I had a brainstorm. I went to their outdoor electricity box and shut off the power. The whooping went on. But in a slightly strained and wheezing sort of way. Battery power had taken over. Finally the battery expired and silence returned. Then the man with the key arrived, we shut the alarm off, and turned the power back on. The quiet was golden, but I'd heard something that showed me the difference between a powerful flow of electricity and a battery—in a word (or two), whoop and wheeze. Compared to God's light, let alone the light of other stars in the Milky Way, the sun is a battery, a rather poor battery. It does the job for us, but it'll expire one day, with one final wheeze.

Getting back to Genesis, we see God "separated the light from the darkness." I would think this goes without saying, but it reminds us that God created darkness as a part of chaos. Now he brings order to chaos by declaring darkness "night" and light "day." In Hebrew thought, of course, night is the beginning of the day. That's why we celebrate the Sabbath, and every other holy day in Israel, at the moment of sundown. Darkness first, then light. The two make a day, a twenty-four-hour day. I know Moses, in the Nintieth Psalm verse 4, says, "A thousand years in your sight are like a day . . ." but I fail to see why people insist that the creative days must have been creative millennia. Creation is an impossibility without God. If God is God, he can create a universe in twenty-four seconds. But it's no issue.

The second day (verses 6 through 8) is a problem. There's talk of water above, water below, and an expanse between. This tells us Hebrew thought was influenced by the thought of the day. Like you and me. We talk of the sun rising and setting, even though we know it's the earth that's moving to and away from the light. I'm not suggesting the Hebrews knew the earth was a revolving sphere, but they did, like us, speak to their generation in terms that were commonly understood. I think an illustration of the current thought about their world would be helpful. Here's the picture. It's a kind of ancient domed football stadium.

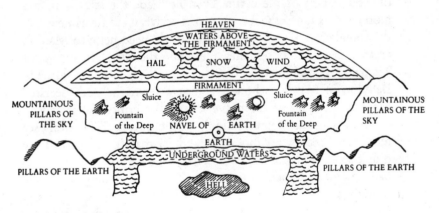

All the Hebrews, all Mesopotamians in fact, would have been card-carrying members of the Flat Earth Society. And why not? They had no airplanes, no satellites, no moon landings to tell them differently. The Hebrews were different, however. They didn't buy everything their neighbors sold about the world.

Perhaps the most common teaching on the market came from Babylon (which means "gate of God"). It's a story called *Enuma Elish* ("When on High").

Seems there were these two oceans, one sweet, the other salty. The sweet one was male, and the salty one female. Their names were Apsu and Tiamat. Apsu was a good guy; Tiamat was a ferocious female. They had a sort of sexual wrestling match that produced some godlings, who in turn produced grand-godlings. These young gods got a bit rowdy, disturbing Tiamat and Apsu to the point where Apsu decided to wipe out the rowdies. But they were saved from destruction by the wisdom of the earth-water god, Ea. Tiamat then decided to attack the gods, who for their part enlisted a god named Marduk to be their general. Marduk agreed on the condition that he be proclaimed king of the universe. The gods went along with this, and he led them to victory. In the process, Marduk killed Tiamat and halved her carcass, one half becoming the firmament of heaven and the other the foundation of the earth. Then he made the stars, sun, and moon and assigned them their places between the firmament and the foundation. The gods thought they'd need help, so Marduk created mankind as servants. He made the first human out of Tiamat's second husband's blood. The gods then built a shrine in Babylon in Marduk's honor, and at a feast, the gods declared Marduk the king of the universe for all eternity. So it ends.

As I said, the Hebrews didn't accept all this. They didn't see matter as preexisting (no Apsu and Tiamat for them!). They didn't see a pantheon of gods. They believed in one God, who had no evil and equal counterpart. They understood the world, though, in flat-earth, firmament terms. Nevertheless, they saw God as Creator and Lord. How he did it and what shape the created world took, ultimately, was not their concern. Their only concern was to communicate to their children the final sovereignty of God. A God who is maker and king of the sky.

The third day (verses 9 through 13) sees a shift from what theologians call immediate creation to mediate creation. To this point God has been creating without the use of preexisting materials. Now he's using materials that he's called into existence, and he's giving them the power of reproduction. First he organizes the water ("under the sky" as contrasted to the "water above it") into seas so that dry ground will appear. After calling the gathered waters "seas" and the dry ground "land," he creates life that will gain its nourishment from the earth. "Let the land produce vegetation: seed-bearing plants and trees on the land that bear fruit with seed in it," he says. The reproductive aspect is implicit in the words "according to their various kinds." The seeds are created and reproduce according to their kind "mediately." A great reminder to us humans that one of our greatest joys and freedoms, sex, isn't our invention or exclusively ours to use as we like. It's God's idea, and his plan relates as much to sex as to anything else.

"Batteries" are the name of the game on the fourth day (verses 14 through 19). Batteries replace the "electricity" of what I call God's "presence-light." Batteries with a physical job to do. Number one, "to separate the day from the night." And number two, to "serve as signs to mark seasons and days and years." So sun, moon and stars appear. And with them, seasons, days, and years. Years upon years, for the batteries still hold their charge.

The fifth day (verses 20 through 23) saw the creation of birds and sea creatures. "According to their kinds" appears again, twice. If I were a biologist, I might interpret these "kinds" as species. But I'm not, so I won't. However, God blesses these creatures and their "kinds" and instructs them to "Be fruitful and increase in number and fill the water in the seas, and let the birds increase on the earth." The stage was just about set for the appearance of man.

The next day, the sixth (verses 24 through 31), was the day for creation of living creatures. These were "livestock, creatures that move along the ground, and wild animals, each according to its kind." And then God said, "Let us make man in our image, in our likeness, and let them rule over the fish of the sea and the birds of the air, over the livestock, over all the earth, and over all the creatures that move along the ground." The author can barely express the awesome moment. So he breaks into poetry:

> So God created man in his own image,
> in the image of God he created him;
> male and female he created them.

An awesome moment indeed! Framed in word pictures of a God who refers to himself as "us," to man's makeup as reflecting "our likeness," to man's relationship with the rest of creation as "ruling," and to man's physical nature as "male and female." You'd think all this would be a bit confusing to the reader. But the opposite is the case. It feels right, quietly comfortable. Almost cozy. Like an old, slightly ragged, but much-loved sweater.

"On the seventh day he rested from all his work" (Gen. 2:1–4a). Why? Because he was tired? I don't think so. He "rested," or stopped, because he "had finished the work he had been doing." His creative work, in space and time, had a beginning and an ending. That's not to say God won't create again. It's simply to say this particular project was finished. (There was another project soon to begin, which would also end. This time with the space-splitting cry, "It is finished!") And he was pleased with the result. Five times he calls his work good. Once he calls it very good. His creation was a complete expression of what he had chosen to do. His work expressed his will.

It's interesting to note that the Genesis account doesn't see the universe as eternal or as the unfolding of some eternal process. Rather, it sees the universe as temporal, with a beginning and an end. Everything that exists in terms of space and time is "post-creation." God's decision to create precedes all matter, all life, all history. He is not the "all." He is before all. That's why theologians refer to his creative work as *ex nihilo,* which is Latin for "out of nothing." He had no preexisting material with which to work. To use a musical analogy, before he arranged the score, he composed the score, without preexisting notes. I like the Revised Standard Version of two Scriptures on this score: "God . . . who

. . . calls into existence the things that do not exist" (Rom. 4:17); and "The world was created by the word of God, so that what is seen was made out of things which do not appear." (Heb. 11:3). He sang our song into being.

Before looking at ways of interpreting this song, let me briefly point out its importance to the Bible. The creation account is presented in various parts of the Bible as historically true. Perhaps this is no more clearly evident than in the Fourth Commandment ("Remember the Sabbath day by keeping it holy" [Exod. 20:8]). Here, and in a few other places, creation is made the basis for the institution of the Sabbath. Creation is also foundational to what God later reveals to be his plan in terms of redeeming (or "buying back") man from his sin. In creating man a free moral agent (as we saw in the last chapter), God had to include the possibility of our saying no to him. This meant creation was implicitly vulnerable to the souring impact of sin. Thus, a plan of redeeming the situation had to be enacted even before sin made its formal entrance. Redemption, then, is predicated upon creation. So the Bible's credibility and the foundational factors in its story of redemption have their deepest root in the Genesis account of creation. For the Bible's sake, to say nothing of ours, it had better be true!

What do we mean by true? Literally true? Scientifically true? Allegorically true? Mythically true? Pictorially true? One of the above, or all of the above? The *literalist* interprets the story at face value. What the Bible says, literally, is good enough; science has no business butting in. In fact, he won't allow for any comparison at all between Genesis and science. The *scientist* (not necessarily a scientist, but someone who insists there is no contradiction between the Bible and science) interprets the creation account as a scientific document and goes through all kinds of contortions to line Genesis up with geology. The *allegorist* interprets the story as a sort of poetic speculation that has deep spiritual meanings. Its value isn't historical but spiritual. The *mythologist*, like the allegorist, interprets Genesis as he would interpret any other fable. But he may surprise you. Some mythologists are deeply

committed to the solid truth that a myth may convey. Sort of
like the *pictorialist*. He interprets the account in terms of its
pregnant imagery. Imagery that may allow for reconciliation of
the Bible and science at some future date. At issue here is not just
truth, but history. History clouded by the interpretive "filters"
of human brains, languages, laws, and traditions. Little wonder
alternate theories abound. Here are four of them.

Dualism comes in two flavors. The first is a belief in two
self-existent principles, God and matter. The second is a belief in
two antagonistic spirits, one good and the other evil. In the first
flavor, God is not matter, and matter not God, but they are
coeternal. Matter, however, is inferior to God; it's an unconscious, negative, imperfect entity, and thereby is subservient to
God. Those who have attempted to understand this type of
dualism see it as an effort to create a hybrid of Christianity and
Greek philosophy. It tries to account for evil's existence and to
do an end run around the forbidding problem of creation occurring without the benefit of preexisting material. It wrestles with
the difficulty of explaining how the purely spiritual (God) could
create, let alone coexist, with that which is impure and phenomenal, as contrasted to spiritual. It can't handle the idea of an
absolute and unlimited God living in both eternity and in space
and time. So the material world, that is, the impure, phenomenal,
space-time universe, is evil. By extension, matter is evil. And
there is a great gap between matter and God. An early Christian
heresy called Gnosticism was dualistic. Its beliefs had very practical applications. Some Gnostics dealt with the evil nature of
matter by attempting to rid their lives of it. They became ascetics,
living a monastic, separated life. Others of them overcame matter's evil by simply disregarding it. They saw themselves as
spiritual, therefore matter had no relevance. This had two logical
results: One, because they still were trapped in flesh and blood
(nasty matter!) and all that could be expected of this evil cloak
was evil, they gave full sway to their carnal, immoral passions.
But their "spirits" (all that mattered) rose to the heavenlies.
What a combination—sex and religion. Irresistible! Two, the

irrelevance of matter led some to suggest it didn't exist for those who were truly spiritual. Therefore, there is no sin, no disease, no pain. It's just a matter of mind over matter. Simple.

The second flavor of dualism was taught by a few Gnostics, but mainly by Zoroastrians and Manichaeans (I include these names just in case you want to check them out in more detail in your trusty dictionary of Church history). They believed that there were two equally powerful but antagonistic spirits—one a good guy, the other a bad guy. They didn't see matter as an evil, self-existent substance, but as the creation of a commitedly malignant intelligence who hates and wars against everything good. Because the outcome of the war was unknown, you were wise to cover all the bases. Keep both warlords happy. The name of the game was superstition and fear.

The Gnostics had something to do with the next theory as well. They were the Syrian Gnostics—joined several centuries later by the Swedenborgians. Their theory was similar to pantheism in that they taught the universe is of the same substance with God, but they differed in that they viewed the universe as a product of a series of evolutions from his being. This is known as the *emanation* theory. An emanation is a piece or part of God's being that has somehow become separated and sent out as independent. Because it has no permanent connection with the original Divine Being, it becomes either degenerate or an active enemy of God. Thus the universe was seen as degraded, actively hostile, and godless.

The third is called the *creation from eternity* theory. It has been held by various philosophers-theologians over the years, most of them obscure. Perhaps the heavyweight among the group is Origen, one of Christianity's early thinkers. This theory sees creation as an act of God in eternity-past (which, of course, is a contradiction in terms). God created the world so he would be God of something. Seems he had an unfulfilled need for significance. So he found his significance, his meaning, in his creation. There are shades of pantheism here, in which God doesn't even exist, let alone gain significance, apart from the universe. One needs only a moment's thought to see this theory making God somehow dependent upon, even in bondage even to, his own world, rather like a mother who lives only for her child or a businessman whose life is his work.

The fourth theory is a key building block in evolutionary thinking. It's called *spontaneous generation.* Creation is just a name for a natural law, the law being that matter has within itself the capability, given the proper environment, of developing new functions and new organic forms. A little bit of this and a little bit of that, combined with a propitious bolt of lightening, and presto!—a living amoeba. But spontaneous generation of life has never been documented. Even if it was, it would still beg the question of who or what invested matter with these life-potential properties. As one theologian said, "Evolution implies previous involution—if anything comes out of matter, it must first have been put in."* When you get right down to it, chickens come *before* eggs.

That's why the Genesis *ex nihilo* factor is so difficult to accept. You don't have eggs without chickens. So it's generally stated you get nothing from nothing *(ex nihilo nihil fit),* unless, of course, there is a God. But if you're not prepared to include God in the scheme, you're left, necessarily, with an eternal universe. At the same time you have to admit the universe is always changing. And change implies some sort of primordial state out of which and by which change is made possible. The question then is, "Was there ever a point when change began?" If there was, you're getting close to the beginning.

In the final analysis we're faced with three views of how the universe came to be. The first is the biblical view, which assumes God. "In the beginning God . . ." The second is the physical view, which disallows any hint of mind or intelligence in the causative universe. The third is the mind-in-nature view, which sees matter as somehow possessing within itself the intelligence or design which does the work of mind in the creation of life. Whereas the biblical view sees a beginning and end to space and time, the

*A. H. Strong, *Systematic Theology,* Judson Press, p. 390.

latter two see the universe as eternal. Genesis presents God as creator of chaos and designer/creator of cosmos out of chaos. The others see chaos transforming itself into cosmos. Like a scrambled egg transforming itself into a chicken.

So why did God create the universe? At this point I'll pick up where I left off in the last chapter. God's glory is the bottom line. Most catechisms declare man's chief end is to glorify God and enjoy him forever. But modern thinking has inverted it. We see the Creator's chief end as glorifying man and enjoying him forever. Maybe the little boy in his Sunday school class had it right: "Man's chief end is to glorify God and annoy him forever."

Before commenting on God's glory as the chief goal of the creation, let's look at what the Bible has to say overall about the why of his creative activity. One reference sets the tone: "The heavens declare the glory of God; the skies proclaim the work of his hands" (Ps. 19:1). Creation is not itself God's glory. Rather, it *declares* God's glory. Or as a theologian might put it, God's glory is not essential, but declarative. So what else does the Bible say? First of all, it says the answer to the why is in himself: "For my own sake, for my own sake, I do this. . . . I will not yield my glory to another" (Isa. 48:11). "The Lord works out everything for his own ends—even the wicked for a day of disaster" (Prov. 16:4). "For by him all things were created: Things in heaven and on earth, visible and invisible, whether thrones or powers or rulers or authorities; all things were created by him and for him" (Col. 1:16). "For from him and through him and to him are all things. To him be the glory forever! Amen" (Rom. 11:36). His will, power, wisdom, and holy name have a lot to do with it, too: "You are worthy, our Lord and God, to receive glory and honor and power, for you created all things, and by your will they were created and have their being" (Rev. 4:11). But the key factor is his glory: "Bring my sons from afar and my daughters from the ends of the earth—everyone who is called by my name, whom I created for my glory, whom I formed and made" (Isa. 43:6b–7). "Then will all your people be righteous and they will possess the land forever. They are the shoot I have planted, the work of my hands, for the display of my splendor" (Isa. 60:21). "Glory to God in the highest, on earth peace to men on whom his favor rests" (Luke 2:14). So whether he's talking about himself, or others are talking about him, whether he's talking about his people Israel, or angels are talking about the birth of Jesus, the bottom line is the same: God's glory. We need to give this some thought. Mainly because it's *his* glory. What about ours? Are we even in the picture?

Relative to the awesome significance of God, we *are* in the picture, but barely—*barely* not only in terms of *hardly* but also in terms of *nakedly*. We're as dust compared to him. So if there's any glory to be handed out, he wears it much better than we do. That's why the Bible teaches it is silliness and sin for us to seek our glory rather than God's. If we do, we're giving ourselves priority, serving the creature instead of the Creator. Mind you, there are always attempts to combine the two glories. I've heard it said the highest end is God's glory and the second highest the good of his creatures. Or it's said the two glories are the same, and God's glory is expressed in our happiness. Further yet, some see God manifesting his glory by promoting our glory.

This is all very interesting. But the bottom line is *God's* glory, not ours. And because he is infinitely wise and good, we can expect his glory will include the best for us. The best, however, is not always the most pleasant—remember your father's words as he bent you, bottom up, over his knee? "Now, Son, I'm only doing this for your own good." I never could figure out what good there was in a spanking. The sobering fact is there may be a lot of sin and sorrow along the way to the highest good. There may be a price to pay.

A big part of that price may be changing your focus. We tend to focus on ourselves. To be self-absorbed. And to the extent we are self-absorbed, we are spiritually dead. For our spirits thrive or die in the context of our relationships or lack of them. The Bible says we need relationship with our neighbor to be spiritually alive. And we need relationship with God. But God comes first. Before ourselves, before our loved ones, before our loved things. Not that he expects us to become monastic nobodies. In fact, the most famous sermon of all time says, "But seek first his kingdom and his righteousness, and all these things [your physical and emotional props] will be given to you as well" (Matt. 6:33). And as "all these things" come our way, we're to enjoy them in an attitude of seeking and declaring the glory of God: "So whether you eat or drink or whatever you do, do it all for the glory of God" (I Cor. 10:31). This doesn't refer to eating as a spiritual exercise. It simply says our focus is God, not ourselves. Our food comes from him. Our health comes from him. Our friends come from him. To God be the glory. Even our life comes from him, "For in him we live and move and have our being" (Acts 17:28a). The Creator is the creature's focus.

But how do we come to grips with our Creator's seemingly insatiable need for glory? Let's try to think it through. First, an illustration. A few days previous to this writing, a Van Gogh painting sold for thirty-five million dollars to a Japanese corporation. This follows a few months of frenetic purchasing of paintings by big spenders for combined hundreds of millions of dollars. Van Gogh must be cartwheeling in his grave! "After all," I can hear him saying, "it's just a painting of a few flowers. I've done much better." So why the big price? Maybe because it's the work of a master. The masters had a genius about them. They were moved by powerful ideals. Ideals which they communicated in prose, poetry, painting, sculpture, or whatever. The strength of and love for the ideal gave power to the painting. A power spanning centuries. You can be sure Van Gogh loved his ideal more than he loved his painting. The picture was just a means of expressing his love.

Robert Browning, the famous poet, once said, "God is the perfect Poet, Who in creation acts his own conceptions." He doesn't paint an approximation of his ideal. He *actualizes* it. What's more, he gives it life. No brittle paint, browning varnish, and rotting canvas for him. His waters teem with fish. His grasses burst with flowers. His man-creatures breathe his breath. Indeed, the entire universe pulsates with life.

But the difference between the poet and God is that one loves an ideal and the other is *the* ideal. His creative act is an act of self-love. He himself is the heart of the cosmos. There is no other heart, no other mind, before him. He is the only being in the universe who can live for himself, for there is none higher than he. Only he is free from submission to some other. Thus, he is the only one worthy of glory. Any "sub-glories" his creatures enjoy are mere reflections.

That's why God's creative work is not only self-love but self-limitation. He submits to no one but himself. In creating the universe and man, he has voluntarily committed himself to the submission of loving us. Thus, the universe symbolizes his self-imposed limitation. Compared to his glory, it is rather dull. The universe can in no way be God's glory, it can only declare it. If creation were God's glory, then he would in some way be dependent upon it. But he's not. He's complete, perfect, dependent on no one.

> Surely the nations are like a drop in a bucket;
> They are regarded as dust on the scales;
> He weighs the islands as through they were fine dust . . .
> Before him all the nations are as nothing;
> They are regarded by him as worthless
> and less than nothing. (Isa. 40:15, 17)

The combined billions of earth and heaven are as nothing before God. Why he gives us value is something known only to him. He could be giving us big trouble. Just ask Noah. Instead, he extends his love. Overwhelming, everlasting, wondrous love. "For God so loved the world . . ."(John 3:16). In response we sing, "Amazing love! How can it be?" That God should love us is the great mystery. Especially when our hearts are continually set against him. Why not just wipe us out? Or wipe us off? After all, as one old theologian put it, the entire universe is but a drop of dew upon the fringe of his garment.

He won't do it. Rather than obliterate us he cries out, "Come, let us reason together . . ." Deep calls unto deep. Heart to heart. Revealing a heavenly irony: if we seek his glory, which is the highest end, then he will be able to effect our highest good. For his glory is the end which includes as sub-ends all the needs of creation. This is why his "need" for glory is not egotistical. In actualizing his ideal, he gives to his creatures the highest good. He paints us in eternal color.

Now for some general comments on the Genesis account. I've already pointed out that Genesis simply assumes God's existence. This should not be seen as mere oversight or literary expediency. It holds a powerful message: to the Hebrew mind God's existence, like life itself, is a given. And he eternally preexists. He is before all. Unlike the religions of their neighbors at that time, the Hebrews had no biography of the Creator. I mentioned *Enuma Elish,* the Babylonian epic. There the original entities were two demonic water monsters, Apsu and Tiamat. They preexisted all subsequent gods, including Marduk, the creator of the world. Marduk had a biography. The entire pantheon (the hierarchy of the gods) had a family tree. Not the God of Genesis. He creates trees. He doesn't grow on them.

The fact that Marduk and all other Mesopotamian gods had biographies is vitally important. It tells us two absolutely key things. First, it tells us the gods were dependent on physical existence—their existence had no meaning apart from the physical universe, which meant their range of movement and influence was limited. They were neither free nor all-powerful. Second, it tells us why magic became so much a part of ancient religion. Beyond Marduk and the pantheon was the preexisting carcass of the female water monster Tiamat. She had a deeper power than that of the gods. Thus, man's destiny was subject, not only to whimsical, adolescent gods but also to a dark power beyond. Even the gods themselves were subject to this primordial force. This meant man had to contrive means to influence those powers beyond the gods. So ritual, incantation, and other devices were developed to appease and manipulate the darker demons.

Genesis tells us God is independent both of physical existence and of magic. He calls things into being. Not by magic incantation (implying there is something—matter, Tiamat, or whatever—to incant) but by all-powerful sovereign will. God is above magic. In fact, his existence declares the impotence of magic. He will not respond to a magician's manipulations. He is no puppet. He is free and wants all his creatures to be free. That's why the creation account is so liberating. He performs his word, not somebody else's. God and magic don't mix.

Mesopotamian magic, however, was continually getting mixed up. Their demon gods, both of major and minor status, were utterly unreliable. You could perform your magic rites perfectly and still see the gods reverse field. You could never count on good overcoming evil. In fact, it seemed that good existed only in terms of one evil being better than another. Evil was the permanent condition. Which meant there was no relationship, ultimately, between morality and individual or corporate well-being. It also meant the universe was essentially without direction, purposeless, meaningless, and vain. Man's history was an endless cycle on a prison-house treadmill.

Enter the God of creation. He is not immoral or, more correctly, amoral. He is totally reliable, orderly, and trustworthy. This doesn't mean he can be completely understood simply by documenting and analyzing his performance. What it does mean is that he operates, on the space-time level, in terms man can understand. The same God who called the world into existence calls all men everywhere to order their lives by absolute demands, "Thou shalt—thou shalt not." But there's more. He frees man from the treadmill. He breaks the prison bars of paganism's vicious time cycle. "Thou shalt—thou shalt not" reflects not only his moral nature but his high view of man as well. He has a plan for man, for society, and for human history. The human impotence of paganism gives way to a thrilling sense of the significance of man.

Genesis doesn't think in terms of a treadmill. It thinks in terms of a destination. In creation terms, time is moving toward a destiny, a culmination. When God said his creation was "very good," he was saying something of profound importance. It meant the universe was essentially good, not evil. It meant man was good. (Sure, man sinned, with cataclysmic consequences, but even in his sin, man was redeemable—thus the story of redemption.) It meant God and man could enter into relationship. We see this crystallized in the covenant relationship God initiates between himself and Abraham. And the apex of covenant is the idea of Messiah and the messianic kingdom, the ultimate destiny of man. Both covenant and Messiah, by the way, are unique Hebrew contributions to religious thought. All because of Genesis.

In conclusion, two things in Genesis stand out worth memorizing: (1) God created out of nothing, and (2) creation is good. Whereas dualism says God created out of something already there and pantheism says God created out of himself, Genesis says God called into being the things which were not in being. Whereas dualism says the universe is evil and pantheism says it's unreal and illusory (in both cases the world is looked down upon, to be gotten out of quickly), Genesis says creation is very good.

Because creation is good, we have a good world to live and work in. We live in the midst of cosmos, not chaos. All the natural world is, with us, a part of God's plan. Indeed, as a poet said, "All creatures great and small, the Lord God made them all." Our existence takes place in a purposeful time-line that had a beginning and extends to a future fulfillment, a future that is new and exciting. Perhaps this is Genesis' ultimate legacy. It's getting ready for a wedding.

CHAPTER 7

God Is No Absentee Landlord

❧ WHEN I was a small child I saw an angel, or so I thought at the time. Here's how it happened. Our little town was in the grip of an arctic chill. Winters were always cold in February. But this was something else. "Sixty below zero!" I heard Farmer Ferguson exclaim as he entered the steaming back door of our neighbor's house. "Saskatchewan don't get much colder'n this." But colder did exist—in our uninsulated parsonage. Climbing into bed at night was like crawling into a king-size ice-cream sandwich. You braced yourself for the initial shock, assumed a fetal position, and stayed very still; slowly your body heat would defrost the sheets. The warm zone, however, extended no more than an inch or so beyond the outline of your body. Any movement while asleep brought on "arctic shock." I learned to sleep in one position for eight-hour stretches. Followed by a lot of early-morning stretches just to get mobile. Oh yes, I also learned not to wet the bed.

One icy morning my brother and I came down to the kitchen for breakfast. Mom looked distraught for some reason, and Dad leaned against the counter, his face set and sober. There were no cereal bowls on the table.

"Hi, Mom, hi, Dad" my four-year-old brother piped.

"Hi, guys." This was Dad. Mom had rushed out, tears brimming her eyes.

"Where's breakfast?," I asked.

"Well, guys, it's this way, We, uh, don't have any breakfast this morning."

"So why not go down to Frazer's and buy some?"

Dad picked away at the frost on the window. So thick it had actually become ice.

"We could do that, except . . . well, we don't have any money right now. But never forget guys, we may not have money, but we're not poor. God will take care of us."

Mom came back in. The four of us sat at the empty table. Dad prayed.

"Thank you, Father, that you promised to care for your children. Thank you that you see our need. We're trusting you for our food. We pray you'll find some way to provide. We love you, Lord. Amen."

Mom made another wet exit. Dad went upstairs to his little study. My brother and I, still somewhat confused by all this, went up to our room to change. I had just got my jeans on when there was a knock at the door, the front door. "That's funny," I said to myself as I rushed down the stairs. "Nobody ever uses our front door in the winter."

The door wouldn't budge. The frost and ice had sealed it shut. Shouting "Just a minute," I grabbed a brick from the makeshift bookcase and chipped the largest ice deposits away. Then, bracing my feet against the door frame and pulling with all my five-year-old might on the handle, I managed to open it with a whoosh of frigid air. Picking myself up from the floor, I looked into the face of an old lady. A face backlit with the diffused glow of sunlight shining through ice-crystalled air. I'd never seen her before. She had three full grocery bags in her frail arms.

"These are for you, Jimmy," she said, handing the first bag to me. As I placed it on the floor, I invited her in. Not just for hospitality's sake, but I was freezing. Bag number two. Bag number three.

"There we go, Jimmy. God bless you." She turned to leave. "Don't go! I'll get Dad. Who are you? I know everybody in town. I've never seen you before. How do you know my name?"

"No, no. It's OK. I'll . . ." I didn't hear her finish. I left her standing there and ran upstairs to get my father. When we returned to the front door, the sun and the cold were still streaming in. But the old lady was gone. We looked up and down the street. She was nowhere to be seen. An hour later, my tummy full of warm breakfast, I remembered Dad's prayer.

Just in case you're wondering, I gave a complete description of the old lady to my parents. They couldn't place her, either. Thirty-five years later they still haven't a clue. "God will take care of us." God had sent an angel to one of his little families in the cold, a warm breakfast from heaven, or so I thought.

Frankly, I still think so. And I've got good theological grounds for thinking this way. The Bible builds a real case for angels. But angels are only part of the story. And that story couldn't be more succinctly expressed than Dad's "God will take care of us." The story is about God's care of the universe generally and of his children specifically. It's called providence.

Providence, the word, comes from Latin *(providere),* which means "to foresee." The corresponding Greek word *(pronoia)* means "forethought." Providence, the doctrine, refers to the preservation, care, and government of God over all his creation. And the foreseeing, forethinking aspect suggests there is, from God's perspective, an end in view. That is, God sees all creation heading for some kind of historical culmination.

Space and time have a date with eternity. Again, from God's point of view, the end totally affects the means. The universe is going somewhere, God knows where, and he stays in the driver's seat. His final goal affects everything and everyone on the way.

That's why providence is the most all-inclusive word in

theology's vocabulary. It has something to do with almost everything the Bible talks about: invisible God, visible world, the relationship between the two, sin, salvation, heaven, hell. Providence relates to all this, for it has to do with God's preparation, care, and supervision of all creation. It's forethought with an end in view.

Forethought can be seen in two ways. It "fore" sees and it "for" sees. It sees beforehand, and it looks out for. It's telescopic and microscopic. Which means that providence encompasses within its scope big and little things, major and minor issues, generations and individuals. Nothing is too huge or too tiny for an infinite and all-powerful God. You might say he's "all-powerful" and "small-powerful."

Just a few technical details before we get going. Theologians often speak of two aspects of providence. They are preservation and government. Then they speak of two kinds of providence: general and special. Preservation relates to creation. Whereas creation calls nonexistence into existence, preservation gives persistence to existence. That is, it extends or causes the continuance of that which was begun at creation. In preservation God provides sustaining power for the created universe. Government relates to the plan of God. Whereas plan has an ultimate end in view, government controls the sequence of sub-ends leading to the final consummation. In government God provides design and control for the created universe. Thus, in preservation God maintains, in government he controls. He both services and drives the car. As for general and special providence, they refer to God's maintenance and control of both the large and the little. He looks out for galaxies and improverished preachers, nations and little old ladies in tennis shoes. He cares. Completely.

Speaking of tennis shoes, here's my game plan for this chapter. First I'll take a fairly extensive look at what the Bible says about providence. Then, a few theories against and/or alternate to the subject. Followed by an overview of how providence relates to free will and sinful behavior. Finally, I'll discuss the fascinating subject of angels, both good and bad, and their role as agents of God's care for his creation. A chapter with "a cast of thousands."

We've seen in former chapters that God is in charge of everything. He is sovereign and has a plan. So what's the difference between sovereignty and providence? Especially as providence includes government. Remember my attempt at describing the difference between predestination and election in chapter 5? I called election generic and predestination specific, generic being inclusive and specific being exclusive. I presented election as the content and predestination as the style of God's plan for us, meaning that election determines the extent of God's family and predestination the course each member will take. Well, there's a similar relationship between sovereignty and providence. Sovereignty is generic, and providence specific. Sovereignty means God is all-powerful and does as he pleases. Providence means he is also "small-powerful" and lovingly does what is best for the world and its inhabitants. The content: God is King. The style: God is Father. He is Lord and Daddy of us all.

So what does the Bible say about our provident Father? So much that I'll quote just a few Scriptures speaking of his care. The bottom line is expressed in verses like this, where he rules the universe generally.

> The Lord has established his
> throne in heaven,
> and his kingdom rules over
> all. (Ps. 103:19)

The universe, of course, includes the earth and its inhabitants, be they nations, individuals, or even animals:

> he makes nations great, and
> destroys them;
> he enlarges nations, and
> disperses them. (Job 12:23)
>
> Before I formed you in the
> womb I knew you,

before you were born I set
you apart . . . (Jer. 1:5)

The lions roar for their prey
and seek their food from
God. (Ps. 104:21)

His providence even controls a lot of what appears to be our
earned successes or deserved failures:

No one from the east or the
west
or from the desert can
exalt a man.
But it is God who judges:
He brings one down, he
exalts another. (Ps. 75:6–7)

Even chance hasn't a chance when it comes to God's providence:

The lot is cast into the lap,
but its every decision is
from the Lord. (Prov. 16:33)

He providentially answers the prayer, supplies the needs, and
grants the protection of his people:

Since ancient times no one
has heard,
no ear has perceived,
no eye has seen any God
besides you,
who acts on behalf of those
who wait for [pray to] him. (Ps. 64:4)

Abraham answered, "God himself will
provide the lamb for the burnt offering" . . .
So Abraham called that place "The Lord
will provide!" (Gen. 22:8,14)

I will lie down and sleep in
peace,

28 *The Decrees and Works of God*

> for you alone, O Lord,
> make me dwell in safety. (Ps. 4:8)

And, surprisingly, his providence even sustains the principle of punishment for the wicked:

> On the wicked he will rain
> fiery coals and burning
> sulphur;
> a scorching wind will be
> their lot. (Ps. 11:6)

So, whether it's the whole cosmos, a lion in the wild, a nation's ascendancy, or an individual's downfall, the Bible sees God's providence in it all. He governs all things and preserves all things. Indeed, as the Israelites in Nehemiah's day put it, "You give life to everything" (Neh. 9:6).

Mind you, there are many in Israel today, to say nothing of both Jew and Gentile throughout history, who see God's role in the cosmos much differently. One of the classic alternate theories to providence is called deism. It flourished in the seventeenth and eighteenth centuries. It acknowledges some sort of creator. But it denies any kind of preserver. Deism says God made the world and abandoned it on the doorstep to make its own way. Rather like a man who makes a computer, plugs it in, and leaves it to fend for itself. The world continues to exist only because of its inherent design, not because of God's holding it together. In fact, God is not even available. He makes no overtures to man. He answers no prayers. He has left us in the care of the laws of nature, for he's too high to concern himself with our low concerns. He doesn't stoop. And stretch as you will, you'll never find him. Which is about as close to atheism as you can get. Providence, replaced by the laws of nature.

Atheism, of course, denies providence in denying God. Regardless of how this world began, its beginning had nothing to do with a creator. Which means matter is eternal, for without God's input nothing can be made out of nothing. That's why you'll hear thoughtful atheists say the cosmos is all there is or was or ever will be. The cosmos is eternal. Sounds like pantheism, where God is cosmos, and cosmos is God. God, replaced by cosmos. And cosmos is held together not by providence, but by its own eternality.

In opposition to deism, atheism, and pantheism is theism. Theism, which is the biblical concept, sees God as both creator and preserver of the universe. This means there is constant contact between creator and creation. He preserves and governs the world according to the laws of nature, not by them. Although those laws don't depend directly upon God for their effect, they do depend directly upon him for their existence, longevity, and consistency. They're not fickle. Gravity keeps both just and unjust firmly planted on the ground. Eventually it will plant us all six feet beneath it.

So whether God has you six feet below ground or six feet above it, we can say, from a biblical perspective, that God is as involved in the natural world as he is in the supernatural. Or as theologians put it, God is both transcendent and immanent. He's above and within the universe. Creation tends to underline his transcendence. Providence stresses his immanence. Pantheism is comfortable with immanence, uncomfortable with transcendence. Deism is the opposite—happy with transcendence, unhappy with immanence. Theism embraces both.

By the way, don't confuse immanence with omnipresence. Omnipresence simply means God is everywhere. Immanence means God is involved everywhere. The former is relatively passive, the latter active. He's present in the world not only dispassionately but passionately. His immanence means he is actively holding everything together by the power of his word. He's involved.

Omnipresence, however, makes me think of a few other qualities of God which relate to providence—love, for instance. Because God is love we can be sure he'll care for what he has created. It seems reasonable to assume that what was worth creating is worth loving. This loving care is providence. Then there's God's unchangingness. He lives in the "certain present."

His plan for the cosmos and its history is certain. He is acting out his plan through creation, preservation, and government. His providence is the plan in action. God has one more quality that relates to providence—his justice. He has established spiritual, moral, and natural law in the cosmos. You and I are constantly falling short of the demands of these laws. Occasionally we have a few blips of righteousness. But God administers these laws fairly and justly. This administration of justice is providence. So his immanence (or involvement), love, unchangingness, and justice are all present in his providence. One might say his providence portrays his character. His character in action.

But how does providence relate to free will and our character in action? If God maintains everything, doesn't that suggest his involvement in our sinful as well as our good behavior? When we sin, is God an accessory after the fact?

As I write these words, two high-profile American leaders are in disgrace. One is, or was, a leading presidential candidate; the other, a television evangelist. Both have resigned because of public disapproval of their extramarital sexual affairs. Both were believers. Before politics the presidential hopeful had chosen to enter the ministry. On his television show the evangelist daily talked of God's love and prayed for the needs of his audience. I don't doubt these men are still believers—perhaps now more than ever. But the question is, what role did God's providence play in the good and bad of their lives? Is God only Lord of the good? What about the dark side?

There's a story in the Bible about King David which makes these questions even tougher to answer. It's in the twenty-fourth chapter of the second book of Samuel. For some reason God was angry at Israel. So he incited David to take a census of Israel's military men. There was something wrong about the idea. Even Joab, David's chief of staff, didn't like it. Nevertheless, the king's will prevailed and the census was taken. Afterward, David was conscience-stricken. Why? We're not sure. Perhaps because the census focused on natural rather than supernatural might. It may have implicitly shoved God out of the way. Whatever. David prays and repents. God speaks to the prophet Gad in response. He gives David three options: three years of famine in his land, three months of fugitive life, or three days of plague. David chooses plague. The plague descends, under an angel's supervision, and seventy thousand people die. David buys some land which includes a threshing floor. There he sacrifices to God, and the plague stops. Strange story. God the inciter becomes God the forgiver. David the victim becomes David the wrongdoer/repenter. And Israel gets caught in the middle. A story majoring on the dark side.

Maybe not. To incite means "to urge on," or "stir up." This suggests there had to be something already within David that God could work on. After all, you can't incite someone to rebel if there's no rebellion in his heart. So God knew there was a growing tendency on David's part to want to be independent, to rely not on God but on the power of Israel's considerable military. God wanted to teach David and Israel a lesson. So he said, as it were, "Come on, David. You want to do it. So do it. Let's get on with it. Let's go," knowing full well he was about to allow David to rediscover, through a tragic experience, a childlike dependence on grace. God was about to show David that Israel's impressive manpower could be decimated in "three years," "three months," or "three days," depending on God's will. "Your choice, David", said God, "but they'll all come to the same end—a paralyzing blow to your vaunted manpower." He was about to provide David another level to his education.

OK. So that's fine for David. But what about those innocent Israelites? Why must they suffer in order for the king to get a master's degree in righteousness? Why must the aspiring president's family and election team be so humiliated? Why must the adoring and needy fans of the evangelist be scandalized? Well, it's like this. You've heard the old adage, "Like father, like son." Maybe you've not heard, "like king, like people," or "like politician, like voter," or "like TV preacher, like TV audience." When high-profile men fall, us low-profilers had better take stock of ourselves. We'd better get our own house in order. As one observer said of the TV evangelist fiasco, "God's just doing a little housecleaning." And if that's true, then we all, big and small, should turn to God with grateful hearts. As much as it hurts, God is providing what we need. His providence wins the day.

King David's son, Solomon, had some fascinating insights. Could be he learned from observing his father. Here's some of what he said about God's providence: "Many are the plans in a man's heart, but it is the Lord's purpose that prevails ... A man's steps are directed by the Lord. How then can anyone understand his own way? ... The king's heart is in the hand of the Lord; he directs it like a watercourse wherever he pleases" (Prov. 19:21; 20:24; 21:1). Sounds a bit like puppetry.

But it's not. Not if we remember two important things about providence. First, providence means God governs all his creation, including man. Second, his control is self-limited in his commitment to govern consistently with our nature and his nature. That is, he won't be untrue to his character, nor will he overrule our free will. But the advantage is definitely with him. He is all-knowing. He lives in the certain present. Thus, he is able to direct all our free choices, good and bad, to his desired end. He stays in the driver's seat. To mix metaphors, he conducts a good symphony. Puppetry is not for him. He's into conducting.

Here's how he "conducts" our evil acts. Some theologians say his providence handles our sinful choices in four different ways. They're called: preventive, permissive, directive, and determinative.

An excellent example of preventive providence comes from the life of Abraham. He had just moved his entire household into the Negev desert. During the move he stayed for awhile in a place called Gerar. The king of Gerar was Abimelech. Abimelech had an eye for beautiful women.

Sarah was beautiful. Abraham was scared. He didn't want Abimelech doing anything rash like killing him just to get his wife, so he and Sarah hatched a plan. They'd tell Abimelech they were brother and sister, which technically was correct. Sarah was really Abraham's stepsister (Gen. 20:12). So they could say they were siblings without telling a big lie. Tongues well in cheek, that's what they did. Abimelech was pleased. He had Sarah in his household in no time, getting her ready for some hot nuptials. All in good faith, mind you. He had no idea he was about to marry a married woman.

But God providentially intervened. He came to Abimelech in a dream and told him he was as good as dead for having taken a married woman into his home. Abimelech pled innocence, which was true. Which was why God said, "I have kept you from sinning against me . . . I did not let you touch her." (All this in Genesis 20.) God, by his providence, prevented Abimelech from bringing disaster to his people. On this occasion he used a dream. He can just as effectively use the preventive influences of age, laws, sex, disease, death, church, culture, parents, or whatever. Conscience can be a great preventer, too.

Withdrawing preventive influences is known as permissive providence. Rather than prevent sin, God gives a green light to the sinner to do his thing. David's census is a case in point. On another occasion God, fed up with Israel's rebellious spirit, "gave them over to their stubborn hearts to follow their own devices" (Ps. 81:12). Once, with regard to the tribe of Ephraim, God said, "Ephraim is joined to idols; leave him alone!" (Hos. 4:17). The Apostle Paul, in one of his sermons, said, "In the past, he [God] let all nations go their own way" (Acts 14:16). In his letter to the Romans he said, "God gave them over in the sinful desires of their hearts to sexual impurity . . . since they did not think it worthwhile to retain the knowledge of God, he gave them over to a depraved mind, to do what ought not to be done" (Rom. 1:24,28). Here nothing stands between the sinner and his sinning. Not even conscience.

Directive providence occurs when God directs the evil acts of men to unexpected ends. He knows the sour notes will be played, but he conducts the musicians in such a way that the cacaphony not only is immersed in, but surprisingly contributes to, the symphony (perhaps, even in the smallest way, by reminding us what discord means). A good example of this is in the story of the Exodus where we read of God "hardening" Pharaoh's heart. He used Pharaoh's shrill music as the keynote for the birth of a nation. (Read about it in Exodus, chapters 4 through 12.) You can be sure Pharaoh hardened his own heart before God added his bit. God just made sure Pharaoh went all the way.

Determinative providence defines boundaries. God won't allow sin to go beyond certain limits. In Job's case God said to Satan, "He is in your hands, but you must spare his life" (Job 2:6). If God gives Satan limits, you can be sure he gives us limits. There is an area known as out-of-bounds. God's providence determines the parameters of our sinning. Because he has an end in view, he determines the quantity and quality of all our sub-ends. Even our deadends.

This sounds a little too personal for some people. They're prepared to acknowledge general providence. God caring for the universe by maintaining general laws is OK. But God caring for the individual? Isn't that going a bit far? Why should God, who's so big, look out for me, when I'm so small? That's just the point. God's big enough to be little. He knows that whole lifetimes sometimes hinge on what appear at the time to be inconsequential events. He knows the value of one life in terms of redeeming a world. That's why he sent us his son. Large doors swing on small hinges.

There are some interesting implications to small-hinge providence—implications for material blessings, accidents, piety, and good works. A contemporary view which has gained wide acceptance in the West is that special providence is tuned to the health, wealth, and prosperity of God's children. When in fact, the opposite is often the case. Special providence may impoverish us in order to introduce true wealth. It may bring us worldly failure, sickly bodies, and even death in order to bring us to good and to God. Jesus said, "Every branch that . . . bears fruit he trims clean so that it will be even more fruitful" (John 15:2). The psalmist put it another way, "Before I was afflicted I went astray, but now I obey your word . . . It was good for me to be afflicted so that I might learn your decrees" (Ps. 119:67, 71).

As for accidents, there may be no such thing, at least in terms of their being for nothing. An accident is called such because it is purposeless. It shouldn't have happened, "and wouldn't had I not been delayed that extra moment before the car came through the red light." Now, as I lie in a hospital bed, my body racked with pain, I contemplate something even more painful: the agonizing awareness that this accident may in fact be serving God's purposes for my life quite nicely. Why? Why not some other way? We'll never know. But trust his providence. As Job said, "Though he slay me, yet will I trust in him." Sounds pious. Mainly because it is. Piety and good works relate actively to special providence. Whereas we're on the receiving end of material blessings (or unblessings) and accidents, in piety and good works we're on the giving end. Active rather than passive. Those who "seek first his kingdom" are the ones who enter God's best. It's only "those who love him" for whom "God works for the good" (Rom. 8:28). Which means we'd better do our best to love God and seek his interests. Special providence has an affinity to committed love. As the song says, "Don't speak of stars shining above; if you're in love, show me!"

But I'm going to speak of stars anyway. At least for a moment. Stars shining over Bethlehem. I was there last night, alone in the Shepherd's Fields. My favorite spot is the traditional site of Boaz's property (you know Boaz, the man who married Ruth, King David's great-grandmother.) His land is on the side of a steep hill about a mile from Bethlehem. It descends to the valley floor in narrow terraces. Each terrace is freshly plowed, and ancient olive trees mark the descending levels. It's rather like a sweeping staircase carpeted with rich earth and olive branches. The air stands still, as though it were anticipating the arrival of royalty, and its perfume is worthy of a king's bedchamber. Everytime I visit I find myself transported from seeing to sighing. It grips you. There's a fabric there. A fabric woven of awesome physical beauty and golden history. Unmarred by time's passing. Crowned with a coronet of the largest, brightest, and "wisest" stars I've ever seen. Stars that have been eclipsed by *the* star; like a young girl touched by the beauty of her mother, somehow gaining added beauty by simple proximity. Stars who shaded their eyes from the brilliance of a moment in history when angels sang, "Glory to God in the highest, and on earth peace to men." A cast of thousands. Singing the most glorious song ever heard in the cosmos. And the place the angels sang was in the area where I was. Last night. Alone. But not alone. For I believe in angels.

So what's an angel? He, she, it (?) is a created being, smarter and stronger than you and I, who serves as an agent of God's providence. Some are good, some are bad. Bad by choice. The bad ones, by the way, serve us and God by modeling a crushed rebellion. But good or bad, they are fascinating beings. Let's look at what the Bible tells us.

Psalm One hundred forty-eight says, "Praise him, all his angels, praise him, all his heavenly hosts . . . Let them praise the name of the Lord, for he commanded and they were created" (verses 2 and 5). The writer to the Hebrews says, "Are not all angels ministering spirits sent to serve those who will inherit salvation?" (Heb. 1:14). Put these two references together, and you've got created beings who, among other things as we'll see, minister to God's chosen. And they're spirits, not flesh and blood. They're much smarter than us, but even their knowledge is limited. "Even angels long to look into these things," says Peter about God's great plan of salvation (I Pet. 1:12). They're also scary, "The guards were so afraid of him that they shook and became like dead men" (Matt. 28:4). Nevertheless, they're not seen in Scripture as superior to man. Strangely, Paul comments that the angels will be subject to some kind of judgment by mankind. "Do you not know that we will judge angels?" (I Cor. 6:3). The judgment may take a while to process; their numbers are overwhelming. "Then I looked and heard the voice of many angels, numbering thousands upon thousands, and ten thousand times ten thousand" (Rev. 5:11; see also Dan. 7:10). They don't procreate (Matt. 22:30), which suggests they have no common character or "national" history. Each one must have been created separately. But like us, they have freedom of choice. Some chose sin—"God did not spare angels when they sinned, but sent them to hell . . ."(II Pet. 2:4). Others chose righteousness and are called "the council of the holy ones" (Ps. 89:7). And God's providence makes use of both good and bad.

Before looking at what good and bad angels do, I want to make a few observations on angels generally. We've already seen they are spirits. This doesn't mean, however, they are omnipresent. They are always somewhere, not everywhere. They're powerful, but not all-powerful. The Bible says they "excell in strength," and gives them names like "principalities, powers, dominions, world rulers." These are creaturely powers, nonetheless. Power that is dependent and derived, subject to the rules of the physical and spiritual world, limited by the will of God. They can't create, perform miracles, act without empowering, or read the mind of man. That's why we shouldn't see angels as junior gods. Their power is merely executive. And they're there to serve.

Angels keep cropping up again and again in Bible history. They reveal God's will to godly leaders, they assist in the Exodus, they guide Israel through the wilderness, they encamp around God's people at dangerous moments, and they even destroy an enemy or two in the process. They really get involved with Jesus—foretelling, announcing, and rejoicing at his birth; supporting him when he is tempted and suffering; staying in the wings at his crucifixion but doing their part at his resurrection and ascension. When Jesus returns and God's people are gathered into his kingdom, angels will oversee the logistics. They look after details.

And what about guardian angels? Are there such things? The idea springs out of biblical references such as, "The angel of the Lord encamps around those who fear him, and he delivers them" (Ps. 34:7). Or, "He will command his angels concerning you to guard you in all your ways" (Ps. 91:11). But the most interesting comment comes from Jesus himself: "See that you do not look down on one of these little ones. For I tell you that their angels in heaven always see the face of my Father in heaven" (Matt.

18:10). Jesus says children have "their angels in heaven." The psalmist says angels "guard" us. Are there guardian angels, then? Why not? If innocence has need of angels, how much more the blighted?

Now a word about blighted angels. They're often called evil, or unclean, spirits. Most commonly they're called demons. These are the ones who sinned and were sent to hell (II Pet. 2:4). We're not told why they sinned. We do have a hint or two as to what the sin was. Like Satan, they were guilty of "conceit" or pride (I Tim. 3:6). And pride has a way of making a devil out of anybody.

These devils work with Satan. Paul warns us about it: "Put on the full armor of God so that you can take your stand against the devil's schemes. For our struggle is not against flesh and blood, but against the rulers, against the authorities, against the powers of this dark world and against the spiritual forces of evil in the heavenly realms" (Eph. 6:11–12). Rulers, authorities, powers, and spiritual forces" all refer to angels. Fallen angels. And as angels they are subject to the same limitations as holy angels. They are dependent on God and act only because he allows them the freedom to do so. They can't overcome or ignore the laws of nature. Nor can they rob man of his free will. In fact, they can do nothing to man without the consent of human will. You've got to put yourself in an agreeable mood or position in order for them to have an opportunity to work their foul deeds in you. This means you can resist them through mental toughness and childlike trust in God. Paul again: "Take up the shield of faith, with which you can extinguish all the flaming arrows of the evil one" (Eph. 6:16). They are intimidated rather easily. At the first sign of resistance they flee (James 4:7). So there's no need for God's children to fear demons. Rather, we should fear God—the demons do (James 2:19). If you've got demon phobia, remember demons have got God phobia.

The irony about bad angels is that even while they're cooperating with Satan, they're working God's plan. The psalmist says,

"He unleashed against them his hot anger, his wrath, indignation and hostility—a band of destroying angels" (Ps. 78:49). God in this case punishes the ungodly by allowing evil angels to do what they want to do, destroy. They're like ravening jackals within feet of their prey, but held back by some superior will. Suddenly that will says, "OK, boys, go to it!" And they do. With a vengeance. Thus God uses Satan. The evil appetite is controlled by God to his own, superior ends. By the way, the jackals aren't able now to rebel against that superior will. When they were yet in their "home" (Jude 6), they had the choice of doing good or evil. Now all they can do is evil. Once they were free. Now they're bound by their own rebellion and have become pawns more than servants of God. Even more ironically, God uses them to good purposes in his children—take a look at the first book of Corinthians chapter 5, verse 5 and the first book of Timothy chapter 1, verse 20. How frustrated they must be. All they want is to consume and use. Instead, they're the ones being used. And one day they'll be consumed(Matt. 25:41).

Then there are the good angels. We've already seen most of what they do in my general overview. There are, however, two things they do which relate to special providence. First, they help and protect individuals. One of many good examples occurs in the disciple Peter's life just as the early Church is getting under way. He was imprisoned by King Herod, who had just killed the disciple James, the brother of John. Here's what the twelfth chapter of Acts says about it: "So Peter was kept in prison, but the church was earnestly praying to God for him. The night before Herod was to bring him to trial, Peter was sleeping between two soldiers, bound with two chains, and sentries stood guard at the entrance. Suddenly an angel of the Lord appeared and a light shone in the cell. He struck Peter on the side and woke him up. 'Quick get up!' he said, and the chains fell off Peter's wrists. Then the angel said to him, 'Put on your clothes and sandals.' And Peter did so. 'Wrap your cloak around you and follow me,' the angel told him. Peter followed him out of the prison, but he had no idea that what the angel was doing was really happening, he thought he was seeing a vision. They passed the first and second guards and came to the iron gate leading to the city. It opened for them by itself, and they went through it. When they had walked the length of one street, suddenly the angel left him. Then Peter came to himself" (verses 5–11). You've heard of angelic visitations, angelic choirs, angelic announcements. Well, this was an angelic jailbreak. Without breaking the jail.

Second, they take a personal interest in individual humans. It's possible to manage a jailbreak at the order of the Lord without necessarily caring about the prisoner himself. Duty, you know. But in the Gospel of Luke we see the interest angels have in our personal histories: "There is rejoicing in the presence of the angels of God over one sinner who repents" (Luke 15:10). They're like celestial moviegoers on the edge of their seats as the drama of our lives unfolds. They're cheering for us. And, from time to time, they're able to jump up onto the screen and become part of the story.

So whether it's an individual human or a cosmos to preserve and govern, God cares for all. Yet there are times, some would say most of the time, when God seems to have left us to ourselves. When in truth it's probably we who have done the leaving— we've left God to himself. Or at least tried to. But what about the apparent "sound and fury" of life, as Shakespeare put it, "signifying nothing"? How does God's providence relate to the "slings and arrows of outrageous fortune"?

If you want to see a picture of "sound and fury," take a look at a bee swarm. I was walking one summer's day through the woods near Lake Kagawong on Manitoulin Island—Canada's, in fact the world's, largest freshwater island. The forest was mainly coniferous. So the forest floor was insulated with a wonderfully soft and fragrant blanket of pine needles. The gently diffused light was punctuated here and there with brilliant shafts of sun that had managed to find gaps in the pine-branched covering overhead. Occasionally a few blue-white flashes pierced the woods horizontally, deflections from the lake, fifty paces or so to my left. The peace was intoxicating. It was one of those times when you are lulled into neutral. You walk, your mind rests, and your senses bathe in a kind of timeless joy. Suddenly the forest opened onto a sun-bathed meadow. A blaze of yellow, purple, and white flowers swept down a gentle slope to the glistening water. It was then I heard the sound of a faint humming. A droning that grew louder as I approached a large pine tree on the very edge of the wild-flowered field. There on a low branch was a thriving mass of confusion. In silhouette it looked like a fat crescent moon. It hummed, droned, and buzzed with pulsating life. A swarm of bees in the wild.

Bees swarm when a colony becomes overcrowded. They leave a hive and fly to form a new colony. Their flight, swarm, and individual goings and comings seem to the average observer to be aimless. There appears to be no rhyme nor reason to their hyperactivity. Yet there is. The bees "dance" for one another. Moving in circles. Moving in figure eights. Circles mean nectar is close at hand. Figure eights mean nectar is far away, and the line between the loops of the eight points the way to the nectar in relation to the sun. They form their new hive. Food gathering, egg-laying, and nourishing of the young occur at remarkable speed. The individual worker bees literally give their short lives for their work. Then, along comes a human bee-farmer. He expertly removes the hive and transplants it on his bee farm. The colony has become colonized. Without their consent, interest, or awareness, the bees have become servants, not just to one another, but to a skilled farmer who provides hundreds of people with honey. They're still acting according to their nature, and to the laws of nature, but they've been directed to a purpose far beyond their understanding. Their "sound and fury" signifies pleasure at hundreds of breakfast tables. Similarly, you and I "strut and fret our hour upon the stage," but are colonized for a greater end than we can imagine. That greater end is called "God's glory."

We don't serve a bee-farmer, however. We serve a God who has made us in his own image and loves us with an everlasting love. He sustains and directs us, as a "colony" and as individuals. He never abuses our freedom of choice. But he uses our choices for his ultimate purposes. He provides our needs. He directs. He disciplines. And sometimes, just sometimes, he sends angels.

CHAPTER 8

Does He Ever Break the Rules?

🐦 MME. ANGELIQUE reminded me of a baby robin. Small, vulnerable, big-eyed, and fuzzy. A fledgling's fuzz is white at the tips, giving it a sort of wise look. A white-headed wisdom, crowning big, deep eyes. But it's so tiny, so fragile. It makes you want to protect it, cup it in your hand, and shield it from all danger. A baby robin has a way of making a hairy-chested man feel maternal. That's how I felt about Mme. Angelique. Like a mother.

Mind you, she was old enough to be my mother. Her oldest son was my age, a fact which never ceased to amaze her, "You're so young, James! How can you be a pastor at twenty-two years of age?" Her second son was a year and a half younger. But they were both rips. Pierre, the oldest, used to take me for one hundred and twenty mile per hour rides in his sportscar. Jean-Guy, his brother, once took me for a ride at the same speed. On his motorcycle! We'd return, breathless, from these flirtations with death to steaming cups of coffee and endless apple pies and chocolate cakes. Mme. Angelique was not about to see her sons, let alone her pastor, expire from low blood sugar. She loved her boys, and showed it. She also loved me. As if I were her third son. She'd draw herself up to her full height, the top of her fuzzy white head reaching my shoulder, and say, "Some day one of my sons will also be serving God in the ministry. Just like you. And the other will serve God by serving the community." And she was right. Jean-Guy became a policeman. A motorcycle cop. And Pierre became a Jesuit priest. Without the sportscar.

One Sunday morning I noticed Mme. Angelique was absent from the service. A pastor gets a unique view of a congregation. From his pulpit he looks out onto a garden of heads. Different shapes, colors, textures, but usually the same pattern because people tend to sit in the same place from week to week. This morning a fuzzy white flower was missing from its place in the garden. The next morning the phone rang.

"Pastor?" It was the voice of a baby robin.

"Yes."

"Would you be so kind as to come over for a moment? I have something important to talk with you about. And I need prayer."

"I'll be right there."

A piping hot cup of coffee met me at the door. The rich, inviting aroma of freshly baked apple pie, too. It was part of the atmosphere, the fabric, of Mme. Angelique's home. Her smile was as ageless as ever. The welcome, warm. But there was a tension, a kind of urgency, in her big eyes. They seemed a bit sunken, as if retreating from some frightening surprise. I took a seat across from her. She got right to the point.

"I went to the doctor on Friday to get the results of the tests," she said.

"Tests? For what?" I asked.

"For my head. I had my head examined," she said, smiling at her own humor. "I've been having severe headaches for months. So I thought I'd better get checked out."

"And what's the story?"

"The story is I've got a brain tumor. Inoperable, too." Before I could say anything, she continued.

"That's why I called you over. The only option is God. I'm in his hands, and I'm prepared to go to meet him, if it's his will.

But I want to give him the opportunity to heal me first. So I'm wondering if you would pray for me."

Her eyes had somehow become clearer and deeper as she spoke. The sunkenness had gone. The baby robin was perched on the top-most branch. Ready for her first flight. Fear fleeing in the face of new horizons.

Even though I was young, I had enough common sense to know there are times when talking is out of place. Sometimes we talk to blunt the blow of devastation or ease the edge of uncertainty, insecurity, and fear. My silence wasn't insensitivity. It was empathy. And in a strange sort of way, respect. Respect for bravery. Awe at the sudden intrusion of death and the just as sudden emergence of nobility of heart. I bowed my head. And prayed.

I prayed for a miracle. The only thing that could save Mme. Angelique was a clear act of God. That's what a miracle is—a clear act of God. God intruding, invading, penetrating his creation to do something his own established laws of nature cannot do. To break his own rules, as it were. Or at least, overrule the rules.

Which raises big questions. Is it ethical for God to make rules only to overrule them? And then to do so on an on-call basis? Doesn't this mean he's whimsical? But what rules does *he* live by? Earth rules? Heaven rules? No rules? Doesn't being sovereign mean exactly that—no rules? Maybe he can't be trusted. Maybe he's more like those old pagan gods than we thought. Maybe Marduk is his middle name.

A lot of maybe's. Maybe before doing anything else I should give you an idea of where I'm going this chapter. First I want to give you a bit of a perspective on where we're coming from when we discuss miracles. You might call it a contextual review. Followed by a look at the possibility and probability of miracles ever occurring. As I usually do in these chapters, I'll present objections to the subject at hand. And then I'll give you a scan of miracles in the Bible. I'll look at signs and wonders, the miracles of Jesus, of his disciples, and of questionable healers, and conclude with a few observations on miracles as they relate to salvation and revelation. And yes, I'll finish Mme. Angelique's story. At the end.

First, the contextual review. As far as immediate context is concerned, we've just come from a chapter on God's providence. There we saw providence as the preservation, care, and government of God over all his creation—succinctly summed up in my dad's "God will take care of us." Providence portrays a higher order working on a lower order. The supernatural on the natural. Providence presents a God whose majesty and magnificence cannot come near to being expressed in the natural order of this little world, "stooping" to care. And as much as we lovingly respond to this excelling love, we know there is so much more in God than we can grasp. After all, he is God. We are merely human, which is the bottom-line setting for our discussion of miracles. The context is human. Miracles don't relate to rocks or trees or galaxies. Miracles relate to men. Only humans have an interest in the supernatural. Perhaps I should qualify that. In most of the human world there is regard for the supernatural. Here in the Western world we've risen "above" the supernatural. Or should that be "below"? Who knows. The point is that God, when dealing with you and me for the sake of his providential purpose, sometimes does an end run around the order of nature. An end-run to a greater end.

There's something else which needs to be remembered when discussing the context in which we consider miracles. Miracles don't relate to heaven. They relate to earth. In heaven there is no distinction between natural and supernatural. It's only here that supernatural has meaning. Miracles present the meeting between the immaterial and the material. You might call them an "immaterial" matter. They have meaning because they occur in a context where natural law generally applies. Like most mavericks, miracles would be run-of-the-mill if there weren't an establishment to be amazed, amused, or abused. And on top of that, an Establishment to be established.

The Establishment, of course, is the kingdom of heaven. And

it comes to us in different ways—sometimes through the everyday processes of nature—for instance, the moisture of the earth becoming the juice of an orange, providing part of our "daily bread"; sometimes through the work of God's Holy Spirit, convincing us of the realities of sin, righteousness, and judgment; and sometimes through events in the world which have no natural explanation. Events brought about by nothing other than a clear act of God. The Westminster Confession puts it this way: "God, in ordinary providence making use of means, yet is free to work without, above, or against them at pleasure." The fact is, no creature can originate life or do anything without the use of means. Even an artist has to use paint, or words, or ideas. He has to rearrange, or manipulate, the established order to "create" something new. So this "without, above, or against" business is a bit unpalatable. Means are our bread and butter. What's more, we Westerners are anti-supernatural in our world view. The only *super* we want is superstars, superglue, or, as one ad agency put it, supernatural British Columbia!

To prove an event miraculous, then, one must prove the absence of any natural means, or cause. A cancer must be cured without medicine, radiation, or natural remission. Paralyzed legs must be made to walk again without surgery or prolonged bed rest. A tortured mind must be instantaneously healed without psychotherapy. Every attempt at natural explanation must draw a blank. We must come face-to-face with an act of God.

That's the direction miracles point us to. God. The Bible is full of examples. Here are a few: "Has any god ever tried to take for himself one nation out of another nation, by testings, by miraculous signs and wonders, by war, by a mighty hand and an outstretched arm, or by great and awesome deeds, like all the things the Lord your God did for you in Egypt before your very eyes? You were shown these things so that you might know that the Lord is God; besides him there is no other"(Deut. 4:34–35). "He came to Jesus at night and said, 'Rabbi, we know you are a teacher who has come from God. For no one could perform the miraculous signs you are doing if God were not with him' "

(John 3:2). "God also testified to it by signs, wonders, and various miracles"(Heb. 2:4). Perhaps the key statement is, "You were shown these things so that you might know the Lord is God." From God's perspective, miracles are a basic form of communication. They reveal him to us. But for some people, belief in miracles is a basic form of superstition. Before I discuss their objections, however, I want to make a few comments about the possibility and probability of miracles.

One day last summer I was snorkeling in the Red Sea. The surface of the sea was calm, and the water clear as glass. Unfolding beneath me as I lazily flipped my flippers was an eerily beautiful garden of coral. I looked down on brilliant yellow dwarf corals, blood-red sea-fan corals, demurely muted mushroom corals, businesslike reef-building corals, delicate soft corals, and an absolute panoply of multicolored fish. Snorkeling in the Red Sea is like snorkeling in an oversized aquarium. I was struck by its magnificence, but I felt a bit like an intruder, which I was. The underwater world is a world of its own. It has its own structure, its own rules, its own "culture." Everywhere in that silent world is an unwritten law, "Do not disturb."

But disturb it I did. I was trying out a friend's waterproof diving watch. The bracelet was loose. So I took it off to make an adjustment and accidentally dropped it. I watched it descend nine or ten feet and land in the middle of some soft coral. Taking a deep breath, I went after it and swam through what appeared to be hundreds of tiny, fluorescent blue fish ascending from the spot where the watch landed. They were about the size of the tip of my little finger, but I could see fury in their eyes. For all I know, my wayward watch disturbed a very important political gathering taking place in that soft coral. Or maybe a birthday party. Would you believe a union meeting? Whatever. The main thing is that life underwater has its own rhythm. Drop a watch into some soft coral and behold the havoc! Havoc wreaked by something, or someone, who belongs to another world—the world above. The world below is in direct contact with the world above, but each has distinctive characteristics, rather like the spiritual world and the material world. The spiritual may be as close to us as beach to waves, or air to water. But there's no awareness on our part of the other unless that other takes the initiative. It's got to drop the watch. Or our union meeting goes on, undisturbed. Oblivious to the world above.

That's why I think it reasonable to assume the possibility of miracles. If we see the laws of nature, the established rhythm, of our world as forever fixed and without a personal God behind them, then we can't think in terms of miracles. However, if see these laws as serving God, rather than God serving them, then we can allow for the possibility of their being altered, interrupted, or suspended from time to time. The swimmer can drop his watch, spear a fish, introduce a new breed of sea life, or create a whole new situation for us to cope with or delight in. And even though all these interruptions may appear miraculous to us, perhaps some of them are not miraculous at all, but simply a revealing of something we don't usually perceive. However, there's no point in becoming connoisseurs of miracles. What we should stress is the existence of a personal God. If he exists and is personal, then miracles are possible.

They're also probable, mainly because God is loving. His love is condescending, from the greater to the lesser, from the perfect to the imperfect. Thus, it's a self-limitation on his part—the old "stooping" theme again. From time to time this condescension will involve action on God's part above and beyond nature. His miraculous intervention will seem to us as an unusual expression of power, an irresistible arm-twisting, a power play—which may be partially true. I think we should expect occasional miraculous backwash as an "occupational hazard" of the greater navigating the sea of the lesser. But it's more than an issue of power overwhelming power. It's an issue of Nature overwhelming nature. That is, the nature of God (which is love) addressing itself to natural law. The natural must bow to the Natural. For there will be moments in God's dealings with us where general providence will not be enough. Special providence, with its angels and miracles, will break the surface tension of the water. We'll see the swimmer's shadow.

But there are objections. I've already referred to the big one—the laws of nature are fixed, they can't be violated or set aside. If in some pantheistic sense God were the laws of nature, or the laws of nature God, this would be true. But God is not the all, and all is not God, including the laws of nature. From a biblical perspective, natural law is like the rest of creation. It's all subject to God. He can suspend, do an end run around, or "violate" at his pleasure any and all law he's imposed on his creation for its greater good. Regardless of how dependable the laws of nature are, we must not forget they are under the voluntary control of a personal God. Natural law determines the outcome of most of life. But its "sovereignty" is executive. It submits to the ultimate sovereignty of God. A God who is subject to nothing, including material and natural law. The architect of free will has left himself free.

I mentioned, three paragraphs ago, that some of what we see as miraculous may, in fact, be simply a revealing of something we don't usually perceive. The implication of this statement is unbiblical, although the bare statement itself does express a truth. For instance, a plane flying over a stone-age tribe may be interpreted by these primitive people as a miracle, when in fact, it is simply the product of advanced minds with advanced technology. The truth is we tend to exclaim "Miracle!" when confronted with a wonder we can't explain. The unbiblical implication is that all unexplained wonders are merely the product of a higher, but natural law. This is known as the "higher law" objection to miracles. It says a miracle is simply a higher physical law at work. A law which we may one day understand.

This, of course, leads us nowhere. First, because it rests on an unproveable assumption—that every physical effect has a physical cause. Second, because natural law cannot create anything outside its realm of established influence. If it could, it would be God. Third, the Bible doesn't talk about higher law. Rather it talks about "the great and awesome deeds" of God. But the real dead end is this: if a miracle is simply the result of a higher natural law, then it's no miracle at all.

Joining the natural-law and higher-law objections is the absolute-God objection. Like the natural-law objection it keys on fixity, or inflexibility. In this case, the absolute rigidity of God's acts. It sees any individual focus on God's part as a sign of whimsy. He can't be influenced by individual petitions or needs. He acts on our behalf, but corporately and eternally. He establishes laws and keeps to them. He never acts extraordinarily. This objection is very compatible with the deistic objection, which suggests that just as a high-tech engineer has no reason to interfere with a computer he has made except to correct a breakdown, so too God has no reason to interfere with creation except to correct a breakdown. And if there is a breakdown, it means God has created imperfectly. Which cannot be. Therefore, miracles (seen as correction of imperfections) cannot be. But if these two objections are valid against miracles, then they're valid against the Bible's teaching of a personal God who involves himself personally in his creation. Which means they're valid against providence, revelation, hearing of prayer, and grace as well. And they're valid against personal relationship—the laws of nature become the mediator between God and man.

The God of the Bible, however, is not a high-tech mechanic, nor some kind of personified natural law. He is an all-powerful, all-present, personal creator and father. He is distinct from this world and its laws, laws which he has imposed. In fact he maintains and controls them in his providence. At the same time he is personally free to overrule them as he sees fit. He normally works mediately, that is, he uses means (natural law). Sometimes he works immediately, without means, but never without meaning. All this, of course, is denied by those who see no difference between God and nature. Denying miracles on the basis of God's power being the same as nature's power has its price, however. It means there are no grounds for distinguishing between natural and supernatural events. To all intents and purposes it banishes

God altogether. He either doesn't exist, or else he's gone on a long vacation.

Now for some Bible. Many of the miraculous acts of God in the Old Testament are referred to as signs. In the New Testament they're often called signs and wonders. First the Old Testament. One of the most famous of signs was Israel's crossing of the Red Sea. As God instructed Moses to raise his staff to divide the water, he said, "The Egyptians will know that I am the Lord." The parting of the waters was to be a sign to Egypt. And to Israel too, for "when the Israelites saw the great power the Lord displayed against the Egyptians, the people feared the Lord and put their trust in him and in Moses his servant"(Exod. 14:18, 31). Notice the revelatory or communication factor here—the sign said God is the Lord and Moses is his servant. This theme recurs consistently. A miraculous sign always points to God and often underscores the authority of the man God uses to effect the sign. Another water-parting sign emphasizes the same point. In Joshua, chapter 3, we read about Israel's miraculous crossing of the flood-watered Jordan river. Joshua prepares the people for the miracle by stressing its sign value. "This is how you will know that the living God is among you" (verse 10). God prepares Joshua by saying, "Today I will begin to exalt you in the eyes of all Israel, so they may know that I am with you as I was with Moses" (verse 7). This time the sign says the Lord is here, and Joshua is his servant. But whichever way the sign puts it, the basic message is that nothing is impossible for God(Gen. 18:14). Signs point to God. We've already seen Moses saying, "You were shown these things so that you might know that the Lord is great and do marvelous deeds; you alone are God" (Gen. 86:10). It's as though signs are more a heavenly public relations effort than anything else. What they happen to accomplish for God's children seems almost incidental.

As for the New Testament, the term *signs and wonders* is used on several occasions. Here are a few examples: "In the last days," God says . . . "I will show wonders in the heavens above and signs on the earth below" (Acts 2:19). "Now Stephen, a man full of

God's grace and power, did great wonders and miraculous signs among the people"(Acts 6:8). In one case the signs are cosmic in nature. They affect the heavens and the earth. In the other case the signs underscore the authority of Stephen, one of God's servants. In either case they point to God. Then you have Jesus' case.

Right off the top I detect a bit of disdain on Jesus' part for signs. At least signs for signs' sake. Look at this: "The Pharisees and Sadducees came to Jesus and tested him by asking him to show them a sign from heaven. He replied . . . 'A wicked and adulterous generation looks for a miraculous sign, but none will be given it except the sign of Jonah' " (Matt. 16:1–4). He saw the demand for signs as a smoke screen concealing a refusal to come to grips with his call for all men everywhere to repent. The only sign he'd give to an unrepentant generation was Jonah's sign— that is, just as Jonah was three days and nights in the belly of a huge fish, so Jesus would be three days and nights in the heart of the earth (Matt. 12:40). The sign, of course, would be what he'd do after the three days and nights. His resurrection would be the ultimate sign of God's power and glory, and of the authority the Father had given the Son. But that's not to say the resurrection sign would be accepted automatically. In one of his parables, Jesus said of his generation's unrepentance, "If they do not listen to Moses and the Prophets, they will not be convinced even if someone rises from the dead" (Luke 16:31). Nevertheless, the main focus of signs is affirmed by this ultimate sign. Remember, a sign or wonder points to God and emphasizes the authority of the sign maker. Whether it's Moses, Joshua, Stephen, or Jesus. In Jesus' case, however, the resurrection sign goes a giant step further. It forever validates the Christian faith (I Cor. 15).

Enough about signs. Except to say a sign is always a miracle, but a miracle is not always a sign. I can say this because Jesus himself often neutralized any sign potential of his miracles by insisting the miracle be kept private, under wraps. Sometimes miracles are to be a personal matter between God and an individual, with no one else in on the secret.

A couple of chapters ago I mentioned Jesus' miracle at Cana. It was his very first, one of eight so-called "nature miracles" (John 2:1–11). When you read it, notice Jesus taking no credit for the miracle. The wedding guests know nothing about it. All they know is, "Everyone brings out the choice wine first and then the cheaper wine after the guests have had too much to drink; but you have saved the best till now" (verse 10). They give the credit to the bridegroom. And for whatever reason, he doesn't pass it on to Jesus. As I said, Jesus often chose to keep a low profile when he performed miracles. He, for one, was unimpressed by the kingdom of heaven invading space and time. He had a healthy perspective. Heaven and earth were both home to him.

What were those eight nature miracles? Here they are in no particular order: water into wine(John 2:1–11); stilling of the storm(Mark 4:35–41); feeding of the five thousand(John 6:5–13); feeding of the four thousand(Mark 8:1–10); walking on the water(Matt. 14:22–33); coin in the fish's mouth(Matt. 17:24–27); and the draught of fish(John 21:1–19). Then there were three miracles where Jesus raised people from the dead: Jairus's daughter(Matt. 9:18–26); the widow of Nain's son (Luke 7:11–17); and Lazarus(John 11). And of course, there were several miracles of healing—lepers, blind, lame, deaf-mute, and demon-possessed people liberated from their afflictions by a word, a touch, or a command from Jesus. Little wonder people were impressed. John put it this way, "He thus revealed his glory, and his disciples put their faith in him"(John 2:11). Jesus was a tough act to follow. But follow him they did.

Jesus' miracles were no stage show, however. Right from the beginning of his ministry he refused to play to his audience. His very first challenge came from Satan himself. There in the wilderness Jesus rejected Satan's tempting him to demonstrate his power as a proof of his divine nature (Matt. 4:1–11). He had nothing to prove, to himself, to Satan, or to anyone else. He wasn't into exploiting his miracle-working power. If there were any promotions agents in his day, he must have driven them to distraction—no posters, no television ministry, no coast-to-coast tours, no books. And there simply was no curing him of his unprofessional tendency to downplay the sensational. I mean, he raises a girl from the dead, and what does he do? "He gave strict orders not to let anyone know about this, and told them to give her something to eat"(Mark 5:43). He lets the grieving friends and family think he was right about her just being asleep (verse 39), and gets her some chicken soup. It's good for what ails you.

But he did stress one point. Again and again. In fact the gospel writers make it very clear that Jesus usually combined his miracles with preaching about the kingdom of heaven. Matthew says, "Jesus went throughout Galilee, teaching in their synagogues, preaching the good news of the kingdom, and healing every disease and sickness among the people"(Matt. 4:23). He didn't mix miracles and magic. Rather, he preached heaven, healed the sick, and in the drama of the moment called for repentance(Matt. 4:17) and granted forgiveness. Indeed, forgiveness of sins was often linked with healing. One good example of this occurs when a paralyzed man enters a crowded house through the roof. His friends, concerned and ingenious, were not about to miss Jesus simply because they couldn't get the man through the door. Jesus, impressed with their faith, says to the paralytic, "Son, your sins are forgiven." Then, in response to some religious critics who saw this as blasphemy, Jesus says, "Which is easier: to say to the paralytic, 'Your sins are forgiven,' or to say, 'Get up, take your mat, and walk'? But that you may know that the Son of Man has authority on earth to forgive sins . . ." He said to the paralytic, " 'I tell you, get up, take your mat and go home!' He got up, took his mat and walked out in full view of them all"(Mark 2:1–12).

So Jesus stressed the kingdom of heaven. Then he would perform a miracle. The miracle was often associated with or responded to by repentance and forgiveness of sins, but there were usually two other ingredients in the process—faith and discipleship. Faith preceded. Discipleship followed. A timid lady, chronically ill for twelve years, after being healed by simply touching Jesus, hears him say, "Daughter, your faith has healed you" (Mark

5:34). Two blind men outside of Jericho cry out to Jesus. He stops, asks them what they want, in response touches their eyes, and "Immediately they received their sight and followed him" (Matt. 20:34). A miracle provides two liberating functions—it's a "window" to the eternal dimension, and it's a turning point in the life of the recipient. You begin to walk a new path. A way leading to God.

Jesus didn't limit the power to perform miracles to himself. The New Testament tells us he sent his disciples out into the world with the express purpose of preaching and performing miracles. Luke says, "When Jesus had called the Twelve together, he gave them power and authority to drive out all demons and to cure diseases, and he sent them out to preach the kingdom of God and to heal the sick" (Luke 9:1–2). The miracles were the accompanying signs which verified the divine calling of the apostles. Luke again: "So Paul and Barnabas spent considerable time there, speaking boldly for the Lord, who confirmed the message of his grace by enabling them to do miraculous signs and wonders"(Acts 14:3). Peter saw miracles as the support necessary to speak the word, or preach, "with great boldness"(Acts 4:29–30). This is why the disciples' miracles had a consistent "signs and wonders" aspect. The disciples weren't Jesus. They were uncertain of themselves, and needed the security of signs in order to keep going. At least, that's how I see it. The miraculous confirmed the disciples' ministry in the eyes of the public and affirmed divine calling in their own eyes.

Paul certainly saw it that way. In a candid assessment of his success he says, "I will not venture to speak of anything except what Christ has accomplished through me in leading the Gentiles to obey God by what I have said and done—by the power of signs and miracles, through the power of the Spirit. So from Jerusalem all the way around the Illyricum, I have fully proclaimed the gospel of Christ"(Rom. 15:18–19). In his eyes, preaching and miracles were partners. One should preach with "demonstration of the Spirit's power"(I Cor. 2:4). In fact, he saw the apostolic ministry legitimized by the miraculous. "The things that mark an apostle," he said, are "signs, wonders, and miracles" (II Cor. 12:12). The preached kingdom had somehow to be actualized in order to become real to people. Miracles personalized that message. They also validated it. To say nothing of validating the miracle workers themselves.

So what about faith healers? Those strange-looking, stranger-acting circus performers appearing at all hours on our television screens. Always yelling, laying hands on people with shouts of authority, knocking them over so they fall down "like a side of beef," as one old farmer put it. Looking mystically into people's eyes or into the television camera with "words of knowledge," reminding you of Madame Fiora, the gypsy fortuneteller who used to appear every year at the third-rate carnival set up outside your town when you were a kid. Do they work miracles? And if they do, does that mean God is validating these weirdos?

Let's look at the plus side first. I think we can safely assume no servant serves perfectly. Simply because he's human, his humanity filters God's divinity. God's light is bent, fragmented even, by the flawed prism of human nature. When shining through us, it is light nonetheless. It may cast things in a sickly hue, like a color television on the fritz, but it still takes a signal out of the air and gives us a picture. Not entirely satisfying, mind you, but a picture at least. Whetting appetite for the real picture. Like some faith healers. Their style hurts the eyes. Watch too long and you get a headache, but at least you can hear the message. The audio is fairly clear. The substance is OK. The focus is fuzzy, however, and can drive you to distraction. Distraction caused by distortion. Little wonder you tire of making do. You either throw the old set out or do without until you can replace it with a new one. You need a clear picture. The clearest available.

Then there's the downside. For a lot of these faith healers the audio is scratchy, the focus is fuzzy, and the substance is bad. There is no message, however distorted, of God. The message, rather, is money. The style is mimicry. They implore their audience to "keep those cards and letters coming in"—moneyed cards and letters, that is. They justify their extravagant lifestyles by teaching that "king's kids" should live like princes. A Rolls-Royce becomes the ultimate symbol of true spirituality. As the Bible would say, these types serve Mammon, or money (Matt. 6:24). Yet they show wounded indignation whenever the cynical public, especially the press, criticizes their money mania. They glare into the TV camera, faces red, necks bulging, and attack their critics with prophetic fervor. They condemn the journalists because they're sinful cynics. Which may be the case—sinful perhaps, cynical certainly. They're also telling the truth.

Which is more than many of these charlatans do. There was a remarkable exposé recently where, in documentary form, a filmmaker infiltrated and recorded the counterfeit "words of knowledge" of a well-known faith healer. To the amazement of his audience and his onstage clients, he told them their names, their addresses, and their physical problems. All on the spot. This must be God! But no. The healer was wearing a microreceiver in his ear. His wife, offstage, was transmitting "words of knowledge" from questionnaires these gullible folk had filled in before the service. That's why I said the message is money and the style is mimicry. They mimic the real thing. Their trade is the jaded, yet real, power of counterfeit. A phony twenty-dollar bill is worth twenty dollars to the indiscriminate. They'll take it in exchange for goods or services. They may pass it on, in good faith, to others, or they may try to bank it and get stung.

Amazingly, some are healed. This tells me God is flexible, not only in terms of circumventing the laws of nature once in awhile but also in terms of circumventing the laws of miracle once in awhile. As I've already said, miracles point to God and underline the divine calling of the miracle worker. When I see people healed in charlatans' meetings, however, I see what I call "fuel-efficient" miracles. That is, a little going a long way—God responding to the recipient's faith, ignoring the antics of the circus performer. Tolerating the juggler in deference to a child's awe at the art of juggling.

The Bible, with an eye to the future, says, "The coming of

the lawless one will be in accordance with the work of Satan displayed in all kinds of counterfeit miracles, signs, and wonders, and in every sort of evil that deceives those who are perishing"(II Thess. 2:9–10). Jesus himself says, "For false Christs and false prophets will appear and perform signs and miracles to deceive the elect—if that were possible. So be on your guard"(Mark 13:22–23). OK, so I'll be on my guard. But what am I looking for? Look for self-aggrandizement in the faith healer. Look for self-promotion, lots of pictures of the healer in his newsletters and news magazines. Look for a message full of self-justification. See this and see a phony. On the other hand, look for a healer with a sense of humor; a guy who downplays his miracles, who has a healthy family commitment and a decided detachment from legalistic spirituality; a man who makes little of religion and much of relationship, whose love for God overshadows everything else. See this and see a saint. Take note of Blaise Pascal's cryptic comment, "Instead of concluding that there are not true miracles since there are so many false, we must on the contrary say that there are true miracles since there are so many false, and that false miracles exist only for the reason that there are true; so also that there are false religions only because there is one that is true." And I say, with all conviction, trust your instincts.

And trust God. Understand that he is telling us something vital when he intervenes miraculously in our history. He's giving us key information about salvation and the kingdom of heaven. Look at Jesus' miracles. Profound implications reside there. For example, his miraculous provisions of food see a day coming when all physical needs will end: "Never again will they hunger; never again will they thirst"(Rev. 7:16). His calming the waters of a storm-stricken lake foreshadows a total victory over chaos: "Then I saw a new heaven and a new earth, for the first heaven and first earth had passed away, and there was no longer any sea"(Rev. 21:1). His healing of sick people implies a day when all suffering will cease: "He will wipe every tear from their eyes. There will be no more death or mourning or crying or pain, for the old order of things has passed away"(Rev. 21:4). His mastery over demons foresees the final destruction of Satan's princedom: "Now is the time for judgment on this world; now the prince of this world will be driven out"(John 12:31). And his raising of the dead suggests a day when death will be forever destroyed: "The last enemy to be destroyed is death"(I Cor. 15:26). The miraculous signals a new day. An age of salvation from death. A new kingdom where the wondrous is old hat.

So Jesus' miracles demonstrate his mastery over nature, health and sickness, life and death. This mastery reveals his divinity, for no one but God himself possesses that kind of power. By healing people from both spiritual and physical disease, he did the work of a savior. Saving men out of the evils and corruptions killing them. When John the Baptist's followers questioned whether or not Jesus was in fact the savior prophesied in the Old Testament, Jesus answered, "Go back and report to John what you hear and see: the blind receive sight, the lame walk, those who have leprosy are cured, the deaf hear, the dead are raised, and the good news is preached to the poor"(Matt. 11:4–5). His miracles were positive evidence that he was who he said he was, the Son of God. That's why we can say his miracles were a revelation of God. Revealing a Father who cares, a Son who lives, and a kingdom that shall never pass away. Thus, Peter can say of Jesus, "Salvation is found in no one else, for there is no other name under heaven given to men by which we must be saved" (Acts 4:12). Jesus himself rested his case on miracles: "Why then do you accuse me of blasphemy because I said, 'I am God's Son'? Do not believe me unless I do what my Father does. But if I do it, even though you do not believe me, believe the miracles, that you may learn and understand that the Father is in me, and I in the Father"(John 10:36–38). His miracles reveal a Savior. A raiser and riser from death. There has been no other revelation in history of such power.

I prayed to this Savior to heal Mme. Angelique. Quietly. Just she and I, sitting on either side of the living room, our heads bowed. And frankly, my faith was small. After the prayer, I left. Over the next several months I saw her frequently. She resumed her seat on Sunday mornings. She baked her pies and cakes, but she never spoke of her tumor. After a year or so, I'd pretty much forgotten all about it. Until a day she phoned to volunteer a few pies for a church social.

"By the way," I said, "how's it going with the tumor?"

"Oh, that! I should have told you. It's gone."

"Gone?"

"Yes. A few days after we prayed about it, I went to the doctor for more tests. He took an X ray and it wasn't there. Boy, was he surprised!"

"Thank God!" I exclaimed.

"Yes, thank God. But please, pastor, do me a favor."

"What's that?"

"Let's keep it between you and me. Our little secret."

"I won't say a thing for, uh, fifteen years," I answered. And I haven't. Until today. Seventeen years later, to be exact.

The Word of God

God Talks about Himself

✥ IT WAS pretty heady stuff for a seventeen-year-old. First there was Allison—a college freshman, the most beautiful girl in town; then there were her friends, also college freshmen, acknowledged by all us high-school seniors as the coolest dudes in town; and the setting, a midsummer's evening, a balmy seventy degrees, and the oldest, most historic, most romantic house in town. The occasion? A discussion of Plato's philosophy. "In depth," I might add, as you would expect from such an erudite crew. Last and by all means least, was I. Present not because of my Platonic expertise, but because of platonic love. I was Allison's "date" at this cerebral enterprise, and I was the envy of every guy there.

The house gave a kind of dignity to the proceedings. A hundred years before it had been the residence of the governor-general of Ontario when he was in the area. Majestic trees and rolling lawns surrounded it with an elderly maturity. The building itself was of a muted gray brick accented with dark green ivy, bedroom gables, and wedgewood blue shutters. Carefully manicured, the walkway swept up to a broad oak veranda furnished with quilted redwood chairs. Chairs fairly reaching out and grabbing you with their appeal. The huge oak doors, trimmed in polished brass, led into a stately foyer dominated by a sweeping staircase. As you stood beneath an ancient chandelier, you were surrounded by large French doors leading to dining room, sitting room, living room, and family room. The furniture had age and depth. The ceiling had a transcendent quality—it was at least twenty feet high. And the hardwood floors were indented with the traffic of thousands of feet over scores of years.

The depth of the house that night was challenged by the imagined depth of the discussion in the family room. The term *knowing enough to be dangerous* is very appropriate when describing students who've just completed their first year of university. The air was charged with academic clichés, profundities, and learned looks. These observations are all in retrospect, you understand. At the time, I was suitably impressed by the vocabulary and authority flying with impunity around the room.

"Let me suggest," said Bob (*suggest* is what you use when you've just finished your freshman year; to *tell* or *say* is too pedestrian), "that your view of the pre-Socratics has prejudiced your view of Socrates."

"I don't see what you're getting at," answered Marsha. At that point the phone rang, and Allison went to answer it.

"Wait 'til I get back, I don't want to miss a thing!" she bubbled. A few moments later, excitement in her eyes, she returned.

"Hey, gang, I've an announcement. I didn't say anything about this before 'cause I didn't know 'til now she could make it."

"Who could make it?" I asked.

"Mme. Sonja, a fortuneteller from Port Stanley! And she'll do all our fortunes for two dollars each. Isn't that great?"

"Such fun! What time's she coming?" asked Maureen.

"In ten minutes. So let's have a coffee. We'll pick up on Plato next time."

"Before we do," said Dave, "let me observe on the course of our discussion so far. I think one thing we agree on is that we all refuse to believe what we don't understand. Right? With the exception of you, Jim" (an aside to me with a definite note of condescension).

"Right!" echoed Al, "the mind's the thing. Reason before anything else. *Cogito ergo sum.*" I just nodded mutely. It was bad enough being the youngest, being envied (Allison's fault), and being the odd man out intellectually, but I was thrown by Allison's announcement. I wasn't keen on fortunetellers.

Twenty minutes later, the air spiced with coffee aroma, the doorbell rang. Mme. Sonja had arrived. She swooped into the room. I say *swooped* because her walk was less a walking and more a gliding motion. She looked and acted the part. Her ageless face had a sort of faceless age—in other words, she had the typical look of a fortuneteller, a look that has been a caricature for women of her profession over the years. You couldn't tell if she was fifty or seventy, but you could tell she was some kind of medium, witch, enchantress, or whatever. The best way to describe her heavy, embroidered garments is "early gypsy." And her voice was cultivated to make hair stand on end. No kidding. She was some performer! Her effect on us all was electric. Plato fled to the shadows. Mme. Sonya was now in charge.

Maybe not entirely. There was something in me that bristled as soon as she entered the room. No, I'm not talking about the hair on the back of my neck. I'm talking about something inside. It was as though my spirit had released a guard dog. I found myself resisting her. Contrary to my new friends' wide-eyed acceptance. They quickly volunteered to have their palms read. As they clustered around her, hanging on every word, making appropriate exclamations—"Yes! Red is my favorite color! My mother always said I'd be a doctor! Oh! How did you know! Isn't this fantastic!"—I found myself slowly withdrawing. Allison turned and caught my eye. I made some feeble excuse to leave.

"You don't like this, do you, Jim," she said.

"No. I guess not."

"Why not?"

"Well, I, uh, look, let's talk about it tomorrow, OK? Just don't take it personally, all right?" She smiled faintly, and I left. The house looked somewhat somber in the moonlight. Almost haunted.

Was I overreacting? Perhaps a bit. But I was also legitimately troubled. Not out of a superstitious fear of fortunetellers, nor simply out of superstition, period. But out of a high view of things spiritual. I knew about evil powers and I feared the consequences of entertaining or being entertained by them. On top of that, I was amazed at the credulity of this group of educated people whom I admired and respected. They had just interrupted a two-hour discussion of truth where they concluded that one should not believe what one does not understand. Now they were laying their lives and minds open, in a naive trust and faith, to the entertaining tip of a potentially destructive iceberg. On one hand they were rationalists who would not believe without appropriate evidence. On the other hand they were superstitious, true believers without any appropriate evidence at all. They weren't practicing what they preached.

In both cases, however, truth was the issue—Plato's theory of knowledge and Mme. Sonja's clairvoyance. Both demanding stage time. Both calling for an audience. For whenever truth is at issue, communication is the name of the game. So the philosopher reasons from the specific to the general, the fortuneteller pontificates from some mystic bag of tricks, and the theologian argues from authority. They all purport to reveal the truth, they call for our vote, but whose truth is truthful? Who really has a revelation?

I'm hoping, in this chapter, to help you understand revelation. We'd all prefer to hear directly from the source of truth, rather than from any self-professed medium. And there is one book that claims to be a direct word from God to his creatures. It's the Bible, the place where God talks about himself. So in my Bible-based exploration I'll discuss the what and the why of revelation and the relationship of both reason and authority to revelation, *authority* meaning the claim the Bible makes to being *the* word from God. In this context I'll comment quite extensively on the subject of prophecy. There are several biblical and common-sense factors in determining what revealer, what prophet, you can trust. I'll show you how to spot a false prophet. But for now, the what of revelation.

In the original Bible languages, *to reveal* means "to uncover oneself." That is, to expose oneself! To take your clothes off. Strip, as it were. This is a vital point. Because it tells us revelation is an active rather than passive process, originating not with the medium but with the source. No amount of spirituality, incantation, magic, or denominational string-pulling will unravel God's garments. Either he pulls the strings himself, on his own initiative, or there's no revelation. We don't discover God. He "dis"-covers himself.

He doesn't dis-cover himself to a vacuum, however. His revelation tells us he knows we have the capacity to receive it. Mind calls to mind, deep to deep, spirit to spirit. He communicates truth to us. Which means he also imparts himself, just as a lover imparts or gives of himself to his beloved. He knows we need to have knowledge of him in order to love him. So he tells it like it is, knowing full well there will be some aspects of his revelation we won't like, knowing he will be rejected by some of us, which hurts. But then, revelation always means vulnerability. That's why most of us prefer to keep our clothes on and our mouths shut.

Mind you, I doubt God has come anywhere near to uncovering himself fully. Maybe we've seen nothing but the soles of his feet. Then again, he may have taken off more than his socks—he's let us see his Son. A Son who said, "He who has seen me has seen the Father." Nevertheless, what we've seen is only a beginning. We've only seen him bent over, stooping. We have yet to see him in his full splendor. To this point he is far beyond our understanding, which brings me back to my gullible friends, palms wide open for Mme. Sonja.

Before her grand entrance, they had announced they believed nothing they didn't understand, a statement only college freshmen could make without embarrassment, for there are so many things we know, or know about, without knowing how or why they are knowable. There's no need for examples here—you can fill in the blanks. Suffice it to say knowledge and comprehension are not the same thing. Sometimes there's a huge gap between the two. In spite of this, however, we all agree something can be unintelligible yet credible—like love, loyalty, or a two-year-old's drawing of her mother. And if we insist that our intellect or experience is the only measure of what is true, we ourselves become unintelligible, but not credible. We might just as well say the earth is flat because we've never fallen off.

When God reveals himself to us, much of it may be above reason, but it's never contrary to knowledge. Truth is truth, and it can't be self-contradictory. So if he reveals his love in his Son, it's believable because we already know God loves us. That knowledge may be intuitive, but it's knowledge nonetheless. If he reveals his moral order in a set of ten commandments, it's credible because we already know God is moral and orderly by observing our own moral nature and the order of the natural world. But whatever it is he reveals, it's consistent with truth. For revelation always includes communication of truth.

As for the why of revelation, I think the most basic factor is found in God's nature. He loves us. Thus, we can assume his love, like ours, demands communication, self-disclosure, voluntary dis-covering. But our assumption is not enough. He's got to show us his love somehow, speak to us with his own voice. The communication we expect must occur. Otherwise he becomes grouped with all the pagan gods—fickle, cruel, and careless. We need to hear, "God so loved the world that he gave . . . " (John 3:16). Or, "Come unto me, all you who are weary and burdened, and I will give you rest" (Matt. 11:28). And our reason, which shows us our selfishness (if only we will care to look) needs to hear, " 'Come now, let us reason together,' says the Lord. 'Though your sins are like scarlet, they shall be white as snow; though they are red as crimson, they shall be like wool' " (Isa. 1:18). For reason and intuition can't sail unaided into the billowing seas of the kingdom of heaven, where waves of trinity, salvation, mercy, and eternal life wash the golden beaches. The ship has the capacity to ply these waters, but it needs a Master at the helm, expertly testing the boat's limits, sailing into the wind of the limitless.

But many people stubbornly insist on sailing in circles. They refuse the hand of the master on the tiller because they refuse to believe in supernatural intervention. They may consider themselves religious, but their religion is established and maintained by reason alone. That is, the onus is on the medium (in this case, reason) and not on the source. The moderates in this group will accept the possibility of divine revelation, but they refuse to accept the authority of the prophets and apostles God used as his mouthpiece. They don't focus on the ocean's horizons, rather they focus on the cultures, traditions, errors, superstitions, and popular beliefs of the crew. They call it higher criticism. I call it not seeing the forest for the trees.

I'm not throwing reason out with the bilge water, however. It has its place on the revelatory voyage. A very important place. First of all, the very idea of revelation presupposes at least two parties—a revealer and a revealee (if there is such a word). There has got to be at least two minds at work—one giving, the other receiving. Reason can't communicate with unreason.

Second, reason is a tremendous guard dog. It's not a medium, but it *is* a filter. Filtering out things like contradiction, for instance. It won't allow us to believe any revelation saying God can do or command that which is morally wrong. It won't accept any revelation contradicting a well-established truth springing from a former revelation, or proven experience, or universal intuition. Reason won't allow us to believe black is white, white black, or right wrong. It bares its teeth at such intrusions. But it does so reasonably, not whimsically—it recognizes the "scent" of God in some things that appear on the surface to be impossible. Like God becoming man in Christ, for example. For it long ago became acquainted with the complex nature of man—at the same time immaterial and material, angel and animal, immortal and mortal. So there's already a basic mechanism for reason to come to grips with "God in Christ."

Third, like a wise judge, it has a high view of evidence. It won't be distracted by anything other than that which is appropriate and adequate to belief. Jesus himself alluded to this when he said, "If I had not done among them what no one else did, they would not be guilty of sin . . . " (John 15:11). As he saw it, the revelation of the kingdom implicit in his miracles provided adequate evidence for belief. Those who chose not to believe in the face of such evidence were "guilty." Those who believed were "not guilty." He underscored this rational exercise of belief and unbelief in his conversation with Nicodemus, "Whoever believes in him [Jesus] is not condemned, but whoever does not believe stands condemned already because he has not believed in the name of God's one and only Son. This is the verdict: light has come into the world, but men loved darkness intead of light because their deeds were evil" (John 3:18–19). Case closed.

So reason is a reliable, indispensable crew member. But it's not the Sailor. He gives commands. The crew obeys. That's why sound theology is based on authority, the authority of the only one who knows the way, the one who writes and keeps the "log," which means we trust his word when his log says he's a person who creates, provides, and redeems. Any other logs teaching something else are to be rejected. Rather than being a rock, they lead to the rocks, to shipwreck instead of golden shores.

Authority, then, refers to the claim of someone who says he's in the know. He speaks from experience, like a parent pulling rank on his child, "I have learned over the years." Or he speaks on behalf of someone else who is in a position of power and has given him his definitive word on the subject, like the U.S. president's press secretary or your neighborhood gossip, who tells you "on good authority" that the local grocer is running around with the new cashier. As you can see, the question relevant to authority is, "By whose authority are you speaking?" Who's the author? Can he be trusted?

The Bible writers claim to be God's emissaries. They speak

in his name, by his authority. So they see their words as God's words. Words which are to be received as *the* word. And they expect God to follow through on what they say he says. These are men, very few of whom knew each other, who have produced a body of material which is absolutely unique. True to the times in which they wrote, but relevant to all times, including ours. So true, that it has been a consistent best-seller for centuries. Without any thought of doing so, it has proven to be the architect of modern civilization in the Western world. A book stressing selfless behavior, providing the time-tested basis for human rights and freedom. But if you'd asked Isaiah or Paul about the long-term impact of their writings, they'd have drawn a blank. As far as they were concerned, their words were given by God for their times, not for the twentieth century.

This speaks to me of authority. When you've got more than fifty writers, writing over the course of fifteen hundred years, producing an organic whole, you've got the product of one mind. The Bible must be what it claims to be—the Word of God, a revelation springing from his certain present. So it's no problem for me to accept and deal with the eccentricities and warts of the individual writers. Paul had a problem with women's rights? Amos wrote from the perspective of a rustic, and Isaiah from that of a courtier? Solomon was bitter with life? John thought he was Jesus' favorite? So what? What impresses me is the uniformity and universality of the timeless message coming through these human filters. I read the Bible, and I hear from God. His Word speaks to me and my generation. What's more, it challenges me to change myself and my world. In preparation for its promise of a new heaven and new earth on the horizon. It leads, I follow, because I trust the Author.

And the Author's style is consistent with the idea of revela-tion. I've already pointed out that revelation places the initiative with the source, not the medium. Unlike other holy books where much is made of the writer or writers, the Bible makes little of its writers and much of its Author. It presents itself, not as the result of man's search for God, but of God's search for man, which means, among other things, that the Bible has a supernatural nature. It presents a God who involves himself in the world, interrupts, intervenes (often miraculously) in order to lead man from destruction to salvation. The process of man's escape from death to life is presented as a series of revelations and revelatory acts. Starting with man's fall from direct access to God, we see God gradually making himself more and more accessible. He looks for someone who will simply believe. He finds such a person, his name is Abram, and God declares him righteous merely on the basis of his willingness to believe (Gen. 15: 1–6). He promises Abram a family that will uniquely become the people of God, a people who will be known as the ones to whom God is "near" (Deut. 4:7). Later, in the aftermath of an unusual wrestling match, he gives them the name Israel (Gen. 32:22–28). Then, he makes it clear that the whole purpose of his relationship with them is that they will be "a light for the Gentiles" (Isa. 42:6). They're to show Gentiles the way to God by dispelling the darkness. Then, when Israel's hope, her Messiah, "the desired of all nations" (Hab. 2:7), comes, "he will be called Wonderful Counselor, Mighty God, Everlasting Father, Prince of Peace" (Isa. 9:6). For he "takes away the sin of the world!" (John 1:29). He does a good job. Not only does he make us "alive" (I Cor. 15:22), but he gives us "eternal life" (John 3:16). But notice— from Eden to Gethsemane, from Adam's hiding place to Jesus' praying place, God takes the initiative. He comes looking for us, calling us, wooing us. For we're either hiding or praying. In either case, we're lost until he finds us.

One of the fundamental ways of finding us, as God takes the initiative, is his use of prophecy. Prophecy (which is not so much "fore" telling as it is "forth" telling) predominates in the Bible as a means of God's uncovering himself. Because of its prominence I want to deal fairly extensively with it, not just because it's so high-profile biblically nor because it's so relevant to the subject of revelation, but rather, because it's so relevant to our times. Historians will look back at the latter half of the twentieth century and declare television as a greater shaper of our times than two world wars in the former half. Church historians will focus in on television prophets. Those men and women, both false and true, who interpreted God's words for the largest audiences in the history of Christendom. For better or worse, the electronic preachers have become the main contact our culture has with God's word, and some of them recently have let us down. Badly. That's why I think we need to reacquaint ourselves with what the Bible says about prophets and prophecy. So we can recognize and respect the good guy and discount the bad guy. We've got to become discerning if we're to continue with a high regard for revelation. No more circus acts, thank you.

To be fair, we would never have seen God's word reduced to entertainment if we hadn't asked for it. We've become far too sedentary and passive in the television age. Our minds have slipped into neutral. Mental stimulation has been reduced to titillation, the lowest common denominator, so prophecy is beaten before it steps into the ring. For there is one thing prophecy doesn't do—it won't tickle the ears. Nor will it shadowbox. More often than not, it blindsides us and leaves our ears ringing. Prophecy, in its barest form, is a word in the mouth. Sometimes feeling like a punch in the mouth!

The Bible really stresses this word-in-the-mouth imagery. Here are several references: "Then the Lord reached out his hand and touched my mouth and said to me, 'Now, I have put my words in your mouth' " (Jer. 1:9); "I will make my words in your mouth a fire and these people the wood it consumes" (Jer. 5:14); "I have put my words in your mouth and covered you with the shadow of my hand" (Isa. 51:16); "My Spirit, who is on you, and my words that I have put in your mouth will not depart from your mouth, or from the mouths of your children, or from the mouths of their descendants from this time on and forever" (Isa. 59:21); "Must I not speak what the Lord puts in my mouth?" (Num. 23:12). This word comes by the initiative of God alone: "Above all, you must understand that no prophecy of Scripture came about by the prophet's own interpretation. For prophecy never had its origin in the will of man, but men spoke from God as they were carried along by the Holy Spirit" (II Pet. 1:20–21).

Nevertheless, interpretation is always a factor in the communication of the revelation, in that the word is usually found in a dream or vision: "The Lord has brought over you a deep sleep: He has sealed your eyes [the prophets]; he has covered your heads [the seers]. For you this whole vision is nothing but words sealed in a scroll. And if you give the scroll to someone who can read, and say to him, 'Read this please,' he will answer, 'I can't; it is sealed' " (Isa. 29:10–11). An exception to these foggy visions is Moses: "When a prophet of the Lord is among you, I reveal myself to him in visions, I speak to him in dreams. But this is not true of my servant Moses; he is faithful in all my house. With him I speak face to face, clearly and not in riddles; he sees the form of the Lord" (Num. 12:6–8). So with a few notable exceptions, the prophets' revelations came by way of visions and dreams. These "riddles" were by the initiative of the Holy Spirit. Word preceded interpretation, rather than the other way around. And, the word in the mouth was sometimes fiery even to the point of "consuming" the audience—an uppercut to the jaw.

Recently, I spoke at a very large church where the minister of music is a friend of mine. The church had just hosted a much-publicized prophetic conference with a high-profile North American prophet as keynote speaker. The crowd was huge, expectations were high, and he didn't disappoint them. Not only did he give sweeping prophecies related to the world and North America, but he also gave several "words of knowledge" to individuals. Not by reading palms, but by the "anointing of the Spirit." Before one of the services he was backstage with the pastoral staff, giving personal prophetic words to each one. "The Lord is showing me," he said to my friend, "that his will for you is being blocked by television. You watch too much. Turn it off, and spend more time in prayer."

A good word. Which would apply generally to almost anyone in North America. But there was a problem in this case—my friend hates TV. Never watches the stuff! Because he's a quiet, soft-spoken sort, he didn't challenge the prophet. "But," he told me, "I had a terrible time taking his public prophecies seriously. His credibility, as far as I was concerned, was shot." OK, so maybe the guy had a momentary lapse. Prophets are only human, after all. But these lapses are a reminder that we should always be prepared to critically examine prophetic words. Intimidation is not a proper means of presenting, nor a proper response to, prophecy. Skepticism is a much better response. Not because we reject prophecy. But because we have a high view of prophecy. We must never forget that even true prophets make mistakes. Nor must we forget that false prophets abound. The human filter must be filtered.

One of the best ways to filter any prophet's words is to know what the Bible says about both the false and the true. Jeremiah provides us with an excellent overview of the recurring factors in false prophecy. They're outlined in verses 9 through 40 of chapter 23. The key comment in this section is verse 11: " 'Both prophet and priest are godless; even in my temple I find their wickedness,' declares the Lord." Here are the factors contributing to the godlessness of the prophets:

1. THEY PREACH A DISTORTED WORD (VERSE 36)

"You distort the words of the living God . . . " says Jeremiah. There are three ingredients in this distortion:

a. *Subjectivity.* "They speak visions from their own minds, not from the mouth of the Lord" (verse 16); "I have heard what the prophets say who prophesy lies in my name. They say, 'I had a dream! I had a dream!' " (verse 25). Notice the false prophets operate under the illusion that dreams are authoritative. It's no concern of theirs that dreams for the most part are a result of subconscious fears, desires, and late-night pizza.

b. *Self-deception.* "How long will this continue in the hearts of these lying prophets, who prophesy the delusions of their own minds?" (verse 26). "They ... live a lie ... " (verse 14). You've heard the old saying, "If you tell a lie often enough, you begin to believe it yourself." And if you want to deceive others, tell as big a lie as possible. History is saturated with those who have deceived and been self-deceived—from Simon Magus, a Christian heretic, to Adolph Hitler, a killer of the Jews. It's interesting to note a major ingredient in the deception and self-deception is sincerity. The Jim Jones massacre in Guyana a few years ago underscores the tragedy of being sincerely wrong.

c. *Materialism.* "Among the prophets ... I saw this repulsive thing: they prophesied by Baal" (verse 13). Perhaps the most attractive aspect of the Canaanite god, Baal, was his availability to the senses. You could always find him—just go to the highest hill in your vicinity, and there he was. A huge rock, conspicuously placed for all to see. He controlled the everyday materialistic concerns of Canaan: the crops, the rain, and personal prosperity. His focus was the here and now, the pragmatic, the practical. As was the false prophets' focus. They dealt in expediency rather than truth, in earthly concerns rather than heavenly. They were secular humanists before their time.

2. THEY SCRATCH WHERE PEOPLE ITCH (VERSE 17A)

"They keep saying to those who despise me, 'The Lord says: You will have peace.'"

False prophets determine their message by consensus—their "dreams" are interpreted in terms of the felt needs of their audience. So their message, rather than "consuming" the hearer, is consumed, greedily, by a voracious consumer. The false prophet is not concerned with the fact that people despise God and his word (their "despising" of God, by the way, is not a function of creed, but a function of greed). He is concerned that they accept his word. He guarantees his acceptance by consulting the polls, giving people what they want to hear, scratching where they itch. False prophets are dedicated politicians. They talk a lot about peace, and play the ratings game.

3. THEY DEFEND THE STATUS QUO (VERSE 17B)

"And to all who follow the stubbornness of their hearts they say, 'No harm will come to you.' "

Following the stubbornness of one's own heart is about as close to a definition of sin as you can get. In this case, sin is a lifestyle, an everyday state of rebellion where God's heart is not considered. The false prophets provide no challenge to change, no fiery words to create discomfort with things as they are, no vision for reform or renewal. Instead, a pat on the head. A grandfatherly stroking of the beard, with a resigned, "Boys will be boys." Everything will work out in the end. In the meantime, bless 'em all. Short-circuiting the law of reaping what you sow.

4. THEY HAVE A LOW VIEW OF GOD AND NEIGHBOR (VERSE 14)

"And among the prophets ... I have seen something horrible: they commit adultery and live a lie."

In our day adultery and lying aren't so horrible. We expect "a little foolin' around" and "white lies" as part of the game. AIDS is horrible. Thus, morality in the eighties is safe sex—do the responsible thing, wear a condom. In a sad sort of way, safe sex means irresponsible sex. That is, sex without commitment, consequences, or long-term implications, be they pregnancy or disease. No-strings-attached sex.

The truth of the matter is that sex has all kinds of strings attached. Physical, emotional, spiritual, and social strings bonding people together. But depending on how you use it, the bond of sex can either be glue or chains. Bonding or bondage. "There's no such thing as a free lunch," says the old adage. It's also true there's no such thing as free sex. It either bonds or it binds. It's never neutral.

The horror of adultery and lying, from a biblical perspective, becomes evident if the meaning of righteousness and justice is understood. When the Bible talks of righteousness, it refers to the fulfillment of the demands of relationship with God. When it talks of justice, it refers to the fulfillment of the demands of relationship with neighbor. And as we've seen earlier both words are translations of the same Hebrew word. *Zadok,* or *zadik,* is usually translated "righteousness" when the relationship is vertical, "justice" when the relationship is horizontal. Righteousness demands a high view of God, justice a high view of neighbor. The height of our view and its impact on our choices determines the extent to which we are righteous and just. The only way to fulfill the demands of righteousness and justice is to love God and neighbor. To love, simply understood, is to seek the highest good. We seek the best for God. We seek the best for neighbor.

Which is why adultery and lying are so horrific. Adultery is blind to the highest good of the involved families. It's even blind to the highest good of a potentially conceived child. (There are, as I see it, no illegitimate children, but only illegitimate parents.) Adultery also ignores God's explicit commandment prohibiting sex outside of marriage. It doesn't see itself as deliberately disobeying. Rather, it lowers God's demands: "He understands. We're only human." And it lowers respect for the wronged spouses: "What they don't know won't hurt them." This lowering of regard for God and neighbor (your husband or wife is your closest neighbor) makes dishonesty and duplicity easier. The adulterers begin to live a lie. Hiding themselves from both God and neighbor. Cutting themselves off from the demands of prior relationships. Limiting themselves to self-absorption.

So Jeremiah sees false prophets adulterating and lying about it. The more they do it, the easier it becomes. Until it's a lifestyle. Their message is neutered by immorality and understandably loses any conviction in terms of addressing the sinful behavior of the times. Conscience gives way to unconscience. And spiritual leadership becomes a joke. As it has in America recently, where the timeless challenge of heaven's kingdom has been reduced to a glitzy soap opera called "Pearlygate."

5. THEY ARE SELF-CENTERED (VERSES 21, 30, 31)

"I did not send these prophets, yet they have run with their message; I did not speak to them, yet they have prophesied ... 'Therefore,' declares the Lord, 'I am against the prophets who steal from one another words supposedly from me. Yes,' declares the Lord, 'I am against the prophets who wag their own tongues and yet declare, the Lord declares.' "

There are two characteristics of false prophets universally common: zeal, and presumption. They run to prophesy, even though they have no heavenly mandate. Eagerness to prophesy is an almost foolproof sign of false prophecy. Reluctance to prophesy is more commonly a characteristic of true prophecy. Then to presume to speak the words of the Lord can, in some instances, be blasphemous. The Lord accuses them of being absent from "the council of the Lord" (verse 18) and being deaf to his word. How, then, can they prophesy? "I did not send them or appoint them," says the Lord (verse 32).

Nevertheless, they prophesy, and justify it by saying, "God told me" (verse 31). They feel the need to pull rank—who can argue with God? I think we should make it a rule of thumb to be positively critical of anyone betraying his insecurity by continually saying, "God told me." Don't be intimidated by the supposed spirituality of such types. Otherwise they'll continue their heady momentum, causing you, and everyone else who'll let them, to forget God's name (verse 27). And I suspect the forgotten name in this instance is "the Lord Our Righteousness" (verse 6).

Ironic, isn't it? The words uttered with the preface, "God told me," cause people to forget the Lord who's supposed to have said those very words. Because the major focus of "God told me" is not "God," but "me." Ego. For the sake of their own self-indulgent spirituality and significance, false prophets confuse and mislead with reckless abandon (verse 32). Indeed, their self-centered message is like "slippery" paths in the darkness (verse 12).

One more point: egotistical people are suckers for other egotists. Gullibility is *very* characteristic of false prophets. "They steal from one another words supposedly from me," says the Lord (verse 30). False prophet A tells false prophet B what "God" is saying, and he swallows it, hook, line, and sinker. With an emphasis on sinker. Then he preaches it as if it were his own revelation. There are three sure signs ego is at work: unwarranted zeal, reckless authority, and gullibility. As anyone in sales will tell you, the easiest sale is from one salesman to another.

So there are the goods on false prophets. From none other than Jeremiah, the reluctant prophet (chapter 20, verse 9). They preach a distorted word, they scratch where people itch, they defend the status quo, they have a low view of God and neighbor, and they are self-centered. So much for the bad news. Now for the good news.

The key word in prophecy is accountability. Whereas a false prophet is accountable to nothing other than the remnants of his conscience (and perhaps an undiscerning board of directors), a true prophet is accountable to both God and history. He believes God is the Lord of history and sees meaning in the universe only in terms of God's involvement. Thus, he subjects any "word" he receives to the discipline of history. He expects his revelation to be consistent with proven revelations in times past. So a vital question we should ask when facing a prophetic word is, To whom is this prophet accountable?

Historically there are three general ingredients characterizing proven prophecy: first, a strong, hammerlike word directed at a present evil and delivered in a style reflecting the personality of the prophet; second, a warning of judgment, often appearing to be insensitive and frighteningly impersonal; third, the promise of hope for the future, depending on repentance in the present. This is why a true prophetic word either explicitly or implicitly has a positive ring. Sure, it tears down, but only because it has vision for a new construction. It condemns in order to renew. And it's prepared to roll up its sleeves for the full term of the building project. It puts its money where its mouth is.

As you would expect, in Old Testament prophecy God's money was with Israel. He had chosen to reveal himself to the world through them, and he had a major task in keeping the filter free from blockage. So his prophets put their finger on one clogging factor after another. In so doing they returned again and again to familiar themes. Themes which have a timeless character and provide a model for "forth" telling the word of God. Let's look at eight of those themes.

I. THE WORD. "THIS IS WHAT THE LORD SAYS"

The Old Testament prophets had a high view of God and neighbor. Therefore, they had a high view of God's word to their neighbor. There was something sacred about declaring it. Indeed, the very act of proclamation was somehow irreversible. It was like adding salt to a recipe. Once it's added, it can't be removed. It's effect is certain. Which makes reluctance on the part of the prophet a part of the recipe. Why? Because they saw themselves not only as the spokesmen of destruction but as the objects of destruction. They were a part of the audience. Thus their reluctance, thus their passion. In their anguished calls to repentance they saw their own salvation in the balance. Their only hope lay in hearing and obeying the word of the Lord.

2. COVENANT. "OUT OF EGYPT I HAVE CALLED MY SON"

The Exodus was the beginning of Israel's life as a nation. Old Testament prophecy remembers God's call to Abram, but it stresses God's deliverance of Israel from Egypt. It continually recalls a covenant relationship which God honored—even to the point of performing miracles (including a remarkable night at the Red Sea) in order to prove his faithfulness. The question then is, God has done and is doing his part in the covenant, why are you (Israel) not doing your part? God is faithful, why are you unfaithful?

3. REBELLION. "THEY WENT FAR FROM ME"

The prophets saw Israel's unfaithfulness, or infidelity, as rebellion. That rebellion was usually depicted as a flight from God. A counterproductive flight. God has only one people through whom to speak, "You only have I chosen of all the families of the earth" (Amos 3:2). So how can he address the nations if his public-address system is out of order? That's why the prophets were so sensitive to even a slight trend toward fleeing from God. They blazed out hotly against any hint of hiding or of flight.

4. JUDGMENT. "THEY SHALL RETURN TO EGYPT"

Whereas the false prophets' moral sins reflected a low view of God's righteousness, the true prophets' stern words of judgment reflected a high view of God's righteousness. They saw judgment as the only way of setting things right. Justice demands judgment. So Old Testament prophecy continually presents God as judge and exile to Egypt as the judgment. If they don't clean up their act they're dead, politically and nationally. They might as well be slaves again. Back in Egypt. Present freedom will be replaced by past bondage.

5. COMPASSION. "HOW CAN I GIVE YOU UP?"

We saw a few paragraphs ago the role ego plays in false prophecy. The presumption of the false prophets was motivated by an unhealthy regard for self. On the other hand, the true prophets were moved with compassion. Their motivation was not self, but love for God and neighbor. And God's love shone through them. For instance, the words "yet you did not return to me" occur several times after various judgments have been proclaimed. This tells us God's purpose in the punishments was positive rather than negative. He wanted his people to abandon their flight and return to him. God knows there's a day coming when, "I will betroth you to me forever ... in righteousness and justice, in love and compassion ... in faithfulness" (Hos. 2:19–20). His love for his people will ultimately triumph.

Before continuing, let's summarize the contrast so far between false and true prophets, by listing their characteristic themes:

TRUE PROPHETS	FALSE PROPHETS
1. The Word	1. The distorted word
2. Covenant	2. Consensus
3. Rebellion	3. Status quo
4. Judgment	4. Immorality
5. Compassion	5. Presumption

So much for point and counterpoint. Now for three themes of true prophecy for which there are no counterthemes in false prophecy.

6. RIGHTEOUSNESS/JUSTICE. "LET JUSTICE ROLL ON"

The false prophets would never have admitted to preaching against righteousness and justice—they were all in favor—but they didn't preach it and they didn't live it. Thus, they led God's children astray. The true prophets bore the anguish of God's heart at the result. One of the most powerful examples of this occurs during the time of two prophets, Amos and Isaiah, who, if not contemporaries, were close to it. Amos spoke out against Israel on a feast day (chapter 5), Isaiah on a fast day (chapter 58). In both cases God's children had the ritual and religious form down pat. They were decked out in their Sabbath-best clothes. But their hearts were naked and dirty. Here's why.

Amos first: "You oppress the righteous and take bribes and you deprive the poor in the courts" (verse 12). Israel had a low view of God and neighbor (they'd been listening to false prophets). Amos accuses them of a view so low that they "turn justice into bitterness and cast righteousness to the ground" (verse 7).

God is offended by this. So much so that he refuses to presence himself among his people, regardless of their laborious preparations and religious ceremony. "I hate, I despise your religious feasts," he says. "I cannot stand your assemblies . . . Away with the noise of your songs!" (verses 21, 23). Little wonder Amos didn't make the "ten most-admired men in Samaria" list. Pity the chief musician!

Then Isaiah: "On the day of your fasting, you do as you please and exploit all your workers" (chapter 58, verse 3). Another version (Revised Standard Version) says, "In the day of your fast you seek your own pleasure, and oppress all your workers." There you have it again—low view of God, low view of neighbor. In Israel, both feast and fast days meant a universal cessation from labor. But no. Isaiah sees only the middle-, upper-middle-, and high-income people in the temple. Other Israelites, the low-income folk, were not there. They were in the factories keeping the economy rolling. God says, "No way!" He wants the entire nation in the house of God. If not, he'll boycott the whole somber affair. Regardless of economic categories, there's to be no distinction between rich and poor when it comes to worship. Oppressing all your workers won't wash. No low view of neighbor allowed. On top of this, God wasn't pleased with Israel's pleasure-seeking. They had reduced an encounter with him to "seeking [their] own pleasure." Israel's worship missed the point. God's pleasure was to be sought, not theirs. And he was definitely not pleased. Only a low view of God sees worship as a means to a worldly end.

So whether it was the crude rustic, Amos, or the elegant courtier, Isaiah, the message was the same. Return to a high view of God and a high view of neighbor—or suffer the loss of God. Isaiah calls for loosing "the chains of injustice," setting "the oppressed free," sharing "your food with the hungry" (verses 6, 7). Amos cries, "Let justice roll on like a river, righteousness like a never-failing stream!" (verse 24). No amount of religion, or subjective "warm fuzzies" in worship, can substitute for bottom-line spiritual relationship. Even Jesus said the bedrock of fulfilling

God's demands was to love him (high view of God) and love neighbor (high view of neighbor)(Mark 12:30–31). If there's a common denominator in true prophetic proclamation, it is this: a call to righteousness and justice.

7. REDEMPTION. "I WILL RETURN THEM TO THEIR HOMES"

Exile, whether self-imposed (by an attempt to flee God's presence) or God-imposed (a "return to Egypt"), is not God's will for his people. Living as he does in the certain present, God has a plan of redemption and wants no one to miss it. That's why the true prophets didn't see judgment as the final chapter. Rather, they saw it as prerequisite to redemption. Redemption against all the odds. Even death. Ezekiel had a vision of dessicated skeletons being given bodies again. Bleached bones breathing with life. "Prophesy to these bones and say to them, 'Dry bones, hear the word of the Lord!' This is what the Sovereign Lord says to these bones: 'I will make breath enter you, and you will come to life. I will attach tendons to you and make flesh come upon you and cover you with skin; I will put breath in you, and you will come to life. Then you will know that I am the Lord . . . O my people, I am going to open your graves and . . . I will bring you back to the land of Israel . . . I will put my Spirit in you and you will live . . .' " (chapter 37). The prophetic word is always given in the context of hope.

8. CONSUMMATION. "A LIGHT TO THE NATIONS"

The pinnacle of prophetic activity is the Messiah. False prophecy announces peace now. The kingdom without the king. Not true prophecy. Rather it looks forward to the establishment of peace by the Prince of Peace. It lives and breathes expectation. Its heart is tuned to a wedding, when God and his people will be united as bridegroom and bride. All true prophecy is preparation for the wedding supper of the Lamb (Rev. 19:9).

So there you have it. A brief overview of true and false

prophecy. "Forth" telling the word of God by God's mouth-
pieces, spokesmen, seers. Men whose character and fruit were
consistent with their message. Between the lines of the last few
pages you've perhaps seen the contrasting character of the true
and the false. Here's a summary:

TRUE PROPHETS	FALSE PROPHETS
Objective	Subjective
Called of God	Self-deceived
Spiritual	Materialistic
God pleasers	Man pleasers
Moral	Immoral
Reluctant	Zealous
Humble	Authoritarian
Skeptical	Gullible

Does this mean we're to become prophecy connoisseurs and make
critical demands of everything puportedly from God? Yes. Do
we castigate the false prophet and adulate the true? No. That
would be to overreact. We're to be discerning, certainly. But we
should avoid the trap of dogmatism. Remember that prophecy
and inspiration are key ingredients in revelation. They are not,
however, the cornerstone of faith. We should focus *secondarily*
on the several factors constituting a true word from God and
primarily on Christ, *the* word of God. All true revelation points
ultimately to him.

Even true prophets are fallible. They speak, however, for an
infallible God. They don't force us to believe, but they confront
us with choice. The choice revolves around relationship: Do we
choose to be with God, or do we choose to be without him? Are
we prepared to accept the demands of that relationship, or is the
cost too high? Will we commit ourselves to seeking the highest
good for God and neighbor? Or will we choose self-absorption?
Our answers will reflect how we read the Bible. We read it either
as a lawyer looking for flaws and loopholes; or we read it as an
heir looking for our inheritance. Because revelation is more than

uncovering, more than communicating. It is the imparting of oneself.

Philosophy and palm-reading, in the final analysis, reveal very little, if anything at all. They may uncover fascinating minds, giving us a Socrates or a Houdini, but they don't give us a Savior, because the only uncovering of eternal value is God's revelation of himself in Jesus. A dis-covering worth discovering.

CHAPTER 10

Can We Trust
the Bible?

⚜ IT'S NOT EVERY DAY you get a phone call about Noah's ark. I was doing a week's fill-in for the vacationing anchorman of a TV news show out of Cyprus. The phone rang in the news room, and I answered. It was long distance from the head office in America. The operator asked for Richard Anderson, the bureau chief. Cupping my hand over the mouthpiece I bellowed his name—roaring, not for the sake of penetrating the paper-thin walls separating the bureau's three offices, but to be heard over the clatter of the UPI and Reuters wire services behind me. "Co-ming!" I heard his British-accented voice answer from office number three. A moment later, bustling and rumpled, he burst into the room.

Last chapter I described Mme. Sonja as "early gypsy." Well, Richard Anderson was "early absent-minded professor." He had that well-slept-in look. A kind of matured dishevelment demanding a soup stain or two as a fashion accessory. He was boundless energy wrapped in crispless drapery. He also had a heart of gold and a razor-sharp mind.

"Hello!" he shouted into the phone (in the Middle East, telephones and shouting go hand in hand). "What's that? Noah's

190

park? Noah's . . . what? James, turn off those silly machines, will you?" Dutifully I pulled the plug. UPI and Reuters were suddenly silent.

"Noah's ark? You gotta be kidding!" At this point I strained to hear the garbled static. To no avail.

"Of course we can make it!" Richard was excited. "Where'd you say Mount Ararat was again? Yeh, we know that. Where in Turkey? Dog-bite who? Spell it. D-O-G-UB-E-Y-AZ-IT. Where's that? On the eastern border. OK. Where's the nearest airport. Oh, brother! You better spell that one too. E-RZ-UR-U-M. Got it. One hundred seventy-five miles! By taxi? Ankara, huh? Connecting flight. What times? OK. All right, well, we'll do our best. We'll try for tomorrow, or the next. OK. We'll send you the tape as soon as we've got it. OK. Bye for now."

"They've found Noah's ark! And they're giving us the scoop! Can you believe it?" He slapped my shoulder, a look of childish delight on his face.

"Who's found it? Are they sure?" I asked.

"Well, it seems so. There's a team of Bible scholars and archaeologists there right now. They expect to uncover the remains of the ark in the next day or so."

"How come they're giving us the scoop?"

"I dunno. Somebody representing this group just called our head office a few minutes ago and gave us the go-ahead. Exciting, eh? Boy! Have I got some scrambling to do." With that he flew out the door calling loudly for his field cameraman.

It took two days before the crew of three left for Ankara. The connecting flight to Erzurum and the drive to Dogubeyazit consumed the third day. So three nights after the big phone call, an exhausted crew of two arrived at the western foot of Mount Ararat (the third member had stayed on in Ankara to settle satellite-linkup details). As they checked into the little hotel, they were surprised to learn that not one, but two discovery teams were hard at work seeking the ark.

One group was looking for the remains of Noah's labors on the mountain itself. The other group was looking in the valley.

They theorized the ark had been washed down the mountain. So one was known as the mountain crew, the other as the valley crew. Our crew, to their great disappointment, discovered over breakfast next morning that they were not welcome to film with either team. The phone call had come from someone associated with the valley team. But, "They had no business calling you," said the team supervisor. "We've got our own film crew, and nobody films but us. Period." He did, however, allow our crew to join the discovery team at the site. They were working on what looked like the outline of a boat's remains buried in the valley floor. "No question," our guys later told us, "it could have been a boat, or something like it. Mind you," they joked, "it wouldn't float too well. The wood has all petrified." Noah's ark? Perhaps. But then, who knows? And at the risk of sounding flippant, who cares?

I know—archaeologists, historians, Bible scholars, even theologians care. Any true biblical archaeological discovery is of great value. That's why I'll qualify my flippancy. My Who cares? is really directed at those who fervently feel such a monumental discovery would "prove" the inspiration, infallibility, and inerrancy of the Bible; people to whom God's word about God's Word is not enough; who on one hand denounce the scientific bias of secular humanism, and on the other hand demand scientific and historic exactitude of the Bible. Talking faith but not walking faith.

Maybe my concern here is a bit unfair, or premature. In order for you to understand where I'm coming from, you need to read the rest of this chapter, a chapter with a basic question: did the writers of the Bible actually write God's word? *The* word? If they didn't, then we can reduce it to intriguing literature. If they did, but partially, then we need all the external evidence (like arks) we can get to help bolster its flagging image. If they did, completely, then we have the final word on God's nature, plan, provision, and expectations. We can trust it completely. Any external evidences happening along from time to time are mere icing on the cake.

So how do I plan to answer the question? First, by taking a fairly extensive look at inspiration. Followed by a discussion of the divine/human element in the Bible. Then a glimpse or two at the person and character of Jesus in the New Testament, with some comments on the moral and historical results of his life as presented there. Finally, I'll make a few observations about infallibility and inerrancy. Instead of traveling to Turkey, we'll talk turkey.

Let's start with a sentence from the Bible: "All Scripture is God-breathed and is useful for teaching, rebuking, correcting, and training in righteousness, so that the man of God may be thoroughly equipped for every good work" (II Tim. 3:16–17). The key term here is *God-breathed.* Theology calls it inspiration. It refers to the work of God's Spirit (technically God's "breath") whereby he breathes into the biblical writers in order to produce the authoritative word of God, rather like a musician blowing into his trumpet, interpreting the mind of the composer and producing the flow of music outlined in his composition.

The music analogy is apropos. The whole point of the agony of composition, the tedium of practice, and the stress of performance is the impact the music has on the audience. All the filters between the composer's mind and the mind of the listener (filters such as writing, practicing, and performing) are attuned to emotive effect, spiritual influence. Indeed the raison d'être of music is the result it produces. Similarly, the focus of inspiration is not the methods which produced the Scriptures, but the impact those Scriptures have on the reader. The Holy Spirit may blow through many different kinds of instruments separately or in unison. And each instrument by virtue of the kind of sound it can produce will give its unique contribution, a clarion note to its time, but also to our time. Because it expresses the mind of one who lives in all times. At the same time.

Another aspect of the music analogy is that the written music is not the music. The notes on the score determine the boundaries of the sounds produced by the various instruments, but boundaries and interpretation are not the same. They are related, how-

194   *The Word of God*

ever. The musicians interpret within the parameters of the boundaries. The music heard by the listener, the sounds stirring his soul,
are a complex of notes, instruments, tuning, skill, conducting,
acoustics, setting, and interpretation, on the production end; and
music-appreciation capacities, emotional and spiritual need, on
the receiving end. To put it another way, music is more than
notes on a page. It's communication from one heart to another,
a message with a flowing symmetry that not only speaks (in most
cases nonverbally) but also stirs. This ability to stir, or to make
alive, is what theologians call illumination. It's a vital factor in
inspiration. For it has to do with making the reader alive to the
message and the message alive to the reader. It opens the ears.

That's why I said in the last chapter that the Bible is a record
of revelation, not the revelation itself. Jesus Christ is the final
revelation of God to man. And until he becomes alive to us and
us alive in him, the Bible is mere notes on a score, or words
without the Word, when, in fact, the Bible sees itself as the living
word. Bringing life to the dead. So when we say the Bible writers
were "inspired," we mean they were moved upon by the Holy
Spirit to record God's revelation (or "uncovering") in such a way
that the same Holy Spirit can illumine (or "make alive") those
words to the reader. Giving him, as he reads, the challenge and
means to be made alive, spiritually, in Christ.

Because the Bible points ultimately to Jesus, there is a timeless
quality to inspiration. Although the writers wrote to their generation, they also write to ours. And their words have the same
authority now as they did then. Two Old Testament prophets put
it this way: "Go now, write it on a tablet for them, inscribe it
on a scroll, that for the days to come it may be an everlasting
witness" (Isa. 30:8); "Write down the revelation and make it
plain on tablets . . . it speaks of the end and will not prove false
. . ." (Hab. 2:2–3). Both Isaiah and Habakkuk see themselves
writing a record of God's revelation in response to a command.
A command from God himself. They see their writings as true
and timeless. And although they never knew God's son as Jesus
of Nazareth, they both looked forward to the day when the

Messiah would rule in righteousness and justice: "For unto us a child is born, to us a son is given, and the government will be upon his shoulders. And he will be called Wonderful Counselor, Mighty God, Everlasting Father, Prince of Peace. Of the increase of his government and peace there will be no end. He will reign on David's throne and over his kingdom, establishing and upholding it with justice and righteousness from that time on and forever" (Isa. 9:6–7); "For the earth will be filled with the knowledge of the glory of the Lord, as the waters cover the sea" (Hab. 2:14). Their music, powerful and timely in their day, was the introduction to a messianic symphony. Revealing God's plan to all men of all times. Conducted by the breath of the spirit, inspiring human instruments to play a divine composition culminating in the glorious presentation of the conductor himself, "Glory to God in the highest, and on earth peace to men" (Luke 2:14).

This doesn't mean all Scripture plays the same note. Most of the Bible says nothing directly or indirectly of Jesus. Take the two books of Chronicles, for instance, or the Song of Songs, or Esther. But take a hard look. Chronicles is theology, stressing three truths providing vital foundation stones for God's ultimate revelation: one, there is an unchangeable moral order designed and maintained by God; two, any community of God's children must worship God in the proper way—that is, with a high view of God; three, God's revelation is a present, living reality. Esther, without once mentioning God, nevertheless presents one very important truth—God will deliver and maintain his chosen people Israel until the day of the covenant's fulfillment. The Messiah will not be the only living representative of the Jewish people when he is revealed. He will come to a people. His people. The Song of Songs simply and beautifully celebrates love, both physical and spiritual. With no holds barred it shows us the high view God has of sex, affection, and loyalty to a loved one. It helps set the stage for the greatest love story every told, a story beginning with the words, "For God so loved the world . . ." (John 3:16). So don't see these books as flat spots or sour notes in the symphony. See them as part of the whole. The beating of a drum or the rumble of a tuba. Not too entertaining on their own. But put them in an orchestra, playing their notes in the right time and place, and they provide a foundational stability. Making the fragile flutterings of a flute speak the language of heaven.

But heaven's a problem because it speaks of the supernatural, and there has been a lot of opposition to the idea of God actually speaking through human vessels. There still is, for that matter. I've referred in past chapters to the anti-supernaturalism pervading our Western culture. In this context it's unpalatable to suggest the Scriptures are the result of God's breath. But the Bible is such an awesome book (the all-time best-seller) and is so foundational to civilization that even the hardest-nosed critics have to come up with some explanation of its genius. So believers and unbelievers alike have come up with what theologians call theories of inspiration. Here's a few of them.

"The Scriptures are inspired just so far as they are inspiring," says the *intuition theory*. Inspiration is human genius applied to religious thought and expression. No divine mind is involved (unless it's the indirect and unconscious intelligence of pantheism). The human mind is the whole story. It discovers truth—there's no divine dis-coverer at work. The Bible writers were no more "inspired" than Shakespeare or Mark Twain, so the theory goes. It's a compelling theory, especially to atheists or pantheists, because it denies a personal God revealing truth, and it appeals to universalists too—those who see all religions as merely different paths up the same mountain. It's attractive because it contains a basic truth, the truth being that there are common denominators in all artistic endeavor—like intelligence, education, and giftedness.

Surely the Bible writers didn't write mindlessly or automatically. Amos, the rustic sheepherder and fruit-picker must have had a hobby: poetry. For he writes powerful poetry. And he must have had some predisposition to writing, unlike most fruit-pickers of his day. This may be one reason why God chose to use Amos as a prophet. In spite of his protests, "I am no prophet, nor a prophet's son" (Amos 7:14, RSV). He may not have been a prophet, but he *was* a poet, and God needed a voice to speak not only to Amos's generation but also to ours. So I've no problem with the intuition theory, as far as natural giftedness goes, but it doesn't go far enough. It won't admit the supernatural, even though the Bible insists it "speaks from God." Without the Holy Spirit's breath, the Bible is no more valid than the Vedas or the Koran or the Book of Mormon. It's purely subjective, with no objective reality. A matter of opinion. Subjectivism in faith, of course, is a dead-end street. It reduces spiritual horizons to our own selfishness, concocting "religion" to suit our self-absorption. As Emerson said, " 'Tis curious we only believe as deep as we live."

Next is the *illumination theory.* My neighbor has two houses—one here in Jerusalem, the other in Toronto. Between his trips here and my trips there we see quite a bit of each other. A few years ago I visited his home in Toronto. After a marvelous kosher dinner (he is Orthodox) he took me into his book-lined study. "I've something special to show you," he explained. Unlocking a drawer in the oak bookcase, he took out a wrapped book. As he removed the wrapping he said, "This is a treasure." And it was. Reverently he handed me a book older than his great-grandfather and more precious than most of the books in his study combined. It was an illuminated Torah.

You're probably aware of what Judaism calls the Torah. It's the first five books of the Bible. And as far as illuminated goes, well, I just discussed it a few paragraphs ago. Illumination refers to "making alive." An illuminated Torah, then, has been made alive. How? By intricate, painstaking, and (in my neighbor's book) gold-leafed artwork in the margins of the text. Each page is literally a work of art, and the artwork is keyed to the content of the Scripture presented on that page. So it takes years to produce an illuminated Torah, but it's worth it. For the illumination draws out the word of God for the reader to see and learn. It's a kind of human and holy endeavor to approximate the work of the Holy Spirit. And I don't doubt some of these illuminators over the ages have been directly influenced by that same Spirit in their artistic endeavors.

The illumination theory appeals to one aspect of what inspiration means, but it errs in making this one aspect, illumination, the whole story. What it says is that the Bible itself is not the word of God, but it *contains* the word of God. It focuses on the inspiration of the writers rather than their writings. The task facing the reader is to "read the writer" more than to read the text. In so doing the word of God hidden in the word of man will come to light.

As I said, illumination is only part of the story. Maybe even half. But fifty percent is not enough. It's fine, and correct, to say the Bible writers were "carried along by the Holy Spirit"(I Pet. 1:21), but what about the Bible's claim to be inspired by God in terms of its text? The objective (the text) and the subjective (the writers) constitute a whole. Inspiration includes illumination and more. It includes truth surpassing human abilities to discover, unless truth dis-covers itself. It includes revelation, a self-impartation of God at his own initiative, whether he can find an artist or not. He may not even settle for someone who can draw only stick men.

That's why a devotional approach to the Bible is not enough. There's more to Scripture than merely finding what appeals to you or what "blesses" you. You've got to come to grips with what offends and angers you as well. Because the objective word of God is bent on unbending you. And change never comes easy. So don't back away from the offensive word. Rather, confront it, wrestle it. God likes a good fight. And it's great when you make up.

Another theory of inspiration is called the *dictation theory*. It says that the Bible writers were pens, not penmen of God. They were automatic writers. No brain in gear, no cultural filter, no historical coloring—just zombielike pencil holders whose only other function was pencil sharpening. In a sense it is an extreme reaction to the illumination theory, in that it stresses the objective word to the point of making it, in its entirety, a verbal communication, punctuation and all. I kid you not, there have been arguments over the years put forward by dictation theorists who insist on the inspiration of the periods, commas, apostrophes, etcetera. Godly grammar.

Now there *are* instances in Scripture where God spoke verbally. In fact, there are several. Here are three: "And God spoke all these words . . ."(Exod. 20:1, introducing the Ten Commandments); "You have not come to a mountain that can be touched and that is burning with fire . . . to a trumpet blast or to such a voice speaking words, so that those who heard it begged that no further word be spoken to them, because they could not bear what was commanded: 'If even an animal touches the mountain, it must be stoned' "(Heb. 12:18–20); "He fell to the ground and heard a voice say to him, 'Saul, Saul, why do you persecute me? . . . I am Jesus, whom you are persecuting . . . Now get up and go into the city, and you will be told what you must do' "(Acts 9:4–6). But there's nothing in the Bible supporting the notion that verbal communication by way of dictation was the norm. Nor does the Bible mask the human factor in Scripture, whether it's variations in style, differences in records of the same event, or occasional discrepancies (see Matt. 20:29–34 as compared to Luke 18:35–43—One beggar or two? Approaching or leaving Jericho? John 6:19—"Three or three and a half miles"; John's not sure. Gal. 2:11–14—Paul and Peter have a big disagreement). Nor does the Bible apologize for using eyewitnesses for much of its content. Dictation doesn't need eyewitnesses. Why not dictate the gospel to some Gentile living in Antioch? And why dictate what the writers already knew, or could have discovered through research (as in the case of Luke, the historian)? Maybe the best example for dictationists to draw on is Balaam's ass(Num. 22–24).

Inspiration, then, is not just natural (intuition theory), but supernatural as well. Not just subjective (illumination theory), but objective as well. Not just divine (dictation theory), but human as well. It's not natural, partial, or mechanical. It's supernatural, complete, divine/human, and it's secondary. Revelation is primary. It precedes inspiration. Oral law preceded the Old Testament, and oral gospel preceded the New Testament. People had faith in Jesus long before the story of Jesus was written. Inspiration follows after truth, by way of God-breathed recording and interpreting. In fact, I think we can safely assume that Christianity would still be true even if inspiration didn't exist. After all, Jesus actually lived, died, rose again, and ascended. Christianity is rooted not in theories of inspiration, but in history.

There is one aspect of inspiration I wish to discuss a little further. It's the combination of divine and human factors in the production of the Bible. First, six verses from the second book of Peter, chapter 1: "We did not follow cleverly invented stories when we told you about the power and coming of our Lord Jesus Christ, but we were eyewitnesses of his majesty. For he received honor and glory from God the Father when the voice came to him from the Majestic Glory, saying, 'This is my Son, whom I love; with him I am well pleased.' We ourselves heard this voice that came from heaven when we were with him on the sacred mountain. And we have the word of the prophets made more certain, and you will do well to pay attention to it, as to a light shining in a dark place, until the day dawns and the morning star rises in your hearts. Above all, you must understand that no prophecy of Scripture came about by the prophet's own interpretation. For prophecy never had its origin in the will of man, but men spoke from God as they were carried along by the Holy Spirit" (verses 16–21).

What is fascinating here is "the word of the prophets made more certain." One could say the inspiration of the prophets gave sufficient credibility to their words, which is true. But here's Peter, himself inspired, saying the prophets' words were not as certain when they spoke them as they are now that "we have seen his majesty."

Peter, James, and John shared the Mount of Transfiguration experience with Elijah and Moses, prophets themselves and representatives of all the biblical seers who had foreseen Christ. There, both prophets and soon-to-be-apostles heard the Father confirm the prophetic focus by declaring, "This is my Son." Look at him, here he is! The hope of Israel, the salvation of the world! In that one moment God proclaimed the veracity and eternity of the divine/human revelation. Both in terms of the divine/human word (as delivered by the prophets and apostles) and the divine/human Word (Jesus himself, the Lamb of God). That's why Peter says we should "pay attention" to the inspired word, as if it were "a light shining in a dark place." The divine/human word, breathed by the Holy Spirit as he "carried along" the writers, will cause "the morning star" to rise in our hearts. So there's been a progressive revelation "rising" from Moses to Jesus, from Genesis to Revelation, and it has come by way of God breathing through man. A Word that can be trusted. Even as Jesus is "the Word made flesh"(John 1:14), so the Bible is the word about the Word made flesh (I John 1:1–4).

This means the Bible was coauthored. Not half and half, but all and all. If we stress the human authorship and downplay the divine, we're sort of like a group of heretics (Ebionites) in the early Church who did the same with Christ. If we stress the divine authorship and downplay the human, we're like another group of heretics (Gnostics) who treated Jesus that way. Either way the Bible loses. We must affirm the Bible as both a human record of a divine revelation and God's record of himself. It's a team effort. With the Holy Spirit as coach. A supernatural coach with a supernatural game plan, coaching a multitude of players.

The key team member, of course, is Jesus. Not that he wrote anything. Surprising isn't it? You would expect the most outstanding personality in history to write at least a pamphlet or something. Like, "Ten Steps to Heaven," or "What the True Church Believes," or "What Mary and Joseph Were Really Like." But no, he didn't write a thing. Instead he looked to his disciples as future writers, and he believed they would be inspired. "The Holy Spirit . . . will teach you all things and will remind you of everything I have said to you"(John 14:26). But he's a key player anyway. Because his life, ministry, and teaching comprise such a large measure of the New Testament text. And he's quoted so often. Not only on general topics but also on the specific subject of how he saw himself. So the Bible gives us an objective/subjective view of Jesus. If it's true, it's another indication of the inspiration and the trustworthiness of Scripture.

When you look at those who wrote about Jesus, however, you don't come away feeling exactly confident. Matthew was a tax collector—a dubious, turncoatish occupation to say the least. Mark, for the first part of his life, was a ne'er-do-well (ask Paul). John was just a kid. And Luke, well, he wasn't even around. He came from Alexandria in northern Africa after Jesus had gone. An accessory after the fact. Then there was Paul, a religious zealot who imprisoned and killed Christians. And who could trust Peter? A man who flirted with cowardice, was a stranger to the truth, and wouldn't eat with Gentiles. Jude was an obscure half-brother of Jesus. James, another half-brother, was perhaps the most trustworthy of the lot. He was the first "bishop" of the early Church and was regarded as a Jew of the Jews by the citizens of Jerusalem. Nevertheless, he denied Gentiles access to the gospel unless they first converted to Judaism. So the New Testament writers weren't the who's who of the book world. Why, the writer to the Hebrews didn't even sign his name.

Yet these writers wrote a story about Jesus too good not to be true. You can be sure they didn't make it up. For one thing, who would expect Jewish men, to whom the concept of a God-man was (and is) blasphemy, to invent such a controversial hybrid? Who of them was capable of fabricating Jesus' teaching or imagining his life and character? As one theologian put it, "It would take a Jesus to invent a Jesus." A Jesus who stood out from the thirty thousand or so young men said to have been crucified outside the walls of Jerusalem during the first seventy years of the present era. A Jesus who stood out and stands out light-years above all other men on the pages of history. A Jesus whose person and character is well documented. How does one account for such a life unless that life is true?

And how does one account for the untold millions over two thousand years who have testified to the personal, living impact

Jesus has had upon their lives? We're not talking fairy tales here. Nor are we talking religion. We're talking personal relationship between man and the Son of man, who said right from the top that such a rapport was possible: "He who loves me will be loved by my Father, and I too will love him and show myself to him . . . we will come to him and make our home with him"(John 14:21,23). In a culture burned by too many false messiahs, there certainly was no inclination to being burned again. They had Jesus nailed as a religious and political nuisance long before they nailed him to the cross. They were ready to pounce on any flaw, any slipup, any plot to immortalize this upstart Galilean. And as his disciples' writings began to appear a few years later, there were plenty of people around who had known Jesus and would have exposed any falsehood in the record. One of the significant facts of history is that Jesus' enemies couldn't produce his body to discount the empty tomb, and they couldn't produce any evidence to discount the written record. They'd been out-coached.

In fact, the success of the gospel in the first three or four centuries is a historical phenomenon. Its acceptance had to do with the personal reality of Jesus to individual believers, certainly. But more than that, it had to do with the integrity of the Scriptures upon which Christian experience was based. This is something you'd expect from a God-breathed text. The Holy Spirit had done more than a good coaching job. More than effective conducting. He had insured a life-giving message for all future generations. In inspiring the writers and the text, he had provided a breath of eternal life for all who would believe. It's quite amazing. Especially in light of the fact that the writers were generally not of the intelligentsia nor of a favored nation. Their Savior was a Jewish criminal, and their gospel, their "good news," was a message of confession, repentance, labor, and self-sacrifice. No wonder one Roman leader called Christians "haters of the human race."

Add to this a definite exclusivity (Christianity was not to be added to the kitty of available religious options, but was "the only way to God"), and you've got a public-relations disaster. Nevertheless, in three centuries Christianity had overtaken the formerly pagan Roman Empire—perhaps the most remarkable religious revolution of all time. Little wonder people began to take inspiration seriously. Only God could produce Scripture so powerful, long-lasting, and true to life.

But there was more than power to convert—there was influence to change. The compelling morality of the Bible challenged the standards, values, and ethics of every culture it encountered. It blazed like a light in the night of pagan morality. Declaring the sacredness of human life, the sanctity of the home, sexual faithfulness, and equality of men and women. Stressing personal holiness, practicing what you preach. And underlying all morality, the lodestone of New Testament teaching, in Jesus' own words, "Love the Lord your God with all your heart and with all your soul and with all your mind and with all your strength. The second is this: Love your neighbor as yourself "(Mark 12:30–31).

The New Testament echoed the Old—above all else, a high view of God and a high view of neighbor. "There is no commandment greater than these." In the world of the Bible writers the individual existed for the sake of the state. They changed all that—their writings, inspired by the Holy Spirit, influenced nation after nation to build a society where the state existed for the sake of the individual. When nations began to see the value Jesus placed on the smallest child or the lowest slave, when they saw Christ dying to save the soul of the weakest widow, when they began to see the equality of man, the world's value systems began to be transformed, and modern civilization began. But it all hinged on the value of the individual. That one lost sheep Jesus came to save. Perhaps this is the eternal legacy of biblical morality—the rediscovery of the individual.

The Scriptures, then, must be inspired. They must have been composed and conducted by the Holy Spirit. Blowing through dusty instruments. Otherwise, God has made an untrue book into the greatest blessing man has ever known. But from what we know of God, he never blesses untruth. He writes no sour music. He's got a perfect ear.

Does this mean the instruments are perfect too? Or does a little dust get in the way from time to time? There's no question the musician is a master. He makes no mistakes, but on occasion the instruments may give an unwarranted squeak or two. Usually in the area of cultural adaptation. Let me give you an example.

Recently I attended a Sabbath service at our neighborhood Orthodox synagogue. Sitting there, my head covered with the required *kippa* (or *yarmulke*), I looked up at the balconies on three sides of the room. There behind discreet curtains sat the women of the congregation. They weren't allowed to participate with the men. It's always been this way, but covering the man's head is a fairly "recent" phenomenon (since about the fourth century). As the service shifted into a momentary lull, I thought of the radical innovation of the early Church.

For the first few decades all the early Christians were Jews. In fact, the big issue facing the leadership in Jerusalem was whether or not a Jewish messiah had any relevance at all to Gentiles. There was a good deal of heated discussion, and occasional division, on the subject. The Judaizers under James's leadership insisted that a Gentile could not become a Christian until he first became a Jew. Thus the circumcision pressure. (You can read about this in Acts.) So as Jews they continued to meet in synagogues, and as their numbers grew they eventually had meetings attended by believing Jews exclusively. Here the radical message of Christianity began to have its effect. In a male-centered culture the early Christians began to see the female as equal to the male, which had a revolutionary impact—for they began to allow women not only to participate in their synagogue-type services but also to pray and prophesy. This is where things get interesting.

Even though the concept of male-female equality was emerging, they nevertheless had a high view of maleness and femaleness. They didn't want roles confused or reversed. They encouraged women to grow their hair long and men to grow beards. A man's "glory" was his woman, and a woman's glory was her hair. And as for a man's head, it reflected the glory of God. That's why an uncovered male head was a must in Jewish worship. If he was bald he had an advantage—the better to reflect God's glory. This is why some of the more devout but hairy men would shave the crown of their heads. (A few centuries later, you see this same phenomenon in the monastic movement.) A service of early believers, then, included a fascinating array of "glories": man's glory, woman's glory, and God's glory. And they were very concerned there be no clash of glories. Everything had to be orderly. Why? "Because of the angels," says Paul.

It was a given, in early Christian worship, that the angels were present in all services. They were seen as "up there," near the ceiling, hovering over the congregation. So they looked down on the tops of the worshipers' heads. Being responsible for maintaining order in the services, the angels were not to be offended. And offended they would be if they saw a man covering God's glory by covering his head or a woman competing with God's glory by uncovering her head. Her glory (her hair) must not be exposed in the presence of God's glory. So if she wanted to pray or prophesy, she had to cover her glory and reflect God's glory. Which was how female head-covering was seen. Her covered head was like an uncovered male head. It reflected God's glory and kept the angels happy.

This is the cultural background necessary to understand the first book of Corinthians, chapter 11, verses 3–16. The passage deals specifically with an ancient Jewish culture, well-established traditions, and a sudden intrusion of Christian liberty. Almost two thousand years later, if taken out of its cultural-historical context, it causes an out-of-place, anchronistic malformation in some well-meaning Christian groups. Women with, as one pastor friend of mine put it, "tea cozies on their heads." So far, however, I haven't seen any men shaving the tops of their skulls.

Nor should they. Just because a passage of Scripture is inspired to guide people through a specific cultural challenge doesn't mean we're to maintain the teaching long after the reason for the teaching has faded away. At the same time we gain a lot by understanding this inspired passage. We're reminded of equality, masculinity, femininity, ministry, angels, and God's glory. Great content needing continual emphasis. Inspired truth without expired cultural baggage.

So there is cultural and historical baggage in the Bible that needs to be recognized as such. It has sat, unclaimed, at the baggage counter for centuries. Its seams are rotted, its buckles rusted away. But like treasured archaeological discoveries, it gives us tremendous help in coming to grips with the real issues facing the early believers. Rather than being thrown out, it needs to be preserved as it is for future generations to appreciate more fully the genius of Scripture. One should not, however, attempt to resurrect it. It won't hold today's clothing. It's an old wineskin. Although the wine has never been better.

Not only were the biblical writers subject to cultural/historical limitations, but they were also subject to theological limitations. Peter puts it well, "Concerning this salvation, the prophets, who spoke of the grace that was to come to you, searched intently and with the greatest care, trying to find out the time and circumstances to which the Spirit of Christ in them was pointing when he predicted the sufferings of Christ and the glories that would follow. It was revealed to them that they were not serving themselves but you, when they spoke of the things that have now been told you by those who have preached the gospel to you by the Holy Spirit sent from heaven. Even angels long to look into these things" (I Pet. 1:10–12). Here we see the Old Testament prophets breathed upon by "the Spirit of Christ" so that they see in advance "the sufferings of Christ and the glories that would follow." But after being pointed in the right direction, they're left on their own to try to find out "the time and circumstances." Their inspiration, trustworthy as it was, was incomplete. In Paul's words, "We see but a poor reflection" (I Cor. 13:12). Even the angels need corrective lenses.

This raises a point vital to any discussion of the Bible's freedom from error (inerrancy) and its authority (infallibility).

In terms of what the Bible writers were able to give us, the Scriptures are entirely trustworthy. Not just because of their inspiration, but because of the One who inspired them. He knows the whole story, and he won't steer us wrong. But it was no easy task. He had to breathe through culture, history, religious predisposition, language, and mind-set. He had to be sensitive to the times even as he orchestrated a revelation for all time and beyond. This is why Jesus is so important. Only when the writings of the prophets and apostles were fleshed out in Christ did they become infallible. More than inerrant, they became undeceivable. For Jesus is, as he himself said, "the way and the truth and the life" (John 14:6). So in terms of the written Word, we have the perfect, living Word alive in the frail, imperfect words of man. Even in language God has to stoop. You might call it baby talk.

Did the Bible writers really hear from God? Yes, I believe they did. They recorded God's dis-covering (revelation) and they gave it their own interpretation (whether it be prophetic or apostolic or both) as the Holy Spirit inspired and illumined them. But I won't insist the human word was somehow zapped into the divine word. I will, though, insist on a divine/human word. The Bible can never be built upon itself. It cannot rest on dictated words and punctuation marks, or arks, for that matter. It must stand on the ultimate and final revelation—Jesus Christ, the cornerstone of the faith.

By the way, I *do* hope those rocks in the valley are Noah's ark. But whether they are or not, they'll never provide a foundation for faith. For that, you need the Rock.

CHAPTER 11

The All-Time Bestseller

❧ YOU CAN'T BLAME the poor guy for changing his name. Wouldn't you do the same if your name were John Gooseflesh? Mind you, you would probably have chosen a name with a bit more pizzazz than Gutenberg. Then again, the name Gutenberg may be the most famous of all names in the secular history of modern man. Why? Because John Gutenberg invented the printing press.

No other physical invention has influenced the history of man like the printing press. Slap down a few bucks for a book, and you've got a window into the mind of a writer and/or the ideas, histories, cultures, imaginations, dreams, hopes, strengths, weaknesses, beliefs, humor, sorrows, triumphs, and tragedies of all time. Books are your link with mankind and with history. They shape our lives. I remember an old teacher of mine once saying, "You grow in two ways—by the people you meet and the books you read." So true. And it all began with Gooseflesh. Here's his story.

In the quaint German town of Mentz lived a boy and his mother. She was a hard-working widow with the unusual occupation of dressing parchments for the writing of manuscripts.

One quiet morning young Johann was carving his name in the bark of a tree. Rather than scraping out the letters, he was carefully outlining and removing them with his knife in order to apply them later to a piece of wood for a nameplate. Carrying the letters to his room, one fell out of his hands just when he was walking past a boiling pot of purple dye in the kitchen/workshop area of their small house. Simply by reflex he picked the floating letter out of the pot and immediately dropped it because it was so hot. To his mother's horror it fell onto one of her freshly dressed parchments. To Johann's wonder, upon picking the letter off the white surface, he saw a beautiful purple *h*. Thirty years later, his name changed from Gansfleish (German for "Goose-flesh") to Gutenberg (his mother's name), his printing press was working in Mentz. The year was 1450 A.D. And the very first book he printed was the Latin Bible. Little did he know his press was changing the world. Nor could he have imagined that the Bible would become the all-time bestseller in publishing history.

In May 1453, Constantinople fell. Hundreds of Greek scholars fled to Western Europe, soon to be established there as teachers of Greek, the language of the rediscovered classics and of the New Testament. The revival of learning in Europe had come. It was the dawning of the Renaissance.

A year later, movable type was invented. Now the presses could begin to keep up with the sudden insatiable demand for books. In 1476 the first Greek grammar was published, followed in 1503 by the first Hebrew grammar. Then, a well-known Dutch scholar named Erasmus published his famous Greek edition of the New Testament, an invaluable tool for the beginning of a great movement in Bible translation. In the foreword to his book Erasmus saw a day when the Bible would appear in the language of the people, "that the husbandman might sing it at his plough and the weaver at his shuttle."

He was anticipating the emergence of a man like William Tyndale, who in a flurry of irreverent Protestant fervor cried, "I defy the Pope, and all his laws; and if God spare me I will one day make the boy that drives the plough in England to know more of Scripture than the Pope does." God spared him, but just for a while. Time enough for him to move to Hamburg in 1524 and, in constant poverty, distress, and danger, manage to complete the first English translation of the original Hebrew and Greek New Testament. Just time enough to smuggle six thousand copies into Britain before being deceived, betrayed, and strangled at the stake. Little wonder some historians refer to Tyndale as *the* hero of the Reformation.

Tyndale's version was followed by Coverdale's (1535), Matthew's Bible, the Great Bible (so named because of its size), the Breeches Bible (in Genesis 3:7 *coverings* is translated "breeches"), the Bishop's Bible, and in 1610 the Douay Version, which became the authorized version for the Roman Catholic Church. The year 1611, however, saw the emergence of the most influential English translation in history, the King James Version. There have been several versions since, some of the better known being the Revised Standard Version, the American Standard Version, and most recently, the New International Version.

Tyndale's work, although the first English translation from the original languages, was not the first available in English. That honor belongs to John Wycliffe, who published a translation of the Vulgate (Jerome's Latin Bible, completed in the latter part of the fourth century) in 1383. Wycliffe, the parish priest of Lutterworth, was a famous thinker and scholar. He was also a bit of a rebel and rather combative.

For his day he had what established church authorities considered to be a totally unacceptable and radical view of the Bible. "The Sacred Scriptures," he said, "are the property of the people, and one which no one should be allowed to wrest from them." He disagreed vehemently with present and past tradition which discouraged people from reading the Bible for themselves (the Church was considered to be the great custodian and expositor of the Scriptures). It was seen as a great danger, even blasphemy, to allow the common man access to the Bible on his own.

Readers of Wycliffe's version were hunted down like animals by church and state authorities. They were burned at the stake with copies around their necks. Man and wife were forced to witness against each other. Even children were forced to light the death fires of their parents. One archbishop complained about "that pestilent wretch, John Wycliffe, the son of the old Serpent, the forerunner of Antichrist, who had completed his iniquity by inventing a new translation of the Scriptures." Can you imagine such a thing being said today? That "pestilent wretch" is now a hero. And rightly so.

Men like Wycliffe and Tyndale have left an awesome heritage to all of us, and if you attempt to study, preach, or teach the Scriptures, your sense of indebtedness becomes all the greater. As one theologian put it, "Other men indeed have labored, and we have entered into their labors." What I am laboring to do in this chapter is give you not an introduction (there are plenty of books available for that), but an *orientation* to this book that men have died for. A rather ambitious project, to say the least. And I don't know if you should try to read the chapter in one sitting. If you do, take a coffee break or two along the way. But please remember as you read, what I'm giving you is a "scouting report," a kind of familiarization which will be of little use to you unless at some point you take time with each book in the Bible itself. It's an attempt to make the Bible less intimidating. So with that in mind, coffee in hand, feet well slippered, a little music in the background, let's go for it. Nice and easy.

GENESIS

Two words characterize Genesis: *beginning* and *covenant*. Beginning has to do with creation, covenant with Israel. And these two words also define the scope of the book. Like the bold, broad strokes of an artist painting a huge mural, Genesis presents, in splashes of color, the creation of the universe, then in careful, painstaking detail, the creation of a people. Background to foreground is portrayed as Adam to Jacob, so in that sense, Genesis is the story of Hebrew origins. The painting includes: creation and the story of Adam and Eve (chapters 1 through 3), Cain and Abel (chapter 4), Noah and the second beginning (chapters 6 through 10), the tower of Babel and the first school of linguistics (chapter 11), Abraham's story (chapters 12 through 23), Isaac and Rebekah (chapter 24), Jacob and Esau (chapters 25 through 28), Jacob and his wrestlings (chapters 29 through 36), and Joseph the dreamer/king (chapters 37 through 50). It ends with Jacob's clan in Egypt. A clan about to become a nation through the miracle of the Exodus.

EXODUS

Whereas Genesis related the beginning of the Hebrew people. Exodus relates the beginning of the Hebrew nation and the Hebrew religion. It can be divided into three: the Exodus itself (chapters 1 through 15), desert wanderings (chapters 16 through 18), and God's instructions to the new nation at Mount Sinai (chapters 19 through 40). This Mount Sinai encounter provides the basis for Israel's status as God's "peculiar people": the Ten Commandments (20:2–17), guidelines for an emerging society (20:23–23:33), and a code of ritual (34:14–26). But the most "peculiar" of all is this: "I am the Lord your God, who brought you out of Egypt, out of the land of slavery" (20:2). Why peculiar? Because it's an introduction to the Ten Commandments (law), while at the same time an eternal proclamation of God's grace (love). It's law and love in one. And it's the basis for all future Old Testament prophecy. Because God delivered Israel, Israel is now his. And she is to live a life of grateful obedience. If she doesn't, she'll have an angry God to deal with. The prophets, on this historical basis, will continually call on Israel to clean up her act.

LEVITICUS

Perhaps this is the reason the Lord says to Moses' brother, Aaron, "You must distinguish between the holy and the profane, between the unclean and the clean" (10:10). Leviticus is known as the priest's manual, and Aaron was the first high priest. In the book God instructs both Aaron and Moses on what constitutes proper ethics and ritual in order for Israel to be clean, or holy, in his sight. Generally, I find it to be pretty dull reading, with a few exceptions like chapter 16, where the Day of Atonement (Yom Kippur) is described; or chapter 23, which outlines the seven festivals of the year. But the dullness is in the eye of the beholder. Look at Bert, Ernie's dour sidekick on the world-famous children's television show "Sesame Street." One of his great excitements is counting pigeons!

NUMBERS

How about counting heads? That's how the book of Numbers starts out (1:1–46). Then it records the organizing of the clans and branches of the tribes, lists various laws, and speaks of the last days before the journey from Sinai to Canaan began (1:47–10:10). An interesting law recorded here relates to those who are "ceremonially unclean" during the Passover celebrations. They come to Moses with their problem, he takes it to the Lord, and the Lord says, No problem. They can celebrate Passover a month later. But anyone who misses one or the other is to be cut off from his people (9:1–13).

Then, in chapters 10 through 20, Numbers records the forty years Israel wandered in the wilderness on her way to Canaan. This period includes several fascinating stories—stories about murmurings and quails (chapter 11); rebellion among Moses' relatives Aaron and Miriam (chapter 12); twelve spies and reports of giants (13–14); more rebellion (16); a walking-stick that became a budding almond branch (17); temper tantrums and water-spouting rocks (20); snakes and adders (21); a prophet and his garrulous ass (22–24); and the choice of Joshua to succeed Moses in the leadership of Israel (27). Moses is about to leave the stage.

DEUTERONOMY

This book is Moses' swan song. It's set in the form of a speech, a sort of last will and testament delivered just before his death and Israel's entry into Canaan under Joshua. Because all the old generation had died in the wilderness, Moses restates the laws given in Exodus, Leviticus, and Numbers. The younger generation has got to be reminded of their fathers' foundation. The main body of the book (chapters 12 through 26) is a recital of laws that are referred to in other parts of Deuteronomy as "this law" or "the statutes and the ordinances." The first eleven chapters of this book and the last eight take the form of a speech by Moses. This speech includes a "song" (32:1–43) and a "blessing" (33). There are two key features: (a) the call for exclusive worship at a central place (12), a suggestion of a "temple" in Jerusalem, and (b) the great statement which was to become Israel's declaration of faith: "Hear, O Israel: The Lord our God, the Lord is one. Love the Lord your God with all your heart and with all your soul and with all your strength" (6:4–5). So in the context of Israel's spiritual history, Deuteronomy is bedrock. In the context of Israel's natural history, it is the first of a series of books (including Joshua, Judges, Samuel, and Kings) which recount the story of wilderness wanderings to Babylonian exile.

JOSHUA

Joshua picks up where Deuteronomy left off. It tells the story of Israel's entry into Canaan. After a few instructions from the Lord, Joshua gives a few instructions to his officers (chapter 1), and then the conquest of Canaan begins (2–12). The conquest includes fascinating stories: Rahab the prostitute and the fall of Jericho (2, 6), Achan the thief (7), and the longest day in history (10). Following the conquest, the land is divided and Israel is settled (13–22). Then, in the hundred and tenth year of his life, Joshua dies, after giving a farewell speech and renewing the covenant with Israel at Shechem (23–24). At this renewal ceremony Joshua utters some of the most memorable words of all Israel's history: "Choose for yourselves this day whom you will serve, whether the gods your forefathers served beyond the River, or the gods of the Amorites, in whose land you are living. But as for me and my household, we will serve the Lord" (24:15). Strong words from a strong man.

JUDGES

The strongest man of all (physically) was Samson. He was one of Israel's judges during the period between Joshua's death and the appearance of Samuel. The book of Judges tells the stories of six major and six minor judges. Samson, whose story is recorded in chapters 13 through 16, is a good example of Israel's roller-coaster life in those days. His spiritual highs and moral lows reflected the national life. Israel was constantly undulating between the heights of spiritual commitment to God (under the leadership of a strong judge) and the depths of moral evil. Up and down. When she was down, she'd be overrun by an oppressor. Under the weight of this oppression, Israel would remember God and repent. Then another judge, a strong deliverer like

Gideon (6–7) or Deborah (4–6), would come along, and Israel would rise out of her bondage for a time. So most of the book is about these cycles of moral declines, oppressions, and deliverances. The final part of the book (17–21) is rather raw reading (the story of the Levite and his concubine in chapter 19 is no children's bedtime story). It ends with the men of Benjamin acquiring wives in cave-man fashion. Reading Judges leaves a bad taste. Maybe the last verse tells us why: "In those days . . . everyone did as he saw fit" (21:25). They did their own thing.

RUTH

Boaz was no cave man. He was a class act. He treated his workmen well ("May the Lord be with you!" was his greeting, and their response was "The Lord bless you!"), and he did the honorable thing with his relative's widow Ruth. The book is a great story of love conquering all. And it has left a lasting legacy to all young bridal couples. How often have I heard a bride sweetly quote, "Where you go I will go, and where you stay I will stay. Your people will be my people and your God my God" (1:16). But there's another legacy. One which the priest Ezra (you'll meet him in a few minutes) would not have liked. It's this: Ruth was a Gentile. A Moabitess. And she was the great-grandmother of King David! Which, if Ezra had his way, meant David wasn't Jewish. So the book was a scandal to some. To others, a little bit of heavenly humor. They can keep their frowns. I'll take the smiles.

SAMUEL

Initially, the books of Samuel and Kings were one book. But human attention spans being what they are, the book was divided in two. Then each division was divided again. One book became four. And the first two were called Samuel, probably because he

was the first major character appearing in the book. Some of
Israel's most colorful stories appear here: Hannah and her son
Samuel (I, 1–2), David and Goliath (I, 17), Saul's Hamlet-like
death (I, 28–31), and Bathsheba's deadly bath (II, 11:2–27). King
Saul was on the receiving end of Samuel's wrath when he heard
these powerful words, "Does the Lord delight in burnt offerings
and sacrifices as much as in obeying the voice of the Lord? To
obey is better than sacrifice" (I, 15:22). This concept blazes out
of the book. It has a timeless ring. Religion must never replace
relationship.

KINGS

In the Hebrew Bible, Samuel is joined by Joshua, Judges, and
Kings in what is known as the "Former Prophets." These books
cover Israel's history from her victory over Canaan to the razing
of Jerusalem in 586 B.C. Kings focuses on Solomon's reign (I,
1–12), the divided kingdom (I, 13–25), and the exploits of wild
prophetic characters like Elijah (II, 7–19; II, 1), Elisha (II, 2–8),
and others like Jehu and Ahijah. There are several fascinating
stories, but the most gripping of all is the contest on Mount
Carmel between God's prophet Elijah and the prophets of Baal
for fire from heaven (I, 18:16–46).

The absolute confidence of Elijah, bordering on arrogance,
is a wonder to behold. He throws out the classic challenge to all
of Israel, "How long will you waver between two opinions? If
the Lord is God, follow him; but if Baal is God, follow him."
He storms about the sacrificial site. He mocks the heathen prophets. He orders twelve buckets of precious water to be thrown over
his prepared sacrifice. He prays. Fire falls. Then he runs about
fifteen miles ahead of a chariot, just to get out of the rain. After
all this glorious victory, he runs again. This time to get out of
the reign, Jezebel's reign.

But there's more to Kings than prophets. There are, as you
would expect, kings. All kinds of them. Some reigning over

Israel, the northern kingdom, some reigning over Judah, the southern kingdom. Most of them reigning badly. As you read you begin to get the impression that the author(s) was somewhat troubled. Troubled with an apparent short-circuit in God's promises. He had promised a dynasty to David, and David's dynasty appeared to be dead. He had led Israel (through the work of the Deuteronomist) to the establishment of a central shrine in Jerusalem. Now both temple and city were in ruins. How to explain it? It must have been the evil reign of Manasseh (II, 21:1–17). After a king like him, what dynasty deserved to survive? Even good king Josiah (II, 22:1–23:30) wasn't enough. After he died in battle at Megiddo, the Egyptian king, Pharaoh Neco, made sure Josiah's inept son, Jehoiakim, got the throne. Bringing more evil to the land. So Kings ends with a tragic, terse sentence, "Judah went into captivity, away from her land" (II, 25:21). The kings had squandered their people and their lands. Now they bowed to the king of Babylon.

CHRONICLES

There's one verse from Chronicles quoted and preached more than all the book's other verses combined: "If my people, who are called by my name, will humble themselves and pray and seek my face and turn from their wicked ways, then will I hear from heaven and will forgive their sin and will heal their land" (II, 7:14). These words were spoken to King Solomon after he had dedicated the temple in Jerusalem. What a dedication! Just the sacrifice alone took "twenty-two thousand head of cattle and a hundred and twenty thousand sheep and goats" (II, 7:5). The words come as a warning. If he walks and rules "as David your father did," the Lord will "establish your royal throne." If he turns away from God, Israel will be uprooted and the temple will become "an object of ridicule among all peoples" (verses 13–22). Just in these few sentences the chronicler shows his perspective. His focus is theocracy, God ruling through chosen leaders. And the ideal for the chronicler was God's rule through David. This perspective shows through in several places as the book records the history of Saul, David, Solomon, and the story of Judah from Rehoboam to the fall of Jerusalem in 586 B.C. Originally the book may have been part of a larger work including Ezra and Nehemiah. As such it chronicled the history of Judah from Adam to the restoration of Judaism under Ezra and Nehemiah. Don't let the geneologies of the first eight chapters throw you. It's a book with tremendous scope.

EZRA AND NEHEMIAH

These books give an overview of Judah after the exile. They tell the story of the return of the Jews from Babylon to Jerusalem. The books revolve around certain leaders: Sheshbazzar, the prince of Judah (Ezra 1:8), under whom the first flow of exiles returned in 538 B.C. to rebuild the temple (Ezra 1–2); Zerubbabel, who supervised the actual reconstruction, beginning in 520 B.C. (Ezra 3–6); Ezra, who introduced spiritual and social reform (Ezra 7–10; Neh. 7:73–10:39); and Nehemiah, cup-bearer to Artaxerxes I, who returned to Jerusalem to rebuild the walls (Neh. 1:1–7:73; 11–13).

The account of the rebuilding is fascinating reading. The narrative holds you spellbound as it describes Nehemiah's efforts in the face of mounting military opposition. When the wall is finally completed, you breathe a sigh of relief. Amazingly, the job was completed in just fifty-two days. It was such a remarkable achievement that "when all our enemies heard about this and all the surrounding nations saw it, our enemies lost their self-confidence" (Neh. 6:16). It's a tremendous example of a small community pulling together with overwhelming success.

ESTHER

In Ruth you have a Gentile female marrying a Jewish man. In Esther it's the other way around: Jewish female, Gentile male. Both cases, however, had a lasting effect on Israel's history. King Xerxes (or Ahasuerus) had a party. A six-month party. With all the nobles, princes, military leaders, and officials of Persia's 127 provinces present. He capped it off with a seven-day banquet for everybody in his capital city. At each bash the wine flowed freely. A six-month drunk followed by a seven-day drunk. The banquet divided the men and the women. Xerxes presided over the men, the beautiful queen Vashti over the women. Suddenly, Xerxes, in his 180-day drunken stupor, orders the queen to come over to the stag party wearing nothing but her crown! Vashti, to her credit, refuses. Which brings crisis to the Persian empire— Xerxes' advisers saw Vashti's disobedience as a dangerous signal to all Persian women that they actually had a say in marriage. You might call Vashti the original women's libber. So Vashti is deposed. Xerxes holds a "Miss Persia" beauty contest, and a Jewish girl, Esther, wins. Then the story gets even more interesting. I won't tell you any more. Suffice it to say, the story of Esther is a timeless example of victory over persecution. That's why the Jews to this day celebrate it (Purim) and remember God's faithfulness.

JOB

Before anything else, Job is a poem about God, but it's also about justice and the meaning of suffering. Job's misfortune is interpreted in classic and timeless ways by his three "comforters"—Eliphaz, Bildad, and Zophar—with an uninvited flurry of invective from a youthful intruder, Elihu. They accuse, Job rationalizes. Indeed, for most of the poem he's on the defensive.

There's lots of talk, mainly of self-justification. Then, when he is finally confronted with the God of the storm, he is silenced (39–41). Job's admission at the end provides a good reminder for all of us when we debate or argue the existence, justice, presence, and meaning of God, "Surely I spoke of things I did not understand, things too wonderful for me to know" (42:3). This is the invaluable treasure of the book: it speaks of an awesome God, high and mighty and mysterious. Refusing to be created in man's image. Riding in no one's hip pocket.

PSALMS

Ever been mad at somebody? Wished they would "go jump in the lake"? Well, that's pretty bland stuff. If you want a real hairy-chested word for your enemy, try a psalm or two. For instance, "Break the teeth in their mouths, O God . . . Like a stillborn child, may they not see the sun . . . The righteous will be glad when they are avenged, when they bathe their feet in the blood of the wicked" (58:16–10).

Ever been in an apologetic mood? But you didn't have the words to say? You wanted something more than a simple "I'm sorry." Try another psalm, like, "I know my transgressions, and my sin is always before me. Against you, you only have I sinned and done what is evil. Create in me a pure heart, O God, and renew a steadfast spirit within me . . . a broken and contrite heart, O God, you will not despise" (51).

Or maybe you're just happy. And you want to tell the world. How about, "Praise the Lord, O my soul. I will praise the Lord all my life; I will sing praise to my God as long as I live" (146:1).

Maybe you're sad. Discouraged. Feeling deserted by God and man. A psalm is in order: "O Lord, do not rebuke me in your anger or discipline me in your wrath. Be merciful to me, Lord, for I am faint; O Lord, heal me, for my bones are in agony. My soul is in anguish. How long, O Lord, how long?" (6:1–3).

There is a full range of human emotions in the book of

Psalms. Psalms, by the way, are simply hymns. In fact, you could say the psalms are the hymnbook of Israel. Compiled over a thousand-year span by authors such as Moses, Solomon, and David. Doctrinally they cover things like sin, salvation, guilt, forgiveness, life, and death. They even talk of Israel's Messiah (2, 8, 16, 22, 45, 69, 72, 89, 110, 118, 132). It's the longest book in the Bible. Perhaps the best known and the most read. And interestingly, here in the last quarter of the twentieth century, there's a revival of singing the psalms. They have an ageless appeal.

PROVERBS

There are three types of people presented in Proverbs: "fools," who don't have a chance to succeed in life; the "simple," who have the potential to be wise but have a long way to go; and the "wise" (or "righteous"), who have their act together and are successful. The book is written from a senior writer to junior readers. Indeed, you almost get the feeling, as you read it, of being in a classroom. There's a kind of Eastern tendency to flowery language and extravagant imagery, but the bottom-line wisdom is indisputable. Here's a great tongue-in-cheek example: "Under three things the earth trembles, under four it cannot bear up: a servant who becomes king, a fool who is full of food, an unloved woman who is married, and a maidservant who displaces her mistress" (30:21–23). The earthy humor is a joy! The writer's feet are on the ground. Perhaps one of his most foundational proverbs is, "A man's ways are in full view of the Lord, and he examines all his paths" (5:21). Proverbs helps us keep our ways pleasing in the Lord's sight. It's sanctified common sense.

ECCLESIASTES

The word best characterizing Ecclesiastes is *meaningless*. That's the conclusion of the writer as he analyzes life, "Everything is meaningless" (12:8). Frankly, there's not much in the book that's encouraging or uplifting. One wonders what role the Holy Spirit had in its inspiration. Unless the whole sorry affair is a setting for two gems that flash out of the darkness with brilliant light: "Remember your Creator in the days of your youth" (12:1) and "Here is the conclusion of the matter: Fear God and keep his commandments, for this is the whole duty of man" (12:13). The writer can't grasp life's meaning, he keeps drawing a blank. But there's something in him, call it an intuition or an instinct, that recognizes the wisdom of being grasped by God. In Ecclesiastes, the ultimate cornerstone of faith is not the enjoyment of life, but the sovereignty of God.

SONG OF SONGS

This is a poem celebrating the joys of sex and marriage, the pleasures of love, and the delights of the natural world. Its high regard for human love gives the reader, by way of analogy, insight into divine love. As far as his creation and creatures are concerned, God is first and foremost a lover.

ISAIAH

Here's a prophet who is an exception to the rule. The rule being that a prophet is usually on the outside looking in (even though he may have a strong sense of identity with his audience). He was well-to-do, a courtier, a nobleman highly regarded by his peers in Jerusalem. He wasn't stoned or exiled for his prophecies, but lived to a ripe old age. The scope of his book is vast. Living through the reigns of five kings, he is able to address all kinds of matters relating to leadership, local situations, international intrigues, battles, idolatries, and captivities. But his most lasting impact exists in his prophecies concerning the Messiah. He looks for a virgin-born redeemer (7:14) whose name will be

"Wonderful Counselor, Mighty God, Everlasting Father, Prince of Peace" (9:6, 7). In spite of his divine nature he will suffer in order to save his people (53); yet for the most part he'll be "despised and rejected by men, a man of sorrows . . . pierced for our transgressions . . . crushed for our iniquities" (verses 3,5). Nevertheless, Isaiah sees the ultimate triumph of this "suffering servant" and speaks glowingly of his kingdom (35:1–10; 65:17–25). One of the things most meaningful to me, however, is the personal insights Isaiah gives us into his own spiritual relationship with the Lord. Such an insight occurs in chapter 6. His total humility in the presence of the Holy is deeply moving and challenging. Isaiah knew more than how to prophesy. He knew how to worship.

JEREMIAH

A hundred years after Isaiah, Jeremiah came on the scene. When he was only fourteen or fifteen years old (627 B.C.), the Lord called him to the prophetic ministry. If he had known then what the prophetic life would mean, he might have chosen to run as far away as possible. His early prophecies were given during the reign of good King Josiah. The nation was in a positive mood. Jeremiah was negative. Then, after Pharaoh Neco killed Josiah at Megiddo and installed Jehoiakim as king, the nation became negative. And Jeremiah became positive—about the nation of Babylon, that is. He prophesied that Judah would be taken captive and exiled in Babylon, and he encouraged the people to acquiesce. They weren't pleased. In fact most people weren't pleased with Jeremiah for most of his forty years of ministry. He was arrested and imprisoned several times, beaten, put in the stocks, thrown in a pit, ridiculed. Why, even his home town tried to kill him. But he persevered and proved to be a true prophet.

Jerusalem fell to the Babylonians in 586 B.C., a few years after the exile had begun. Against his better judgment, to say nothing of his will, Jeremiah was caught up in a flight to Egypt where he spent the rest of his life. His book, which was dictated to a secretary named Baruch, is a collection of sayings, prayers, oracles, poems, hymns, proverbs, visions, and stories. He is powerfully eloquent, especially when he attacks false prophets (23:15–40). But his most significant prophecies relate to a "new covenant" (31:31) and "a righteous Branch, a King who . . . will be called: The Lord Our Righteousness" (23:5–6). Maybe one of the outstanding lessons of Jeremiah relates to the price of being true to one's beliefs. Integrity costs. But it also pays.

LAMENTATIONS

Jeremiah wept a lot. He was emotional as well as persistent, and he was poetic. Lamentations (which in the Hebrew Bible is *How?* the characteristic beginning of a funeral dirge) is a series of five poems. The first four consist of twenty-two stanzas, each stanza beginning with the successive letters of the Hebrew alphabet. Each poem is a response to Judah's downfall in the Babylonian invasions of the early sixth century B.C. The third poem tries to put a good face on the catastrophe—seeing the sovereignty and goodness of God behind it all (3:22–40, 55–66). Here in Israel and wherever observant Jews live throughout the world, Lamentations is read on the ninth of Av (which usually falls somewhere in July or August), the day of remembering the destruction of the temple by Titus in 70 A.D. In spite of the doleful nature of the book, there is a positive note or two. One of them relates to patience and perseverance in suffering: "The Lord is my portion; therefore I will wait for him" (3:24). You don't wait for someone you don't expect to arrive. There's more than a hint of optimism here—there's overcoming faith.

EZEKIEL

You find the book of Ezekiel hard to follow? Join the club. There's an old Jewish story of an aged rabbi who said he would set out to explain Ezekiel fully. The rabbinic council who heard the boast promptly ordered three hundred barrels of oil for his study lamp. They knew he'd never finish the job, and they were right. Ezekiel was a dreamer, a visionary, and an abstract writer. He was also a bit of a character. He was into illustrated sermons. One time he lay in the same position for more than a year, eating bread baked over a fire fueled by human excrement (chapter 4), just to emphasize a point.

He was a young contemporary of Jeremiah and he lived in the original Tel Aviv, on the Kebar river in Babylonia. He prophesied to the Jews in exile. Four visions dominate his book: the storm cloud (1–3), the eating of a scroll (2:8–3:3), the coming destruction of Jerusalem (9), and the dry-bones resurrection of the nation (37). The book ends with a detailed description of the temple and the land of Israel in the messianic age (40–48). Initially, with his wheels within wheels (chapter 1), Ezekiel seems a little "spinny," but as you read further you begin to see a prophet with genius rising beyond his eccentricities. Little wonder he's called a "major prophet."

DANIEL

You thought Ezekiel was hard to understand. Try Daniel! If it's any consolation, the book is known as "apocalyptic literature," which means symbolism, colorful imagery, and mystery. Underlying apocalyptic writing is hope. Hope for some kind of drastic divine intervention in history to terminate present evils and bring in a new age of godly rule where justice and righteousness prevail. The only other apocalyptic book in the Bible is

Revelation. In both cases a period of persecution provided the incubation for mysteriously expressed hope. Daniel is best known for lions and fiery furnaces, but beyond these quirks of life in Babylonian exile, the book looks forward to God's ultimate vindication of his people. Apocalyptic and future hope go hand in hand.

HOSEA

Hosea had a bad marriage. His wife was unfaithful to him, again and again, and flaunted it. She continually sought new sexual excitement and had a hankering after luxury, but in her pursuits she was pursued, by her loving and faithful husband. Hosea's marriage was a microcosm of God's marriage with Israel. The book is about Israel's continual cultural and spiritual pursuit of Baalism, and God's faithful pursuit of his adulterous bride. It may be the greatest hymn to God's faithfulness written, both for the eighth century B.C. and forever.

JOEL

Written after the Babylonian exile, the book of Joel is divided in two, with a messianic future view in the middle. The first part (1:1–2:27) is about an invasion of locusts, the second (3:1–16) concerns judgment in the nations. The conclusion (3:17–21) continues the optimism of the middle section (2:28–32). Joel sees the locust attack as an act of God (2:25) foreshadowing a divine attack on the soon-coming day of the Lord. He calls vigorously on Israel to return to God. This call contains one of the most powerful images from the pen of a prophet, "Rend your heart and not your garments" (2:12). And his view of a future outpouring of the Spirit (2:28–32) was a vivid picture hundreds of years later when Peter preached the church's first sermon (Acts 2:17–21). Joel's mouths of locusts and Peter's tongues of fire had a common denominator: a messianic day when "everyone who calls on the name of the Lord will be saved" (Joel 2:32; Acts 2:21).

AMOS

Like Joel, Amos was captivated by the "day of the Lord." As he saw it, the destruction of Israel was inevitable because "the lion has roared" (3:8). His warnings, however, fell on deaf ears. Jeroboam II of Israel had ended the 150-year war with Syria. Israel was experiencing unprecedented prosperity in the eighth century, as was Judah under Uzziah's leadership, but the prosperity was accompanied by gross moral decay and Baal worship. So Amos, the shepherd and fruit-picker, left the ruggedly pastoral environs of Tekoa to blast Israel. On the way he took shots at Damascus, Gaza, Tyre, Ammon, Moab, and Judah (1–2). His prophecies have the bone-crunching power of a lion's jaws. He casts his eyes disdainfully on the luxury-addicted nation and accuses it of turning "justice into bitterness" and casting "righteousness to the ground" (5:7). They "trample the poor" (verse 11) and "oppress the righteous" (verse 12). That's why the Lord "hate[s] . . . despise[s] your religious feasts," that's why he "cannot stand your assemblies" (verse 21). Until "justice roll[s] on like a river, righteousness like a never-failing stream" (verse 24), Israel will stand under God's condemning justice. Religion must give way to relationship—love for God and love for neighbor. This is the ringing cry of Amos, the first to put his prophecies in writing, and the first to protest against religion as an opiate, dulling hearts and minds to injustice.

OBADIAH

This is the shortest book in the Old Testament, a blunt denunciation of Edom (the people whose patriarch was Esau, Jacob's brother). The central message, apart from Edom's certain and total destruction, is the justice and sovereignty of God. He won't tolerate rebellion indefinitely, and he will, if he chooses, utterly destroy a godless nation. "The Lord has spoken," says Obadiah (verse 18). The destruction will occur because there is a day coming when "the kingdom will be the Lord's" (verse 21).

JONAH

Jonah's a fun book, so well known; but apart from the entertainment, it's a book wrestling with the mystery of God's mercy. It caricatures a narrow-minded Israelite worldview as a foil for the sovereign freedom of God. God is Lord and Father of all men, even Assyrians. Several centuries later Paul asked, "Is he not the God of Gentiles too?" (Rom. 3:29). Indeed, the Lord doesn't want "anyone to perish, but everyone to come to repentance" (II Pet. 3:9). Ninevah repented, Jonah sulked, and the Lord was merciful.

MICAH

Micah (a contemporary of Isaiah, Amos, and Hosea) addresses himself to both the northern kingdom of Israel and the southern kingdom of Judah, and he focuses on the two capitals, Samaria and Jerusalem, as the centers of spiritual rottenness. When he talks of the "rulers of the house of Israel, who despise justice and distort all that is right," building "Zion with bloodshed, and Jerusalem with wickedness" (3:9–10), he's applying a timeless maxim. The end does not justify the means. Zion must be built according to God's plan, not man's. God's plan includes the Messiah. So in the middle chapters (4, 5), Micah addresses the future messianic kingdom. The famous "swords into ploughshares" passage is here (4:3), and the "ruler over Israel" from Bethlehem is also here (5:2). As is the case with genuine prophecy, Micah concludes with a message of hope: "The day for building your walls will come" (7:11).

NAHUM

Jonah would have loved Nahum. Then again, it may have given him further reason to pout. One hundred and fifty years after Jonah's temper tantrum over God's soft heart, God finally has had enough with Ninevah's sins. Assyria had been hassling the Hebrew kingdoms on and off for over two and a half centuries. She was even now at the height of her power, but her end was near. Nahum announces what Jonah would have loved to see, without any fish stories.

HABAKKUK

After Josiah was killed at Megiddo, Pharaoh Neco placed Josiah's second son, Jehoiakim, on the throne. In 604 B.C. he and Judah were forced to submit to Babylon; then three years later he rebelled, dying when Nebuchadnezzar besieged Jerusalem in December 598 B.C. We read in II Kings 23:37, Jehoiakim "did evil in the eyes of the Lord." Habakkuk's book is mainly against Jehoiakim and his evil, but it ends with a hopeful note, "Yet I will rejoice in the Lord" (3:18). Like all the other true prophets, Habukkuk saw beyond the present evils to a glorious vindication of God's justice and righteousness.

ZEPHANIAH

Zephaniah didn't have much good to say about anybody—Judah, Jerusalem, and all nations everywhere. He was downright negative. But he was scared, frightened of the approach of an unnamed menace (Scythians, perhaps) whose destruction must be averted. That's why he calls together a solemn assembly of Josiah's people "before the fierce anger of the Lord comes upon you, before the day of the Lord's wrath" (2:2). After the prayer meeting's success (the threat was averted), he leads the people in a joyful celebration. This hymn (3:14–18) is followed by a stirring promise: "At that time I will gather you; at that time I will bring you home. I will give you honor and praise among all the peoples of the earth when I restore your fortunes before your very eyes" (verse 20). So after a blasting, Zephaniah gives a blessing. Another typical prophet for you.

HAGGAI

Haggai, on the other hand, is not a typical prophet. Why? Because he's almost entirely focused on a present opportunity to do good. He denounces very little evil and encourages the people simply to build the temple. The book is dated somewhere around 520 B.C. Haggai was one of Ezra's right-hand men in rebuilding the temple (Ezra 6:14). You might call him the public-relations/ sales director of the project. He was a practical enthusiast motivated by hope.

ZECHARIAH

Haggai had been prophesying for about two months when Zechariah began his prophetic ministry. Whereas Haggai was very practical, Zechariah was more visionary. He was captivated by visions and enamored of the future messianic age. You may, with everyone else, find it tough to unravel his visions, but there's something you shouldn't miss: his focus on the unchanging grace of God. A key word from the Lord occurs in chapter 8, verses 14 and 15: "Just as I had determined to bring disaster upon you and showed no pity when your fathers angered me . . . so now I have determined to do good again to Jerusalem and Judah." As Zechariah saw it, the bludgeonings of past prophecy will give way to the blessings of future glory. God the disciplinarian is also God the lover (1:14–17).

MALACHI

Malachi, like Haggai, is not so typical either. Unlike the preexilic prophets, he believed proper religion would produce proper relationships. The right religious ritual would create justice and righteousness. Whereas most of the prophets would denounce the combination of sin and religion, Malachi would say proper religion is an antidote to sin. If you focus on your religion, you won't focus on sin. And because the priests of Malachi's day were responsible for religion, he calls on them to perform their tasks properly (2:1–7). The temple, completed in 515 B.C., had been around long enough (it was now about 450 B.C.) for the priests to become sloppy and corrupt. It's time for a change, says Malachi. Return to the Lord, and he'll return to you (3:7). Little did he, or anyone else for that matter, know what form that return would take. Just four hundred years later.

MATTHEW, MARK, LUKE, JOHN

These four books, known as the Gospels, have one purpose— to tell the story of Jesus. Matthew and John write from their personal experiences as disciples. Mark also writes from personal experience. He was probably in his early teens when his family was closely associated with Jesus and his disciples. His parents' home seems to have been Jesus' headquarters when Jesus was in Jerusalem. Luke writes from the perpective of a historian. He was a physician from Alexandria and wrote Jesus' story by gathering his material through primary and secondary sources. Their stories differ in style and order of presentation, but not much in substance.

You will notice different traits, however—like Matthew stressing Jesus as the Christ, citing more than 130 different passages from the Old Testament to prove his point; or Mark making explanations of things you'd expect a Jewish audience would have no need of, thereby implying he wrote his Gospel for the Gentiles. (It makes sense, when you remember he spent his formative ministry years traveling with Paul and Barnabas.) Luke, for some reason, emphasizes Jesus' ministry to those who needed it most—Samaritans, Gentiles, publicans, and sinners. (Only in Luke does Jesus eat with Zachaeus; and a Samaritan shows up a priest and a Levite.) John, however, underlines the "sign" aspect of Jesus' ministry as it relates to the "hour" which "is coming and now is" in the broader context of the judgment polarizing believers and unbelievers in the "last day." But the other three would agree with John. They wrote "that you may believe that Jesus is the Christ, the Son of God, and that by believing you may have life in his name" (20:31). They tell the greatest story ever told.

THE ACTS OF THE APOSTLES

Acts is the second book written by Luke. It's a continuation of his history, concerning itself with the impact of Jesus' life on the world at large. As such it is a history of the early Church. It's full of so many interesting stories and fascinating characters that one's mind can be somewhat boggled by it all. You've got Jesus' ascension (1:9), the Day of Pentecost with fiery tongues and other tongues (2), the failure of early communism capped off by the death of two liars (4:34–35:11), Saul's conversion (9:1–22), Cornelius (the first Gentile convert) accepted into fellowship (10:1–48), an angelic jailbreak (12:1–19), a shipwreck (27:13–44), and on and on.

One of its most fascinating aspects, however, is its record of the struggle early Christians had with the concept of Gentiles as believers. Their first and protracted philosophical problem wrestled with the relevance, if any, the Jewish Messiah had to Gentiles. It was quite a boxing match, with the knockout blow delivered to Peter by way of a large sheet dropped on his head full of "unclean animals" (chapter 10). Reluctantly, the church leaders began to accept Gentiles. But James, the first bishop, was slow to change his convictions. He insisted Gentiles had to be circumcised and become Jews before they could become Christians. So it's a book of powerful everything—conversions, lies, intrigues, visions, jailbreaks, healings, and convictions. There's nothing bland about Acts. Acts is action.

ROMANS

This is a heavy book full of weighty doctrine, but in terms of an orientation to the book, I think there are a few verses in the first chapter which are vital to everything that follows. Here they are: "The gospel he promised beforehand through his prophets in the Holy Scriptures regarding his Son, who as to his human nature was a descendant of David and who through the Spirit of holiness was declared with power to be the Son of God by his resurrection from the dead: Jesus Christ our Lord" (1:2–4); and "I am not ashamed of the gospel, because it is the power of God for the salvation of everyone who believes: first for the Jew, then for the Gentile. For in the gospel a righteousness from God is revealed, a righteousness that is by faith from first to last, just as it is written: 'The righteous will live by faith' " (verses 16–17). In these three sentences Paul presents: the integrity of prophecy and the inspiration of the Scriptures; Jesus, his human nature and his divine nature as underscored by his resurrection; the saving power of God in Christ; the universal nature of the gospel (Jew and Gentile); and the relationship between righteousness (and/or justice) and faith.

As you read the rest of Romans, you'll see these ideas developed. When you run into difficulty (as you will from time to time with all of Paul's books), consult a few good Bible commentaries. There's one chapter you should get to know—chapter 12. I call it Paul's "sermon on the mount."

CORINTHIANS

In the Greco-Roman world, to call a person a Corinthian was to call him a drunk. "Living like a Corinthian" was a slang term for unbridled hedonism. Corinth was a city dominated by an eighteen-hundred-foot peak called Acrocorinth on which a famous temple to the goddess of love, Aphrodite, was built. It had a full stable of sacred prostitutes for the multitudes of observant tourists.

Paul was Corinth's first missionary. After establishing a church there, he left it in the hands of local leadership. Gradually the hedonistic atmosphere eroded the morality of the church community. Things got so bad that a delegation from Corinth sought Paul out in Ephesus to get his advice. Disturbed by what he heard, Paul wrote his first letter to the Corinthians. A little later Timothy reported slow progress in Corinth, so Paul wrote a second letter. The letters are a mix of moral teaching and doctrinal teaching, with a good measure of self-defense thrown in. I say self-defense because, as you would expect, Paul's long absence from Corinth had given his detractors lots of time to undermine his authority.

His moral teaching addressed subjects such as incest (I, 5), lawsuits between believers (I, 6), and marriage (I, 7; II, 6). His doctrinal teaching included the preaching of the cross (I, 1), eating food offered to idols (I, 8, 10), the Lord's Supper (I, 11), the proper use of spiritual gifts (I, 12, 13, 14), and the resurrection (I, 15).

As far as self-defense is concerned, you'll encounter it here and there throughout the entire work. Just remember when you read Corinthians that it's addressed to a pleasure-seeking, worldly city culture. A culture with more than a residual presence in the life of the church. Remember also, there are some specific subcultural concerns (like women's head coverings and men's hair length) which aren't quite on the same level as the Ten Commandments or the Sermon on the Mount.

GALATIANS

Paul knew what he believed, so much so that he was prepared to consign anyone (including angels) who taught a different gospel to hell (1:6–9). A different gospel (verse 6) is the issue. There were two. One was teaching the Galatian believers they had to become Jews before they could become Christians—after which, they had to observe all the laws and traditions of Judaism. The other was teaching a kind of libertinism, where the field was open to sexual sins as long as you were part of the "in crowd" who had secret knowledge of God. These two groups were known as the Judaizers and the Gnostics. In both cases freedom was the focus—on the one hand too little, on the other hand too much.

Paul, rather than striking a balance between the two, paves a highway above them both. He presents freedom as it really is in Christ. That's why Galatians has been referred to as the Magna Carta of the Christian faith. Take your time with this book. It's a classic.

EPHESIANS

Here's a book some have called the "divinest composition of man" and "the most heavenly work." No question it's got great style, and an even greater message: unity. Not just generic unity among all members of Christ's "body," but specific unity among Jewish and Gentile believers. In the early years of the Church there was a distinct tendency toward Jewish-Gentile division. The "inferior" ones in this case were the Gentiles, for they were the add-ons, the Johnny-come-latelies. So Paul makes a point of stressing the fact of Gentile equality with Jews in the new creation of God's household (2:19). We're all part of the same building, he says (2:21), and Jesus is the cornerstone. This unity focus is the main feature of Ephesians (2:11–4:16). Even his comment about wives and husbands (5:22–33) is an analogous attempt to discuss the meaning of unity in the church. Maybe the most quoted part of Ephesians is the passage talking about spiritual warfare and spiritual armor (6:10–18). But the most important relates to Jew and Gentile "being built together to become a dwelling in which God lives by the Spirit" (2:22).

PHILIPPIANS

Philippians is full of great quotes, such as "To live is Christ and to die is gain" (1:21); "Whatever was to my profit I now consider loss for the sake of Christ" (3:7); "Forgetting what is behind and straining toward what is ahead, I press on toward the goal to win the prize for which God has called me heavenward in Christ Jesus" (3:13, 14); "Whatever is true, whatever is noble, whatever is right, whatever is pure, whatever is lovely, whatever is admirable—if anything is excellent or praiseworthy—think about such things" (4:8), and "I can do everything through him who gives me strength" (4:13).

One reason for the memorable quotes related to the lack of need for correction in the Philippian church. Paul didn't have to spend any energy on negative things. He could be joyful, thankful, and full of praise, for this was his most trouble-free congregation. Not only were they spiritually mature, but they faithfully supported Paul financially (4:18), which was even more reason for joy. Theologically, the greatest contribution of Philippians is the poetic passage describing the incarnation,

God becoming man in Christ (2:5–11). This book leaves a good taste.

COLOSSIANS

A major factor in the Gnostic heresy was its downplaying of Christ's humanity. Jesus couldn't have been a man, they said, because men are flesh and blood. And flesh is material, which means, as they saw it, flesh is evil. How could God, who is holy, take on flesh, which is evil? So they spiritualized Jesus to the point where relationship with him had nothing to do with the here and now, and everything to do with the by-and-by. That's why the Gnostics had no concern about sexual immorality. What else can you expect from evil flesh? Rather, they emphasized the heavenlies, the mysteries, the angels, and the secret knowledge available to the truly spiritual.

This book is an attempt to counteract the Gnostic influence in the Colossian church. You'll see a lot of emphasis on Jesus as both God and man. He's not only "the firstborn over all creation" but also the creator of all (1:15–16). "He is the head of the body, the church; he is the beginning and the firstborn from among the dead, so that in everything he might have the supremacy" (verse 18). The key verse in the entire book is, "For in Christ all the fullness of the Deity lives in bodily form" (2:9). He is fully God and fully man. That's why the Colossians have no need of religious ceremony or the mediation of angels (2:16–19) as auxiliary powers. Believers "have been given fullness in Christ, who is the head over every power and authority" (2:10). When Christ is your Lord you have need of no other. So "let the peace of Christ rule in your hearts . . . Let the word of Christ dwell in you richly . . . And whatever you do, whether in word or deed, do it all in the name of the Lord Jesus, giving thanks to God the Father through him" (3:15–17). Quit playing the mystic and start trusting the Master.

THESSALONIANS

Both the first and second books of Thessalonians deal with the return of Christ. The first letter is written to assure believers that those who have already died in the Lord will not miss out on Jesus' return, but will in fact come with him (4:13–18). The second letter is written to counter a bogus letter claiming Paul believed the day of the Lord had already come (2:1–4). He opposes this counterfeit, showing there are many events yet to occur before that great day.

TIMOTHY AND TITUS

Both were young men trained by Paul for the ministry. These books are called the pastoral letters because they're written by a senior pastor to junior pastors. When you read them, you'll see that most of the material relates to combating Gnosticism, especially its matter-spirit dualism. So Paul insists on "one God and one mediator between God and men, the man Christ Jesus" (I Tim. 2:5); the goodness (rather than the evil) of the material world (I, 4:4); the bodily reality of Christ (I, 3:16); the inspiration of the Scripture (implying the completeness of Scripture—thus, no need for extra-biblical visions and "what is falsely called knowledge" (II, 3:15–17; I, 6:20); and he plainly accuses the Gnostics of not really knowing God at all (Titus 1:15–16). Scattered throughout is a good deal of practical, fatherly advice. They're especially good reading for both those in the ministry or those considering the ministry as their future calling.

PHILEMON

Paul met Onesimus, a runaway slave, while he was in prison. It turns out that Onesimus's master, Philemon, was a convert of Paul's (verse 19). So Paul writes Philemon to ask him to forgive Onesimus and then release him to serve Paul. It's a very human and touching call for help. Church history tells us that Philemon responded positively and Onesimus became an influential church leader.

HEBREWS

This is a book, written to Hebrew believers, which speaks of someone "much superior to the angels" (1:4), "worthy of greater honor than Moses" (3:3), and the "guarantee of a better covenant" (7:22). Hebrews shows how Christ has become the ultimate high priest who "entered the Most Holy Place once for all by his own blood, having obtained eternal redemption" (9:12). There's no further need for yearly days of atonement. In Christ everyday is atonement day. If you're Jewish, or familiar with Judaism, you'll appreciate the radical message of this book. It's earthshaking.

JAMES

James wrote to keep believers' feet on the ground. No lofty themes here. Just "pure and faultless" religion defined in terms of looking after "orphans and widows in their distress" and keeping "oneself from being polluted by the world" (1:27). It's written for believers who talk faith but don't walk faith (2:14–26), who give preference to the wealthy (2:1–7), who blame God for their temptations (1:13), who gossip (3:2–12), and who get into fights (4:1–12). A verse capturing the essence of the book is,

"Do not merely listen to the word, and so deceive yourselves. Do what it says" (1:22). James would probably have said "Amen!" to the famous line in *My Fair Lady* which goes, "Don't speak of stars shining above; if you're in love, *show* me" [italics added].

PETER

The first book of Peter is addressed to believers in Asia Minor who were facing persecution. It's intent is to encourage: "Encouraging you and testifying that this is the true grace of God. Stand fast in it" (5:12). The main body of the letter (1:3–4:11) has been seen not only as an encouragement to persecuted believers but also as a manual of instruction for new converts. Its spirit is captured in 1:13, "Therefore, prepare your minds for action; be self-controlled; set your hope fully on the grace to be given you when Jesus Christ is revealed."

The second book of Peter is written to confront certain "lawless men" (3:17) who are probably Gnostic teachers. He says they "never stop sinning; they seduce the unstable; they are experts in greed—an accursed brood!" (2:14). He reminds his readers of the prophetic and apostolic witness upon which their faith is built (1:19; 3:2), encourages them to be familiar with Paul's teaching (3:15–18), and calls for Gnostic knowledge to be replaced by a true knowledge of Christ (1:3, 5–8). He wants to stimulate them to wholesome thinking (3:1). You might say the slogan of the first book of Peter is "Stick to your faith"; and the slogan of the second book of Peter is "Stick with your faith." Be sticky and stuck, not in the mud, but "in the grace and knowledge of our Lord and Savior Jesus Christ" (II, 3:18).

JOHN

The first book of John is also written against Gnosticism. Right off the top John talks of the physical presence of Jesus—a seeable, hearable, touchable reality (1:1–4). Using striking contrasts—light-darkness, truth-lie, commandments-sin, love-hate of the Father and of the world, God-Satan—he discusses the true meaning of "walking in the light" (1:7) as it relates to such things as the world, antichrists, love, spiritual discernment, and eternal life. The second book of John also addresses the Gnostic problem. Written from one congregation to another (personified as "the chosen lady and her children"), it warns against "deceivers, who do not acknowledge Jesus Christ as coming in the flesh" (verse 7). The third book of John is simply a memo to Gaius about an upcoming interview concerning Demetrius. John commends Gaius for the hospitality he has shown to "the brothers, even though they are strangers to you" (verse 5). A notable point in each of the three letters is the emphasis on love—the love of God, the love for God, and the love of brother for brother. It's not surprising this should come from the pen of the one who, in his gospel, revealed to us that "God is love."

JUDE

Jude gives one final blow against Gnosticism. He refers to the Gnostic teachers as "certain men whose condemnation was written about long ago." They've "slipped in among you" and even as they teach, they "pollute their own bodies, reject authority and slander celestial beings" (verses 4 and 8). He encourages his readers to shun Gnosticism and to "build yourselves up in your most holy faith and pray in the Holy Spirit" (verse 20). The best-remembered part of Jude is his conclusion (verses 24 and 25). It has become a classic doxology.

REVELATION

Speaking of doxologies, here's the doxology of the Bible. A doxology with a difference—rather than disengaging you from some holy encounter, it engages you in holy expectation. Like Daniel, it is apocalyptic literature, which means, among other things, that almost anything goes in terms of its interpretation. Some say it was written just for its own generation, others say it outlines the history of the Church, while yet others say it outlines the events surrounding Jesus' return. Then there are those who say it's purely a spiritual book with all kinds of possible typological and symbolic applications. Maybe the best approach is to understand the basic factors in apocalyptic writing generally, and then try to make some sense of it all.

There are four foundational factors in apocalyptic writing: (a) First, there are two divisions in time: the present evil age and the future godly age. Present evil is about to give way to a future glory in which Satan will be destroyed and Israel will enter her inheritance in a new heaven and earth. (b) The present age will end traumatically and suddenly. (c) The end is near. (d) The end will be characterized by natural catastrophes (plagues, famines, earthquakes, floods, etc.) and cosmic irregularities. With these in mind you then see at least the set for a cosmic drama. A drama in which Satan's reign over this present age is in its death throes and Christ is at the door. Through a veritable kaleidoscope of imageries, symbols, and abstractions the audience finds its excitement mounting as the drama unfolds. And one's thirst for life, eternal life, is sharpened. Intuition reaches beyond reason, and your heart thrills to the words "Behold, I am coming soon!" (22:12). You find yourself straining forward, reaching out for contact with the coming reality—a reality you've lived, however partially, through your commitment to God's past revelations and inspired word.

Suddenly the most sublime words of all come rolling out of the heavenlies. A divine invitation just for you. "The Spirit and the bride say, 'Come!' And let him who hears say, 'Come!' Whoever is thirsty, let him come; and whoever wishes, let him take the free gift of the water of life" (22:17). The whole point of the Bible suddenly becomes clear. A cry from deep within the heart explodes out of us, "Amen! Come, Lord Jesus!"

Conclusion

CHAPTER 12

A Man with
an Experience

❧ I'LL NEVER FORGET the funeral at which one of the official mourners was a dog. It took place during the dead of winter in an unheated hall. My father was the officiating clergyman, and the arrangements were under the casual management of the Jordan River Undertakers. Most families buried their dead without the expert inefficiency of the River, as the locals called them, because they were not only inept, they were expensive. They were also ill-equipped. Their only vehicle was an eighteen-year-old 1936 Desoto hearse. No clergy car, no family car. The minister had to ride in the hearse with the casket while the funeral director, A. K. Broodle, drove. And this funeral, Dad's first in the area, nearly drove him nuts. Appropriately, the name of the unincorporated village was Nut Mountain. Mind you, there was no mountain (this was *flat* central Saskatchewan) and no nuts (of the edible persuasion). Just the craziest funeral ever.

The day didn't start well, mainly because our 1947 Pontiac wouldn't start at all. To the car's credit, the temperature was thirty degrees below zero. Dad finally solved the problem by lighting a wood fire under the Pontiac's oil pan. Although this is not recommended cold-weather starting procedure, it worked, and got us to the hall on time. When we arrived, the hall was smothered in a blue-white cloud of carbon monoxide. Because of the subzero temperatures the grieving friends and relatives had left their car motors running. And the frosty air, with never a breath of breeze, caused the exhaust gases to linger ever so nonchalantly in an ever-increasing poison cloud around the frigid hall. Dad uttered a kind word of amazed disdain (something like "Look at those dummies!") and turned off the car's engine as a kind of protest—which was a mistake.

Walking through the cloud to the front door, we heard loud shouting and wheel-spinning from behind the hall. The hearse was stuck in the snow-filled back alleyway. A team of horses was attached to the front bumper, trying to pull it out.

"Gee! Gee! No, haw! Haw! Haw!" (These were left and right instructions to the horses.)

"Now A. K.! Now! All right, ease up on the clutch. Nah! It ain't gonna work. Car's too heavy."

"Maybe we should remove the casket," said A. K. Broodle.

"Yep. That might do it."

So as we watched in amazement, A. K. Broodle and three burly men in bright plaid mackinaw jackets removed the casket and wrestled it across thirty feet of waist-high snow to the back door of the hall. At one point, to catch their breath, they sat the pine box on top of the snow, and one of the pallbearers added to the general pall of smoke by hand-rolling and lighting a cigarette. It was a scene worthy of a Norman Rockwell painting.

From inside the hall, the back door was to the side of a crude platform. We had just walked down the center aisle when a muffled, "I think it's a bit stuck with ice," preceded three shoulder-breaking thumps followed by the whole door crashing off its hinges. The startled mourners on the rough benches saw an equally startled A. K. Broodle, three pallbearers, and a casket bathed in smoky sunlight. The fourth pallbearer, who had entered the hall by more conventional means, rushed forward to help his fellow laborers place the casket on the two sawhorses in front of the lectern. The viewing was about to begin.

Without any formal announcement the mourners stood and filed down the aisle to view the deceased. Their breath, steaming out of mouths and nostrils, added to the haze. Their feet, shod in an assortment of boots, were coated with unmelted snow and frozen wood shavings from the dirt floor. As they solemnly viewed the departed, I managed, from my front row seat, to catch glimpses of the dead between the mackinaws of the mourners. He looked a little blue to me. Mind you, the living were blue, too, with cold, but there was a major difference—the mourners were filling the air with visible crystallizing breath. Some of the warmer-blooded ones were even emitting vapor from their be-toqued heads. But the blue loved one steamed not at all.

About a third of the people had filed past the casket when there was a commotion at the front door.

"Get him, Sandy!"

"No, you get him."

"Let's both get him!" Two of the pallbearers suddenly dove for something below our craning line of sight. There was a terrible din of thumps, grunts, thrashings, and yelps, then a loud yiping and bared-teeth barking. The family dog had come to pay his respects.

With a ruffled dignity he walked away from his would-be captors and threaded his way through legs and boots to the casket, where he took his place beneath his departed master, dutifully sniffing the remaining mourners as they passed by. Occasionally, a friend would whisper, "How ya doin', Mickey?" and the dog would thump the sawhorse with his tail in recognition. A few times he sniffed and growled, and the growlee's viewing would be more hurried, a muted view-and-run.

The viewers were all seated when, through the uninsulated walls, we heard A. K. Broodle saying, "OK, folks, this way, please." The front door opened and in walked the bereaved family. In the lead was the deceased's large wife. Behind her was the small, bald, worried-looking brother-in-law. After him came several children and grandchildren. As soon as she entered, the bulbous spouse began to wail. I'd never heard anything like it and didn't again until fifteen years later when I first heard a jet engine start up. Her volume and pitch increased with each step down the aisle, and she began to flail her arms and lean backward. The diminutive brother-in-law placed his hands on her back, not only to brace her from falling but to defend himself from a horrible fate. He had the presence of mind, when they reached the front, to steer the windmilling siren to the right and out the bare-hinged door. We saw neither the spouse nor the brother again, although we did hear the wife for a time, her voice fading into the distance.

The funeral service itself was fairly straightforward. There were just a few quirks. When we rose to sing "Abide with Me," the organist gave a mighty push with her booted foot on the reluctant pump pedal and broke the bellows. There was a not unnoticeable amount of foot-stomping and arm-clapping in efforts to increase body temperatures, and a general shivering. In fact, you might call it a quaking. Then, as Dad pronounced the benediction, Mickey stood, stretched (with an accompanying yawn), sniffed, briefly chewed an artificial flower, and sauntered out the naked back door.

The interment was to take place twenty miles away at the family plot. Forty-five minutes later we were all there. A long line of cars, motors running, were stretched over about one hundred yards of single-lane country road. Because it took some time for those in the last cars to get to the grave site, Dad and the pallbearers waited before removing the casket from the hearse. When they did, someone jumped out from the crowd with a Brownie camera. "Hold it!" she cried. So Dad and the mackinawed pallbearers froze for a moment. All five of them grinning like Cheshire cats. "What do *you* do when someone suddenly points a camera at you?" Dad later asked my somewhat miffed mother.

Some of the more practical mourners made the interment a bit more colorful than usual. As Dad stood at the head of the grave (it had taken the local grave diggers two days to chisel through the snow and frost), these pragmatic ones were trying to turn some of the cars around. They succeeded in getting the first car stuck. So while Dad intoned, "Forasmuch as it hath pleased Almighty God to take unto himself the soul of our brother here departed," the background was full of spinning tire sounds, grunts, expletives, and loud directives.

"No, no, Al! Rev the engine, pop the clutch, we'll shove..."

"Earth to earth..."

"Watch the Ford! Oh, nuts! The bumper's scraped Fred's fender!"

"Dust to dust..."

"OK! Let's try again."

"Ashes to ashes. In sure and certain hope..."

"Now you've done it! The motor's overheated. Rats!"

"... of the resurrection from the dead."

When it was over, Dad shook hands with the family members and returned to the grave to get his hat. He had placed it on a snowdrift while he prayed. All he saw was a boot-shaped hole where his hat had been.

Later, as we drove back to Nut Mountain in the hearse, A. K. Broodle said, "Say, Reverend, did you leave your motor running?"

"No. Should I have?" asked Dad, his violated hat somewhat askew on his head.

"Of course you should have."

It took Dad half an hour to find enough wood for a fire. Another half hour later we were on our way home.

A month or so later the lady with the Brownie camera showed up at our door. She had a picture to show Dad.

"See what I mean, Reverend?" she asked, a hush in her voice.

"Yeh, I suppose so," said Dad.

"It's a halo, a presence. This picture is a sign that Albert was a saint. Just like my dream."

"Your dream?"

"Yes. Before Albert died, maybe a week or so, I'm not sure, I had this dream about him. He looked like an angel. All full of light and shining. He spoke to me and said I was to be a missionary to Africa. I wasn't too sure. I mean I was afraid—you know, snakes and cannibals and all. But now that I've seen this picture, well, I think it's a sign. What do you think? Should I go to Africa?"

"Why are you asking me?"

"Well you're in the picture and all. And, well, you're a pastor. You should know."

While Dad dealt with this naive soul, I looked at the picture myself. Sure enough, there was a kind of halo, or aura, around Dad, the casket, and the pallbearers. Radiance and silly grins. I knew what caused the grins, and I had my suspicions as to what caused the halo. It looked very much like frost on the lens.

In this chapter I want to talk about frost on the lens. Paul, referring to what we're able to comprehend of the kingdom of heaven, said, "Now we see but a poor reflection" (I Cor. 13:12). The King James Version says, "For now we see through a glass, darkly . . ." Our lenses are fogged. But a lot of people disagree. Almost as soon as the early Church was established, there were those who claimed they had had special revelations of the heavenlies. They had secret access and secret knowledge. They were known as the Gnostics. You've seen, in the last chapter, how many New Testament letters were written to combat Gnosticism. People who mistook the diffused light of a frosty lens as a halo, an aura, a special dispensation from God. People who imputed divine authority to their personal experiences with light. Knowing full well that a man with an experience is never at the mercy of a man with an argument, they fully embraced mysticism and perverted the gospel of Christ. They failed to recognize that a man with an experience must always subject it to the authority of God's word.

So what I plan to do is give you an overview of Gnosticism. I'll discuss (a) the general traits in historical Gnosticism; (b) a key factor in Gnosticism; (c) Gnostic tendencies today; and then (d) a New Testament response to Gnosticism. I want not only to inform you but also to warn you. Apparent special sight can sometimes be very deceptive. What you see is not necessarily what you get.

The fundamental error of Gnosticism was not subjective mysticism but rather its view of Jesus. The two are closely related, mind you. I'll discuss that a little later, but for now suffice it to say there have been two classic mistakes throughout history whenever Christians have attempted to explain the person of Jesus Christ. One is very practical—"Jesus simply couldn't have been God"; and the other, very mystical—"Jesus wasn't really human at all." Yet the Bible presents Jesus as fully God and fully man. He has two natures united in one person. Most believers have little sympathy for mistake number one, but they do have an affinity with mistake number two. This shouldn't surprise us for, historically, this dehumanizing of Jesus has always been a major problem for the Church. The movement to unman Jesus has been and still is the work of Gnosticism.

Early Gnosticism was built on the teaching of several outstanding personalities. A Syrian, Simon Magus, regarded himself as Father, Son, and Holy Spirit. He saw himself as having descended to earth through many heavens. This idea of several levels of heavenly existence between God and man became fundamental to Gnosticism.

Another teacher, Saturninus, taught that the Supreme Deity is completely unknown. He made spiritual beings who in turn made the world. When making man, their product was animated by "a spark of life," which is the element Christ saves in good men. Christ came to wipe out anyone hostile to the Supreme Deity. But Jesus' coming was not physical, because every material thing is evil. He just seemed to be human.

Marcion taught that there were two gods involved in the world. One was Jesus' father, the other was the Creator of the Old Testament.

Valentinus taught that there were several aeons or emanations or angels between the Supreme Deity and the earth. The twelfth and lowest of these was the female Sophia, whose instability caused her to fall into outer darkness where she conceived spontaneously and gave birth to a premature infant who became the creator of our universe. Jesus was sent down to redeem Sophia and mankind by collecting "spiritual seeds" and restoring them to the "fullness of spiritual being."

Philo of Alexandria taught the preexistence of the soul and the prison house of the flesh. Man must somehow escape the flesh and be etherealized to union with God.

So these founding fathers of Gnosticism introduced the basic tenets of their mystic view of Jesus and the world: several levels or aeons between God and man; two gods; the evil of matter; the flesh as the bondage of the soul; and Jesus, the unmanned superangel.

As Gnosticism grew, several characteristic traits emerged. First was *exclusivism,* the view that only a select few had special knowledge of the truth. This knowledge *(gnosis)* was superior to faith and was the possession of the more enlightened. One Gnostic theologian, Ptolemaeus, divided men into three categories: pagans; everyday Christians; and Gnostics, the truly spiritual ones. They were Christendom's spiritual giants.

The second trait was *self-righteousness,* which related to their view of all matter as evil. They saw denial of the flesh as the path to God. And as is always the case with self-denial systems, a number of legalisms or do's and dont's become standard issue.

Third was *immorality.* Ironically, their denial of the flesh as the path to God led them to immoral behavior. Because their focus was the spiritual world and because they saw all matter as evil, some of them developed an indifference to the physical world. Self-denial became matter denial; that is, they began to deny the reality of the physical world. Which rendered sexual morality irrelevant. "How can any law or behavior make what is evil become good?" they asked. All flesh is evil, so what can you expect from the flesh but evil? So they were able to live comfortably with immorality (denying its reality) during the week and with great praise and worship on Sundays.

The fourth trait was *mysticism.* Because they believed Jesus to have been only spiritual and not physical, it meant the man who died on the cross was an optical illusion or a fake, and salvation was gained through something other than blood sacrifice. That something else was the superior knowledge of the mysteries of the heavenlies. So Gnostics became committed spiritualizers, vision mongers, and mystics.

Perhaps the key factor in the popularity of Gnosticism was the general dissatisfaction second- and third-generation Christians had with the simplicity of the gospel. People wanted something new, more complex, higher. Indeed, the Gnostics rather disdained childlike faith in a simple gospel. Their big thing was "to know the depths," which John (in Rev. 2:24) turned against them by calling the depths "the depths of Satan." In their lust for depth they were getting in deeper than they'd planned. They were knocking on the gates of hell. A pretty serious charge. But then, messing with Jesus' nature is pretty serious business.

That's why Gnostic tendencies in the Church today need to be seen for what they are. Speaking personally from my vantage point here in Jerusalem, where a cross section of the Christian world is always coming, going, or passing through, I see three Gnostic traits in the ebb and flow. In the first place, I see Jesus being unmanned. There's a spiritualizing of Jesus to the point where many Christians don't really believe Jesus was "tempted in every way, just as we are—yet was without sin" (Heb. 4:15). How could he be? He was God's Son!

Thus, the reality of Jesus' overcoming the temptations of the flesh through the power of the Holy Spirit loses its relevance and impact on us as we fight our moral battles. Jesus doesn't relate to sex problems or money problems or indulgence problems because he's not seen as having been curious about or tempted by any of these things. Which means this fleshless Jesus can't relate to you and me in our fleshly needs and desires.

Rather, we exult in his deity. But we don't rejoice in his humanity. We've developed the tragic habit of ignoring the incarnation (bringing it out of mothballs at Christmas—"God in man is now residing"). So we've dehumanized Jesus. This may be one reason why the Church has become dehumanized. We praise and worship with gusto, while one third of our world starves to death. We treat people as objects, participate in the occasional sexual dalliance now and again, and sanctify it all with intense adoration of a short-sighted but glorified Jesus. We talk about achieving "fleshless purity" in our endeavors for God. "I want no flesh in this ministry of mine, I want to minister purely in the Spirit." Well, that's not only a Gnostic idea, it's also asking more of ourselves than the Father asked of the Son, in whom "all the fullness of the Deity lives in bodily form" (Col. 2:9). Let's face it, the flesh-spirit ratio in ministry has got to be at least fifty-fifty.

In the second place, I see a lot of Christians putting this world and themselves down. Fleeing worldliness is seen as equivalent to fleeing the world. The implicit message: this world is evil, the flesh is evil, and it's all under the sway of an evil power—the black equal of a white God. People are giving too little credit to themselves as creatures of God and too much credit to Satan, as though he were not himself a creature but an equal of God. Satan is seen as all knowing, all powerful, and all present in this world. He's given credit for every evil thought, plan, and action, when in fact, he's only a creature himself, without omniknowledge, omnipower, or omnipresence. With all due respect to Flip Wilson, "The Devil *didn't* make you do it!" He can't make your choices for you. *You* make your choices for you. Satan is a defeated foe. Jesus made sure of that. And as for the world, you're in it whether you like it or not. No amount of spiritual gianthood will make you any less dusty a pilgrim or any less qualified for God's grace.

In the third place, I see many believers opting for what I call insider religion—insider faith, insider community, insider jargon; nourished by more teaching, more "new" material, more tapes, books, seminars; flattered by the latest word on what praise form is best, what prayer ritual is most irresistible. It is as if God is the manipulated victim of those who have a secret knowledge of his magic. The gospel is reduced to a complicated bag of spiritual tricks and power maneuvers. We shouldn't be surprised that, in the pentecostal and charismatic arm of the Church, the "word of knowledge" has become *the* spiritual gift of the eighties.

And so we dehumanize Jesus, we devalue his created world, we desimplify the gospel. Gnosticism is alive and well. And the New Testament, with its attack on Gnosticism, has never been more relevant than it is today.

The New Testament gets down to earth. Literally. The incarnation sees God reducing himself, stooping to our level, and becoming one of us. It resists any attempt of ours to reverse the process. It won't allow us the proud privilege of becoming gods. Paul combated early Gnosticism in Colossae by getting one thing straight off the top: "For in Christ all the fullness of the Deity lives in bodily form" (Col. 2:9). *Bodily* form. We're talking flesh and blood here. He also presents Christ as creator, sustainer (in whom *matter* and all creatures and all events "consist and have their being"), and reconciler. He has reconciled us to the Father in history through physical blood shed on a wooden cross. Gnosticism emphasizes mystery. The New Testament emphasizes history.

Some in Corinth thought themselves wise. They were prone to disputing, speculating, and professing knowledge. (" 'We all possess knowledge,' as you say," says Paul in one manuscript of the first book of Corinthians (8:1). They believed they could "fathom all mysteries and all knowledge" (I Cor. 13:2). "So what?" says Paul, in effect. "It only puffs you up." (Have you ever looked at a "puffed up" anything?) The only thing God is impressed with is love (I Cor. 13).

In Ephesus, young Pastor Timothy was having a hard time of it with the Gnostics. They were, among many other things, living immorally while soaring on the wings of spiritual experience. Paul warned Timothy that they were tragically self-deceived. They have "a form of godliness but deny . . . its power" (II Tim 3:5). This means the New Testament expects our faith to be expressed in our morality, lifestyle, values system, and culture, in the broader context of our love for God and neighbor.

It's called practicing what you preach. Maybe the bottom line on Gnosticism comes from John. "This is the spirit of the antichrist, which you have heard is coming and even now is already in the world" (I John 4:3).

We must never forget the Bible *insists* Jesus existed as a real man. He was "born of a woman, born under law . . ." (Gal. 4:4; see also Phil. 2:7). He shared in the same flesh and blood as fallen humanity (Heb. 2:14), and in those days of his flesh he "offered up prayers and petitions with loud cries and tears . . ." (Heb. 5:7). He "grew in wisdom and stature, and in favor with God and men" (Luke 2:52). He "became obedient to death—even death on a cross!" (Phil. 2:8). And after his resurrection he appeared bodily to his disciples and gave the greatest blow to Gnosticism in the entire New Testament: "Touch me and see; a ghost does not have flesh and bones, as you see I have" (Luke 24:39). So get your feet on the ground. God did.

I heard a story once of an old Christian woman whose age began to affect her prodigious memory. She had had a lifelong experience of God's presence, which was rooted not in her spiritual victories, visions, or mystic "warm fuzzies," but in the word of God. She had committed much of the Bible to memory. As her old age eroded her mind, she eventually could quote only one verse, "I know whom I have believed, and am persuaded that he is able to keep that which I have committed unto him against that day" (II Tim. 1:12, KJV). Eventually part of that disappeared, and she would quietly repeat, "that which I have committed unto him." Finally, as she hovered between life and death, her children noticed her lips moving. Putting their ears to her mouth, they heard her whispering, ever so softly, the only word of the Bible still in her memory, "Him. Him. Him." She had lost the whole Bible except one word, but she had the whole Bible in that one word. Him. No fantasy, but a reality.

Fantasy and reality. Sometimes one wonders which is which. I stood last Christmas in the Shepherd's Fields outside Bethlehem, taping a broadcast for Kol Israel (Israel State Radio). As the crew and I set up the equipment beneath the dignified olive trees growing in Boaz's terraced orchard, our bodyguard cocked his Uzi machine gun. The sudden tension quickly subsided as the suspicious intruder at the end of the field turned and called to an unseen flock of sheep. The broadcast taping began. First question: "Tell us, Jim, why did you choose this spot for our Christmas broadcast?"

Why indeed? None of the deeply imbedded symbols are there—no snow, no Christmas trees, no lights, no pageantry, no music, no crêche; just sunshine, olive trees, wild flowers, bird-piped peace, a cave or two, and Bethlehem nestled on the hill, just a mile away.

"O little town of Bethlehem, how still we see thee lie." Remember 1958, Sudbury, Ontario, the old Glad Tidings Tabernacle on Alder Street. Packed church, the tallest Christmas tree a prairie boy had ever seen, musty old blue velvet curtains hiding the platform. Christmas concert time.

"OK, Jimmy, don't forget to sing loudly. There's lots of people out there. Now!" Curtains groan, part reluctantly, and we shepherds sing, "How silently, how silently, the wondrous gift is given!" The staccato of machine-gun fire on the hills gives way to the bleating of sheep. The shepherd looks at us curiously, draws on his Marlboro cigarette, and walks away.

Marlboro cigarettes: a raw-boned cowboy on a horse, the universal American symbol. Shepherds buy symbols. A wisp of tobacco smoke carried on the wind whispers a fantasy—a shepherd on a horse, his sheep are range cattle, bravely weathering the wintry blasts of the North American prairies. "Shepherds in your fields abiding, watching o'er your flocks by night."

The fantasies persist. The North Americans mimic the shepherds, and the shepherds mimic the North Americans. But as I stood in those fields, my memories finally broke through the layers of accumulated symbols to the moment when the Lord Jesus reached down to me, a boy of five in a rough-hewn church camp. There the reality gripped me. Even as I wander the fields of Bethlehem today, the greatest moment in all my life tells a story of sunshine, bluebottle flies, wood-shaving floors, a lady called Grace Brown, and a church camp in Watrous, Saskatchewan—my story a mere blip in the great story, the Incarnation. "God in man is now residing."

INDEX

Abraham, 46, 53, 58, 70, 121,
132
Abram, 174, 183
Abimelech (king of Gerar),
132–33
Accidents, 135
Acts of the Apostles, 234–35
Adam, 46, 174
Adonai, 77
Adultery, 179–80
Agnosticism, 27–28
defined, 27
AIDS, 179
Amaziah (king of Judah), 61
Amos, 60–61, 173, 185–86,
196–97
Amos, Book of, 229
Anderson, Richard, 190–91
Angelique, Mme., 143–45,
160–61
miracles and, 143–45,
160–61

Angels, 136–40
attributes and limitations of,
137
Bible on, 136–37
fallen angels, 138–39
guardian angels, 137–38
help and protection offered
by, 139–40
interest in humans, 140
Anthropological argument,
20–21
Anthropomorphisms, 41
Anti-God theories. *See*
Unbelief
Antitheologians, 5
Apathy, 92–93
God's Plan and, 92–93
Apocalyptic writing, 244
four factors of, 244
Apsu, 108, 119
Arianism, 79–80
Arius, 79

communication barrier and,
4–5
language and, 4–5
See also Theology
Theology
defined, 5
head knowledge, 6
heart knowledge, 5
as "image" not reality, 8–9
as puzzle, 5
right and wrong and, 6–7
self-limitation as student of,
7
self-repression as teacher of,
7
three guidelines in teaching,
8
See also Theologian(s)
Thessalonians, 240
Tiamat, 108, 119
Time and space, 55
Timothy, 257
Timothy, Book of, 240
Titus, Book of, 240
Torah, 197
Trinity, 63–80
analogies and, 66
Arianism and, 79–80
Athanasian Creed and,
64–65, 66
Bible and, 65–66, 72–75,
75–76
C. S. Lewis on, 67–68
Holy Spirit and, 71–72
Isaiah and plural personality
of God, 74–75
Jesus and the Father as one,
70

misrepresentations of, 79–80
plural personality in Old
Testament, 72–75
as presupposed in New
Testament, 75–76
Sabellianism and, 79–80
sonship of Jesus and, 69–70
Truth, 52, 170
Tyndale, William, 210–11

Unbelief, 22–35
agnosticism, 27–28
atheism, 24–27
materialism, 29–31
pantheism, 32–34
secularism, 29–31
skepticism, 27–29
See also Existence of God
Unity of God, 49–50

Valentinus, 253
Van Gogh, Vincent, 117

Westminster Confession, 147
Westminster Shorter Catechism,
101
on God's Plan, 101
Word, the, 79, 183
as theme in prophecy, 183
Word of God, 43, 172–74
Wycliffe, John, 211–12

YHWH, 77

Zadik, 61–62, 180
Zechariah, Book of, 232–33
Zephaniah, Book of, 231–32
Zoroastrianism, 113

BIOGRAPHICAL SKETCH

James Cantelon, a clergyman living in Jerusalem, has been a pastor for eighteen years as well as a free-lance broadcaster for the last sixteen. Forty-eight years old, he is married and has three children. After pastoring in three Canadian cities—Montreal, Sudbury (where he established and hosted a top-rated radio talk show for three years), and Toronto—he moved to Israel in 1981. For the next two years he broadcast two shifts per week at a radio station in southern Lebanon, three miles north of the Israeli border. During this time he also established two programs for Canadian youth in Israel—one, "Kibbutz Shalom," a program for young adults working as volunteers on Israeli kibbutzes and the other, "Campus Shalom," a study program for students at the Hebrew University in Jerusalem. In the summer of 1983 he founded the Jerusalem Christian Assembly. Cantelon, who has guest-hosted a Canadian national Christian television variety program on several occasions, has written for several Canadian magazines including *Faith Today* and since moving to Israel has wrote articles for the Toronto *Star* and the Jerusalem *Post*.